NATIONS IN ARMS

OSPREY
PUBLISHING

Barney White-Spunner

NATIONS IN ARMS

FIVE ARMIES THAT MADE EUROPE

OSPREY PUBLISHING
Bloomsbury Publishing Plc
Kemp House, Chawley Park, Cumnor Hill, Oxford OX2 9PH, UK
Bloomsbury Publishing Ireland Limited,
29 Earlsfort Terrace, Dublin 2, D02 AY28, Ireland
1385 Broadway, 5th Floor, New York, NY 10018, USA
E-mail: info@ospreypublishing.com
www.ospreypublishing.com

OSPREY is a trademark of Osprey Publishing Ltd

First published in Great Britain in 2025

A catalogue record for this book is available from the British Library

ISBN: HB 9781472872982; PB 9781472872999; eBook 9781472872975;
ePDF 9781472872951; XML 9781472872968; Audio 9781472873002

25 26 27 28 29   10 9 8 7 6 5 4 3 2 1

Plate section image credits and captions are given in full in the List of Illustrations (pp. 7–9).
Maps by www.bounford.com
Index by Alan Rutter

Typeset by Deanta Global Publishing Services, Chennai, India
Printed and bound in Great Britain by CPI (Group) UK Ltd, Croydon CR0 4YY

Osprey Publishing supports the Woodland Trust, the UK's leading woodland
conservation charity.

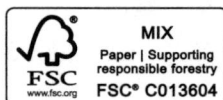

MIX
Paper | Supporting
responsible forestry
FSC
www.fsc.org   FSC® C013604

To find out more about our authors and books visit www.ospreypublishing.com. Here you will
find extracts, author interviews, details of forthcoming events and the option to sign up for
our newsletter.

For product safety related questions contact productsafety@bloomsbury.com

Contents

List of Illustrations

Constantine in York, where he was proclaimed emperor. His portrait on coins suggests this may be quite a good likeness. (Photo by: Education Images/Universal Images Group via Getty Images)

Christian propagandists majored on Constantine's supposed dream before the Milvian Bridge in which Christ urged him to conquer under the sign of the Cross. Constantine may have been converted before he died, but he certainly was not a Christian in 312. (piemags / Alamy Stock Photo)

How Christians saw the Milvian Bridge and possibly, in later years, how Constantine saw himself. (Peter Horree / Alamy Stock Photo)

Romans never forgave Constantine for not making their city his capital. They got their revenge by making his 'Arch' a less than subtle insult. (iStock / Getty Images Plus)

We get the most realistic idea of what Roman emperors looked like from their coins. Here Diocletian is portrayed in all his serious majesty before he went off to grow cabbages, while Constantine is full of youthful energy. (Photo by Ann Ronan Pictures/Print Collector/ Getty Images)

And Maximian's image appears to justify Lactantius' less than flattering description. (Photo by Heritage Art/Heritage Images via Getty Images)

While his son, Maxentius, would appear to belie his later reputation. (Photo by Heritage Art/Heritage Images via Getty Images)

Solid evidence that Constantine was not a Christian at Milvian Bridge. This coin from 318 shows Sol Invictus, the Sun God, on the obverse. (Photo by Heritage Art/Heritage Images via Getty Images)

Sultan Mehmet portrayed by Gentile Bellini. While the artist was staying in Istanbul, he had an argument with the sultan as to what a decapitated head looked like. Mehmet cut the head off an attendant slave to prove his point. The horrified Bellini fled back to Venice. (Photo by Fine Art Images/Heritage Images/Getty Images)

A stylised portrayal of Janissaries in action, depicting both the uniformity that was achievable by regular troops and their development of musketry. (Photo by Universal History Archive/Getty)

The world on the last day. The final assault on Constantinople on Tuesday 29 May 1453. For centuries afterwards, Greeks regarded Tuesdays as inauspicious. (Photo by The Print Collector via Getty Images)

A stylised but accurate view of the siege. The fall of Constantinople stunned the Western world. (Photo by Leemage/Corbis via Getty Images)

Oliver Cromwell – outstanding general, religious zealot, dictator and one of the founders of the modern British army. (Photo by VCG Wilson/Corbis via Getty Images)

Dynamic and effective as Cromwell undoubtedly was, much of the inspiration behind the New Model Army, and hence the contemporary British army, was Thomas Fairfax. (incamerastock/Alamy Stock Photo)

Cromwell's military genius resulted in his reorganisation of the cavalry which became the *arme blanche* of the New Model Army. He modelled his regiments on those which had been successful in the Thirty Years' War. (Photo by Hulton Archive/Getty Images)

Gerhard Johann von Scharnhorst – field soldier, patriot and superb administrator whose vision allowed the German enlightenment to take practical form. (Artexplorer/Alamy Stock Photo)

Chief of staff to Blücher at Waterloo, Neidhardt von Gneisenau was one of the very first practitioners of the new Prussian staff system and the greatest proof of its effectiveness. (Yogi Black/Alamy Stock Photo)

The Prussian *Landwehr*. The three-tier system that Scharnhorst and Gneisenau built was short lived but proved to be one of the most effective models for a national army. (Photo by: Bildagentur-online/Universal Images Group via Getty Images)

George Marshall was responsible for taking the US Army from 19th in the world in 1941, ranking below Portugal, to fielding 69 divisions in Europe and 22 in the Pacific within three years. (Photo by: Universal History Archive/ Universal Images Group via Getty Images)

Famous for his irascibility, George Patton was arguably the most effective of all the Allied commanders in the Second World War. (Bettmann/Getty Images)

The story of how the US Army was sent to war in 1942 with inadequate battle tanks is an extraordinary saga. The M3 shown here, the unhappy result of inter-branch army disputes, was totally outclassed by the German models it confronted in North Africa. (Photo by Fox Photos/ Hulton Archive/Getty Images)

It was rapidly replaced with the Sherman, which although equally outclassed, was produced in such numbers that eventually mass won over capability. (Photo by Fred Ramage/Keystone/Hulton Archive/Getty Images)

While the Germans produced technically advanced tanks like the superlative Panther, shown here, they were never able to manufacture enough of them, nor harness the necessary logistic support, to give them battlefield superiority. (Photo by: Photo12/Universal Images Group via Getty Images)

The ultimate tank of the Second World War, and of the folly of the German production system, was the immensely capable but chronically unreliable Tiger. It is estimated that there were only ever half of them available for combat. (Photo by ullstein bild/ullstein bild via Getty Images)

List of Maps

Chapter One

What is an Army?

*'You may not be interested in war but war is
interested in you.'*

Leon Trotsky[1]

Sadly, war is inevitable. Many of us who have had the privilege
of being born in Western democracies after 1945 have been
spared having to confront war directly. This has created a
false optimism that future generations may not have to suffer
its terrible embrace, much as we also hoped as a generation
that pandemics had been consigned to history. Those who
live in other parts of the world have been less fortunate. In
the last three-quarters of a century, many in South-East Asia,
Africa and the Middle East have had to confront both war
and pandemics regularly, but it is only since Russia invaded
Ukraine in February 2022 that war has become seen as a
present threat in the rich European liberal democracies.

This is regrettable, by any measurement of human values,
and negates the feeling that life will inevitably get better
as humankind progresses. War does not, of course, negate
societal progress – in a rather macabre way, it can actually

give societies an impetus to rebuild – but it is a sad fact that the 20th century was the bloodiest in history. It is impossible to come up with a precise figure, but certainly more than 100 million people lost their lives through conflict, with some estimates as high as 187 million, or over 10 per cent of the world's population before the First World War. Many distinguished people have attempted an explanation as to why humans fight each other. Arguably no one has yet done so compellingly nor is it the purpose of this book to try to do so. My starting point is that war is a sad but unavoidable part of the human condition which, given that we cannot get rid of it, it is our duty to minimize the consequences of.[2] Just as aggressors will use armies to pursue their interests, so responsible governments need armies to defend theirs.

Sadly, it looks as if this present century may rival the last in terms of war and bloodshed. This points to two things. First, human nature remains violent. Not only is modern conflict hideously costly in life, but the violence of war itself has not diminished. There is a certain rather revolting smugness in thinking that a strike by a remotely controlled missile is somehow less horrific than a Roman legion massacring a village, but the effect on the unfortunate recipients is much the same. It is also sadly true that warfighting on a battlefield when armies meet is as nasty, primitive and destructive as it has always been; there is again little difference between how a 4th-century BC tribesman speared his rival whose bones were found on Salisbury Plain and a Russian conscript knifing a Ukrainian in 2025. The battle of the Somme in 1916 is often cited as being the ultimate example of how hundreds of thousands of lives were wasted for minimal territorial gain. A life for every yard was the criticism levelled at the army commanders; around Bakhmut, in 2025, that figure is one Russian life for every 19 inches.[3]

Secondly, the inevitability of conflict means that societies, and therefore states, need armies. Societies must be able to defend themselves. A state may not be interested in war but, in Trotsky's sinister words, 'war is interested in you'. It is totally plausible and logical to think that war will not happen, but sadly it is wrong. Aggressors see war differently. There was a reasonable and genuinely held belief that the demise of the Soviet Union in 1989 had greatly reduced the threat to world peace in general and to Europe in particular, thus allowing a substantial post-Cold War peace dividend. There was a corresponding feeling that armies were becoming something of an anachronism, and the inevitable triumph of liberal democracies meant that eventually you wouldn't need an army because there would be no enemies to fight and no threats to combat. It was felt that it was as important for armies to reflect social change as for them to be operationally coherent. Governments across the Western world measured success by how much they could save on defence budgets.[4] They were again simply following a pattern set for millennia that when there was no war, you did not need a large standing army. When threats emerged, you re-armed. If you were the aggressor, you did so first to steal a technological and readiness advantage over your rivals; if you were less aggressive, you re-armed late and generally lost, at least in the early stages of a war. Sadly, we are now entering one of those dangerous periods when war hovers menacingly in our world, clearly and horribly defined in Ukraine and Gaza, more a lurking spectre in Western Europe. Sweden, Finland, Poland, the Baltic States, Germany, Hungary, Czechia, Slovakia, Romania, Bulgaria and Turkey are all restructuring and re-equipping their armies, as are many nations in Asia and Africa; the UK has just published a major defence review, and the Trump administration in the USA heralds further changes to US defence commitments. We are entering a period when a nation will once again be defined by its army. States are now forced to reconsider what part of their national resource they are prepared to devote to the protection of their citizens even though the threat may be imminent as opposed to immediate.

But what is an army? Originally societies gathered together to protect themselves. Every man, and sometimes woman, in a group was required to take part in the defence of the group whether village, tribe or, later, state. Over time this principle became refined so that each group was required to produce a quota of fighters, such as the Anglo-Saxon *fyrd*, a principle later extended into the British county militias. It also became corrupted as the better off found ways of delegating their service to those less fortunate. However, the idea remained that every member of a society should participate in its defence, although admittedly that was a principle that became complicated as rulers fought wars to further their own interests. Yet the fundamental point remained, and, although armies were to become less representative and more professionalized, when a state faced existential threats, such as France after 1914 or Russia in 1941, the whole nation was mobilized. Contemporary politicians misunderstand this, clumsily citing conscription as a tool for engineering societal change. By doing so they obscure the fact that the most fundamental purpose of government is to defend the state when it is threatened and that every member of that state should in some way contribute. History shows us that the vast majority understand this and are prepared, if not actually happy, to participate. It is for government to provide the means for them to do so.

Take, for example, Lithuania, a Baltic State of 2.8 million souls which finds itself uncomfortably situated between Russia and the Russian enclave of Kaliningrad which used to be Königsberg, once the capital of Prussia and scene of some of the most vicious fighting in 1945. Since 1990, when Lithuania gained its independence from the Soviet Union, its citizens have enjoyed the benefits of living in what has become a prosperous liberal democracy. They hoped that this time it might last, unlike the last time they celebrated independence in 1918. Lithuania is a member of NATO and relies on its NATO allies under Article V of the North Atlantic Treaty, which says that an attack on one is an attack on all. However, they are taking no chances, and every part of Lithuanian society is preparing to mobilize. They intend to deter any future Russian aggression, and if Russia does invade, yet again, they are determined to defend every inch of their native soil. It wasn't what they had hoped for back in 1990, but now they see it as inevitable if they are to have a chance of survival.[5]

One way governments have discharged their fundamental duty to protect their citizens is to create professional armies that could also be used in circumstances when the state is not existentially threatened, or to further other interests. Being structured, armed and trained organizations, armies could also be used as police forces, as guards, to enhance the prestige of a state and, most importantly, could act as a core when there was a requirement to expand. They could also act as the repository for technological innovation. Sometimes these 'professional' armies were full time, as in most European states, or sometimes they were part time, such as in Sparta or later Prussia, but they were still part of the standing army, as opposed to being reservists who might be called up in times of crisis.

Much as the fundamentals of warfare have not changed over the last two millennia, so the fundamentals of how a society defends itself and organizes its army have not changed much either. Weapons and communications are self-evidently constantly changing, but the roles and structures of armies are much the same now as they were in classical times – although this truism can be vitiated by the sheer complexity of modern warfare. Successful armies historically have been those that have structured themselves around these fundamentals rather than just being re-modelled versions of what went before. Restructuring an army is a difficult thing to do. It requires someone with the authority and confidence to do so, for them to have the political support and to be strong enough to override the traditionally conservative instincts of those in command. Restructuring also tends to happen during a crisis, when time is short and measured thought a rarity. The natural tendency is to develop what is there, which can have obvious advantages but can also lead to reinforcing failure. What most successful armies have in common is that although they are constructed against a specific threat, which is self-evident and which demands action, they are also flexible enough to adapt; this flexibility comes from having been built on the foundations of those same core principles.

So what are these principles? There are many that could be said to apply, but for the purposes of this book I have rationalized them down to five. The first is to maintain an effective fighting force that can succeed in combat – or 'warfighting', as it is more usually referred to. This force must be clearly identified, trained and equipped so that it is ready to fight. Traditionally these forces have been made up of young men on the basis that they have been fitter, more malleable and more resilient than older men, and it is only recently that women have been encouraged to serve in fighting units.[6] The issue of age has become something of a sacred cow for governments. When the average life span of a man was between 30 and 40 years, it made sense to recruit soldiers in their late teens and early twenties. However, as life expectancy increases and medicine and fitness improve, the logic in not recruiting old men and now women is less obvious. The average age of the Ukrainian soldiers fighting against Russia is somewhere over 40, approaching 45. However they are constituted, successful armies have protected their fighting force from other, more routine, duties to ensure that they are properly trained. The size of such forces has obviously varied hugely over the centuries, but an overriding principle of the armies examined in this book is that they first created, and then sustained, their combat troops. Critically, they trained them. A force trained for the most demanding operations can adapt to perform less demanding ones, but it must always be kept ready to fight at the highest end of the spectrum of combat. If it is not, then it will lose. And training allows armies to adapt; wars never progress as they are expected to.

Secondly, successful armies establish a relationship with the nation and the society that spawns them. They are not seen merely as a tool of government, although a small sector of society will always regard them as such, but as servants of the nation. This may seem self-evident to citizens of some Western countries, but achieving a balance between the organization which has a monopoly of lethal force and the government to whom it answers has long taxed both rulers and generals. Should an army have its own voice and see itself as semi-independent of government, holding to the wider values of the society it represents, or should it be entirely subject to its own government? In the time it has taken to write this chapter, we have seen the army in Bangladesh take the former view, while that of Venezuela sided with its government against the people. Even in stable European democracies, government ministers rage when generals take an independent line. We may argue that ministers are entitled to do so, possibly because we are subjective in believing in the strength of our democratic systems, whereas if democracy becomes threatened, which is not impossible, then might we be actually grateful that an army may refuse to deploy onto our streets? Conversely, a system that allows an army too much power and results in periods of military rule, such as the Rule of the Major Generals during the Protectorate in England, only diminishes an army's utility, as it becomes seen as divorced from its core purpose. Within these criteria, an army must be affordable. Armies that consume too great a proportion of the national resource become a burden to their society and soon become unsustainable, witnessed by the fall of the Soviet military in 1989. Spending on armies may have to surge in wartime, which is to be expected, but their steady state running costs should be within limits that a society judges appropriate.

Thirdly, soldiers in successful armies are respected by their nation, which ensures that they are looked after. Service must be seen as honourable. History offers a vast range of examples where soldiers have been greatly respected, such as Sparta and the armies of the Roman Republic, but even more where they have been treated as what Wellington referred to as the 'scum of the earth'.[7] There is, however, a danger in history becoming revisionist in how it judges the degree of respect and the standard of care afforded to troops by applying contemporary standards. Wellington's army was, by the standards of the early 19th century, well cared for. That said, successful armies are those whereby societies honour those who defend them. Equally, armies must abide by a code of conduct that ensures they earn that trust and respect, and again there are numerous examples of armies that have failed miserably to do so.

Fourthly, armies that succeed have the flexibility to adopt and use new technologies. This may seem to be a statement of the obvious, but the times that an army has been defeated and its nation destroyed because it has been unable or unwilling to alter its methods and structures to understand and absorb new technologies are as numerous as the stars in the sky. Too often an army thinks it has the monopoly of knowledge and is unwilling to work with industry to harness its intellectual power to the national effort. We are in danger of entering such a period today.

Lastly, a nation must be able to equip and sustain its army. This is not so much a question of logistic support to fighting troops, which is more a function of combat, but rather one of maintaining the necessary industrial base to meet an army's needs. There is a tendency to think that this is more of a modern problem. In fact it was, for example, as difficult in comparative terms – given the facilities available – to supply Hannibal's army in Italy in the Punic Wars as it was the U.S. Army in the Pacific in the Second World War. However, what is different today is the multi-national nature of manufacturing, which means that it can be very difficult for armies to carry sufficient spares and replacement equipment without vast budgets. How to solve this is one of the biggest issues now facing contemporary armies, evidenced by Ukraine, which has had to beg for weapons and munitions internationally. Is the lesson therefore that nations should maintain sufficient domestic defence production capacity so that they can be self-sufficient in a world where it may not be politically or practically possible to buy stocks when you need them during a war? In the past, that is exactly what successful armies did. How should a contemporary army deal with this so that it does not find itself in the position British forces did during the Falklands conflict or as the unfortunate Ukrainians do today?

Designing contemporary armies also takes these principles to new levels. It requires an awareness not just of the military threats that nations face but also the wider threats to their societies. Whereas in the past, armies were not always so concerned with dealing with issues such as environmental threats, pandemics or mass migration, modern armies have been regularly diverted from their core functions to deal with these issues simply because there is no other organized or competent body that governments can call on. In the early 2020s, for example, the Australian Army spent more time dealing with flooding than training. Yet defending against these threats is as important as defending against conventional military threats, so a society must be organized to deal with them. This is why going back to first principles matters. These threats menace everyone in a nation, so a government should draw on a wide cross-section of society to combat them. The skills required to deal with pandemics and flooding, for example, are not necessarily those owned by soldiers. But they are skills widely available across many different age groups if they were organized in such a way that they could be used. It is, if you like, a contemporary application of the Anglo-Saxon *fyrd*.[8]

Taken together, these issues mean that governments need fundamentally to rethink how they 'do armies' so that they can both succeed on battlefields that are as brutal as they have ever been and also combat these emerging threats. This challenge is not new. Nations have faced similar challenges many times, but they have not always dealt with them successfully, success in this instance meaning armies not just achieving short-term victory on the battlefield – essential a prerequisite as that obviously remains – but rather being able to defend the long-term interest of the societies that spawned them. What this book sets out to do is to look at five armies that have met the challenge successfully, to show what links them, and by doing so identify those common and unchanging traits that underpin success. The five armies selected also represent a historical continuum, being linked chronologically in that they successively all played a major part in shaping Europe. They do not all represent the principles identified above in their totality – some actually represent an antithesis of them at various stages in their development – but taken together they do show the overall value of those principles.

The first is the late Roman army after Constantine the Great's re-organization from AD 306. By the middle of the 3rd century AD, the Roman Empire was in crisis. In AD 260, the Roman Emperor Valerian was defeated by King Shapur of Persia at the battle of Edessa, taken prisoner and thereafter used as a human mounting-block by Shapur until he died, after which his skin was stuffed and preserved in the Persian king's palace. The last Roman emperor to come from the traditional Roman aristocracy, Valerian's chaotic reign was followed by a succession of ten emperors in 24 years, almost permanent civil war and the creation of rival empires until, in AD 284, an Illyrian farmer and successful soldier called Diocles took power. Ruling as the Emperor Diocletian, he began to stabilize the Roman world, dividing it into East and West and appointing three co-emperors in what became known as the Tetrarchy. This arrangement was to prove intrinsically unstable and brought renewed civil war until Constantine, son of the Western Tetrarch, reformed his army, defeated his rivals and re-united the empire with its capital at Constantinople. His reforms would last for 1,100 years.

Secondly, as the Eastern Empire faded, the vestiges of Constantine's legions fell victim to the Ottoman army. Reformed in the early 15th century after its devastating defeat by Tamerlane in 1402, it went on to take Constantinople and to push and then hold the borders of the Ottoman Empire, from the Danube to the Tigris, for 300 years. Much of the structure of modern Western armies is of Ottoman origin. It was the army and its conquests that enabled the Ottoman state to flourish; once the army began to decline so did the empire, unable to penetrate deeper into Europe as the Central European powers, whose armies owed so much to what they had learnt from the Ottomans, gradually surpassed them.

Third is Cromwell's British army, which started life as the 'New Model Army', created in 1644 as the parliamentary forces restructured themselves at the nadir of their fortunes during the British civil wars of 1642–51. One of several European armies restructured in the middle of the 17th century after the chaos and devastation of the mercenary armies employed in the Thirty Years' War, the New Model Army was, despite severe organizational failings, quickly successful on the battlefield. Subsequently commanded by Cromwell, it became effective in combat and efficiently administered, even though its operations in Ireland were reprehensible. Its political views are particularly interesting, as is the way it was transformed into the Royalist army after the Restoration of the monarchy in 1660. It was the first regular British army, and British armies ever since have been modelled on it.

Of the other Central European armies created in the mid-1600s, the most effective, and arguably the one that took the most from the Ottoman model, was that of Prussia. Yet it was its devastating defeat by Napoleon at Jena in 1806 that caused its most fundamental overhaul. The Prussian army's rebirth after Jena in 1806, led by Gerhard Johann von Scharnhorst, shows how a nation was mobilized to support a cause, how this spirit was organized into a formal structure, how command was analysed, doctrine written and how the army became the most respected element of national society. Chapter Five discusses the military success of that model but also how later it tried to subvert civilian control. Comparison will be made with Napoleon's army, which neglected the basic lessons, leading to a century of French military failure, and how it was other armies that consolidated the lessons of Napoleon's campaigns.

Lastly, Chapter Six looks at the army of the United States of America. In 1941 the American army was ranked 19th in the world, behind Romania and Portugal, although just ahead of Bulgaria. In three years it used the lessons of its European counterparts to build a force capable of fielding 69 divisions in Europe and a further 22 in the Pacific. From this it built itself into the world's leading expeditionary force – a position it has never relinquished, despite Vietnam – an army designed to operate overseas rather than at home, and mobilized American industrial power to do so. Now taken as the apogee of armies, the world's most powerful military is constructed along the lines identified by Constantine and the Ottomans, by Cromwell and by Scharnhorst.

What all five armies have in common is that, although they were reacting to crises, they considered in depth what defence of the nation involved and were all prepared to be radical, not just adjusting the capabilities they inherited. It goes without saying that they were all successful on the battlefield. That is, after all, the basic function of an army, and they were organized so that they could prosecute war with all its brutality. They were successful not just in interpreting and prosecuting strategies in support of the governments they served but also in being respected by and responsible to their societies. They were seen by many, although never by all, as representative of the values those societies embraced and as pursuing strategies that enhanced and supported the wider aims of the nation or empire. They were all also able to adapt and modernize, thus ensuring their longevity. Such an analysis must therefore exclude armies which, at first sight, may seem to demand inclusion, such as the French army under Napoleon. Tactically one of the most innovative and successful armies ever fielded, it ultimately served only the vanities of a regime and left France enfeebled for a century.

There are, of course, other armies that I could have included, such as the Israeli Army which, however controversial its operations may appear to some, meets most of the criteria for a successful army. However, it is difficult to discuss in the midst of current events when emotion can distract from objective analysis.

This book is not about battlefield tactics. Many, many books have been written about how General X should have done this, or Emperor Y that, as they manoeuvred against each other. A few are even helpful and there is an enduring debate about the 'revolution in military affairs' which is, by definition, cyclical. Strong armies, successful armies, can stand tactical defeats. Success on the battlefield is, of course, core to the point of an army, but a successful army is one that defends its national interests over an extended period. Historians often criticize the British Army during the Second World War, comparing its performance very unfavourably with that of the German Army. This is curious. The German Army certainly won tactical victories, but these came at unsustainable cost. It never won a campaign, and by 1945 the armies that emerged triumphant were those of the Western Allies. Germany lost sight of the core principles on which its army had been founded, something explored in Chapter Five.

This is rather a book about the nature of armies. Despite armies having operated in conjunction with navies for millennia, the study of navies is a separate subject, and the nature of a navy is subtly different to that of an army. The book will touch on air forces, given that several air forces such as the United States Air Force and the British Royal Air Force started life as part of their respective armies, but it does not pretend to be an authoritative study of the air arm.

I hope you will find it both an enthralling history – and much of it might be less well known to Western readers – but also a timely reminder that we no longer have the luxury of regarding the need to defend ourselves as being in some way outdated. You may not agree with the politics of the protagonists, but that is not the point. Much as you may despair of Constantine's moves towards Christianity, deplore the spread of Islam into Europe, hate everything that Cromwell stood for, believe that Prussian militarism was responsible for that most lethal 20th century and that American interventionism is not a force for good, I ask you to put your feelings aside while you read and concentrate instead on the breadth of vision and scale of achievement those armies represent, and ask yourself whether perhaps we should not now be thinking along the same lines.

Chapter Two

The Army of Constantine, 312

'in hoc signo vinces' ('In this sign, conquer')
As seen in a vision by Constantine prior to the
Battle of the Milvian Bridge, AD 312

Flavius Valerius Constantinus, better known as Constantine the Great, was proclaimed emperor by his army in York in AD 306. His father, Constantius Chlorus, was Diocletian's Tetrarch in the West. His mother was Helena, who would later claim to have found the True Cross. We do not know where Helena came from, with theories ranging from her being the daughter of a British chieftain to a Bithynian innkeeper's daughter. Contemporaries would also cast doubt on the validity of her marriage to Constantius. Whatever her origins, she became a devout Christian and one of the most powerful women in the empire. During his 31-year reign, Constantine would re-unite Europe, convert the Roman Empire to Christianity and move its capital from Rome to Byzantium, renamed after him as Constantinople. Whether he actually became a Christian himself is possible; what is beyond doubt is that he possessed exceptional skills as an army commander, as a military administrator and as a strategist. It was the army that was his authority and his power.

Constantine was proclaimed emperor as the Roman Empire was slowly emerging from its mid-3rd century nadir. In AD 260 the Emperor Valerian had been defeated by the Persian King Shapur.[1] He had been taken prisoner, reputedly used as a human mounting-block until he died, after which his skin was stuffed so it could be put on display in Shapur's palace. His successor was his son Gallienus, whose 'genius was destitute of judgement' and who 'attempted every art except the important ones of war and government. He was the master of several curious but useless sciences, a ready orator, an elegant poet, a skilful gardener, an excellent cook, and most contemptible prince.'[2] For the next 30 odd years the empire was 'reduced to the lowest pitch of disgrace and ruin from whence it seemed impossible that it would ever emerge' and 'was significantly reduced by invasions, rebellions, famine and plague'.[3] There were ten emperors in 24 years between AD 260 and 284, and rival empires emerged in Gaul and Palmyra. Power was with the army, which proclaimed its popular commanders then did away with them when they no longer served their purposes. Rome lost its relevance, if not its sense of self-importance. Valerian and Gallienus were the last two emperors to come from a patrician family, while their successors were soldiers whose authority came from the army not the senate.

The Roman Empire in the last half of the 3rd century was considered to be in two parts. The Western half comprised Europe west of the Rhine and the Danube, together with the North African littoral west of Egypt. The Eastern half was Europe south of the Danube, so modern Greece, and the western Balkans, Turkey, Syria, Palestine and Egypt itself. Its eastern border, where the Roman and Persian empires met, was in continuous flux, occasionally stretching as far as the Tigris. In AD 284 a soldier called Diocles, who had risen to high command, was proclaimed emperor by his troops on the Danube and subsequently defeated the Emperor Carinus, who had only lasted a few months. Diocles came from humble origins, his father rumoured to have been a freed slave, and he took his name, subsequently aggrandized to Gaius Aurelius Valerius Diocletianus, from his mother's birthplace in Dalmatia. He had risen steadily through the ranks due to his military competence and had become governor of Moesia, roughly equivalent to modern Serbia. He proved to be as adept politically as he was as a soldier and set about consolidating his rule and restoring some stability to the fractured empire. He appreciated that this was beyond the scope of one man, first establishing a co-emperor, Maximian, in Milan, ruling the Western Empire, while he governed in the East first from Sirmium in Moesia and later from Nicomedia just south of the Bosphorus in Asia Minor. Calling themselves rather immodestly Jupiter and Hercules, even such divine association did not prevent the task of government and recovery proving too great for two men. Consequently, they both appointed sub-emperors, again one in the East, Galerius, who answered to Diocletian, and Constantius Chlorus in the west, reporting to Maximian. The four emperors, the senior now calling themselves 'Augusti' and the junior ones 'Caesars' after their illustrious predecessors, were known as the Tetrarchy.

Able a statesman as Diocletian, as he is better known, undoubtedly was, choosing co-emperors was not a skill in which he excelled. Maximian was a fellow soldier who 'was born a peasant, ignorant of letters, careless of laws, the rusticity of his appearance and manners still betrayed in the most elevated of fortune the meanness of his extraction'.[4] Galerius had been a herdsman 'with a native barbarity and a savageness foreign to Roman blood'. His outward appearance 'corresponded with his manners. Of structure tall, full of flesh, and swollen to a horrible bulk of corpulency; by his speech, gestures, and looks, he made himself a terror to all that came near him.'[5] Despite this seemingly intimidating demeanour, he was nevertheless competent but jealous of his position and, having married Diocletian's daughter, saw himself as his natural successor. His specific responsibility was the Danube frontier, confronting the 'Barbarians' or the German tribes who lived to its north and east. Maximian's Caesar, Constantius Chlorus ('the Pale'), so called because of his very pale complexion, was another officer from Moesia. Allegedly he came from imperial stock, his mother claiming to be the niece of the Emperor Claudius II who ruled briefly in AD 268–70, although this story was most likely exaggerated in the telling when Constantine needed to prove some ancestry. Regardless, he was also competent if brutal, and had been governor of Dalmatia, throwing in his lot with Diocletian when he overthrew Carinus. His responsibility was Gaul and Britain. Like Galerius, he was forced to divorce his wife, Constantine's mother Helena to whom Constantine was devoted, and marry Maximian's daughter.

Constantine was born in Naissus, now Nis in Serbia, probably about AD 282.[6] He grew up in his father's household, although Constantius was mostly away campaigning. In 287 Carausius, a soldier from what is today Belgium, who commanded the Roman fleet in the English Channel, rebelled and established an independent empire in Northern Gaul and Britain. Coming so soon after the last rogue empire in Gaul, which had only been finally defeated in 273, this was a serious blow, not least because Carausius was a capable commander whose domination of the sea made him difficult to combat. With Maximian busy fighting in Spain and North Africa, it fell to Constantius to lead operations against Carausius and his successor, Allectus. Basing himself in Boulogne, he built a second fleet, but it was not until 296 that Britain and Northern Gaul were back under Roman control. Consequently, Constantine did not see much of his father. In 297 he was sent with his mother to Diocletian's court, by now at Nicomedia although in fact mostly itinerant, as the east of the empire was as unsettled as the west. For the next five years of seemingly endless campaigning, Constantine served as an officer in Diocletian's army as the senior Augustus attempted to restore order to the Eastern Empire. He was a naturally gifted commander who, although obviously helped by his father being a Tetrarch, had risen by 305 to be a *Tribunus Ordini Primi* – the most senior rank of Tribune. Diocletian also liked him and saw his military ability.

Constantine saw service in Egypt, where Diocletian was suppressing a rebellion and which resulted in the siege of Alexandria and the slaughter of a large part of its population. However, he would also have witnessed Diocletian's efforts to restore stability to the shattered province and especially his care to preserve its ancient Greek culture. While Diocletian remained in Egypt, he sent Galerius to subdue the Persians, resurgent under a new king, Narses, who had invaded the Roman client kingdom of Armenia. Constantine accompanied him, probably against Galerius' wishes, although again he distinguished himself in the field. From the Persian frontier Galerius redirected his army against the Carpi, invading Roman Thrace, now Bulgaria, from north of the Danube.

Consequently, by his early twenties Constantine had gained extensive military experience not just against poorly organized rebel groups such as those in Egypt but against organized armies like the Persians. He had also seen how Diocletian used and controlled the army, imposing his authority on it after the instability of the previous decades, and how, although the nature of the Tetrarchy prevented him insisting on unity of command, he had begun to make reforms to its structure and roles. These were initiatives that Constantine would later develop. Constantine had also seen a lot of the world. He left little by way of personal records, but he did write that in his youth he had visited both Memphis and Babylon.[7] In 301 he had also got married in Antioch, to Minervina. We know very little about Minervina other than that she died in 303, the same year as Constantine's adored son Crispus was born so it's possible that she died in childbirth.

Constantine had also witnessed two other significant societal trends. The first was that although agricultural production across the empire was increasing on land that was actually farmed – archaeological evidence shows a growing number of grain storage facilities – more land was being left fallow because of the endless warfare, and people were leaving the countryside for the safety of the cities. These were actually reducing in size physically, abandoning their suburbs and concentrating their populations behind reconstructed defences, despite having to absorb more people. The average size of a late empire city was just 18 hectares; an extreme example was Amiens in Gaul, which reduced from 100 hectares around AD 200 to a mere 10 hectares a century later, although the new military cities such as Trier, which would become Constantine's capital in the first part of his reign, grew to 285 hectares, and Milan, Sirmium, Thessalonica,

Nicomedia and Antioch were also rapidly expanding.[8] It would seem that it was becoming increasingly clear to a man of Constantine's character that the endless civil wars were preventing the empire from realizing its economic potential, something he valued certainly from its ability to pay tax and also from the general well-being of its people. He had also witnessed Diocletian's catastrophic attempt to control inflation – his Edict on Maximum Prices issued in late 301, which attempted to set maximum prices for a whole range of goods and services and which caused chaos in the markets. Although it was soon withdrawn, the lesson that economic stability was as necessary as military superiority was not lost on him.

The second movement which profoundly influenced Constantine was Christianity. Although he may have been baptized on his death bed, he was certainly not a Christian while he was emperor, although he is often portrayed as such because contemporary historical sources were written by Christian eulogists such as his tutor Lactantius and Eusebius of Caesarea. Both their accounts were written to propagandize the Christian religion rather than offer objective history. It is also possible that Minervina's family were Christian; many well-to-do Antioch families were, and maybe the reason so little is known about her is that the Diocletian persecution was in full swing at the time of her death. Galerius was a particularly unattractive advocate of taking harsher measures against the Christians.

What Constantine probably saw in Christianity was a movement that could unify the empire under a code which – generally – encouraged people to live peacefully together, to adhere to a strict model of behaviour under a hierarchy of priests and to be obedient to one all-powerful central authority.

He had been brought up to worship Sol Invictus, the Invincible Sun, whose cult his father had championed and to whom the Christian world has cause to be grateful as it preserved Sunday as a day of rest. The concept of worshipping one all-powerful God as opposed to the quarrelsome Roman pantheon was therefore not unnatural for him; many contemporaries saw Sol Invictus and the Christian God as the same being. Constantine's early coins show Sol Invictus on the reverse, although it is known that he also dabbled in Mithraism, then a popular cult amongst senior Roman officers, which shared many similarities with Christianity. It was particularly widespread in Britain. He was probably also close to and impressed by Tiridates, the young king of Armenia, who had rallied his country under the Christian banner to drive out the Persians. Yet it appears that what mattered to Constantine was not the theological arguments that underpinned these various religions but rather their impact on governance. He understandably declared himself disinterested in the various intricate Christian quarrels in North Africa, the Donatist controversy. He was also clearly preoccupied with other, more pressing matters when he was presiding over the Council of Nicaea which proclaimed the divinity of Christ as being consubstantial with God the Father. It is unlikely that he actually believed in the outcome of Nicaea but rather felt it politic to go along with the majority, which was led by the North African faction in the Christian church – staunch supporters of the divinity of Christ, who threatened to cut off the grain supply to the empire should they fail to get their way.

In February 303 Diocletian announced an edict against the Christians which led to an 18-month persecution, the last in a long line of attempts by the state to disrupt what was now a powerful and popular sect. Diocletian was known to dislike this new religion which he believed polluted the purity of the empire, but even so this was a strange move. It may have been prompted by Galerius, who also held a particular dislike of Christianity but who believed that Constantius, still preoccupied in Gaul, was sympathetic to Christianity, as was Constantine. Galerius thought that it would strengthen his case and that of his family to succeed Diocletian if he could discredit them. The persecution in the East was savage, with churches destroyed and scriptures burned. Christians lost their legal rights and there were numerous executions. It was, however, enforced half-heartedly in the West and there is in fact little evidence that Constantius did anything about it, which may have played to Galerius' coming success.

Later in 303 Constantine accompanied Diocletian and Maximian to Rome for their Vicennalia, the celebration of their 20 years in power. Maximian had already started work on the massive complex of the Baths of Diocletian, to be seen to be doing something for a city which, although increasingly marginal, was still officially the capital of the empire. Diocletian and Maximian staged a triumph in the manner that successful commanders had done for centuries, but 'it was less magnificent' than those that had gone before.[9] Diocletian disliked Rome, saw the senate as irrelevant and the Praetorian Guard, so long arbiters of power, as militarily ineffective. For their part, despite their smart new baths, the Romans resented Diocletian's increasing use of the trappings of royalty, such as wearing a diadem, something he had copied from the Persians. However, their real resentment was that the Augusti had made their capitals at Milan and Nicomedia, rendering Rome increasingly irrelevant. For Constantine the lesson was exactly that; the centre of the empire had shifted to the east and to North Africa.

Events would come to a head in 305 when Diocletian took the unusual step for a Roman emperor of abdicating. He had been seriously ill after the Vicennalia, and when late that summer he appeared in front of his troops at Nicomedia, 'he was so pale and emaciated, that he could scarcely have been recognised by those to whom his person was most familiar'.[10] He had secured Maximian's agreement to retire at the same time, or at least he thought he had. Announcing that Galerius would succeed as Augustus in the East, he appointed as his Caesar Galerius' son-in-law, a relatively unknown soldier called Maximinus Daia. In the West, Constantius would be Augustus, but instead of appointing Constantine – who, as his son and a man who had distinguished himself, was expected to be appointed – he chose a man called Severus. He was another friend of Galerius', who had been the army's paymaster, an appointment from which, as with many of his successors throughout the centuries, he did very well indeed. If the chroniclers had been rude about Maximian and Galerius, it was nothing compared with their judgements on Daia and Severus. Daia was 'a young man, half-barbarian' totally 'unfit for the charge of public affairs', while Severus was described as 'that dancer, that habitual drunkard, who turns night into day and day into night'.[11] Diocletian then retired to his roots on the Dalmatian coast, building a massive palace near Salona, modern-day Split, where he famously spent his remaining years growing cabbages. Maximian retired, at least temporarily, to a villa near Rome.

Constantine was present in Nicomedia to witness Diocletian's strange pronouncement and now found himself in the distinctly hostile atmosphere of what had immediately become Galerius' court. Taking the three-year-old Crispus with him, he fled quickly to join his father Constantius in Gaul, arriving in Boulogne at the end of the year, and sailed with him to Britain where he was to suppress the Picts who were raiding south over Hadrian's wall. By January 306 they were both in York, and after a successful campaign that spring Constantius died in July. Constantine was now proclaimed emperor by the legions in York. The 'distinguished comeliness of his figure, his strict attention to all military duties, his virtuous demeanour and singular affability, had endeared him to the troops and made him the choice of every individual', and he needed little encouragement to declare himself Caesar without reference to Galerius.[12]

By the early 4th century, Roman Britain was fairly settled. Constantius' campaigns had been successful so that, having put down the Pictish rebellion, the island was generally peaceful. It was one of the more integrated societies across the Western Empire, with the propertied classes seeing themselves as part of the Roman administration. Britain had benefitted from having three legions permanently stationed there: II Augusta behind Hadrian's Wall and VI Victrix in York; a third legion, XX Valeria Victrix, was based in Chester. They had all been there for some time; II Augusta had originally come over with Agricola, which made for continuity of security, and most of the soldiers were by this stage British. VI Victrix had originally been raised by Octavian in the civil war following the assassination of Julius Caesar. Others came and went, such as during Carausius' rebellion, but otherwise the south of Britain was quiet.

Constantine therefore decided to move from York to Gaul, first to Colonia Agrippina, modern Cologne, on the Rhine, where he had a bridge constructed and from where he was well placed to deal with the 'barbarian' tribes east of the river. Later he moved to Augusta Treverorum, now Trier, which would become his capital and where his great basilica is still in use. Galerius grudgingly accepted the inevitability of his self-proclamation, but otherwise Diocletian's careful plan for his succession was disintegrating. Maximian's son, Maxentius, had declared himself Caesar in the West, and using his father's North African army seized control in Rome and southern Italy. Maximian came out of retirement to assist him. In 307 Galerius sent Severus to confront them, but he was defeated by Maxentius' experienced army and executed. Maximian subsequently fell out with his son and made an alliance with Constantine, to whom he married his daughter Fausta. Initially the marriage did not seem to be a successful one, there being no children for nine years. Later, possibly forced by dynastic pressures, there would be five. Ultimately, it would end in tragedy.

Diocletian was eventually persuaded to come out of retirement to chair a summit to sort out the in-fighting, which was held at Carnutum, between Vienna and Bratislava on the Danube.[13] Maximian promised once more to retire, and another long-term friend of Galerius', Licinius, was made Augustus in the West. Constantine was confirmed as his Caesar, but by this stage the concept of the Tetrarchy was too broken to be effective. Diocletian returned to his cabbages. The newly elevated Licinius prepared to move against Maxentius, but one of the tribes who lived north of the Danube, the Sarmatians, attacked south across the river and he and Galerius were forced to divert their army to deal with them.

As Constantine surveyed the empire from Trier, he must have already decided that the only way it would achieve the cohesion and prosperity he sought was for it to be re-united under his rule. There are several theories as to his motivation. The Christian eulogists would have us believe that he had already decided to convert the known world to Christianity, something they saw as logical and inevitable. Others point to Constantine's belief that he was the true emperor because of his alleged descent from Claudius II, although it is hard to believe that an intelligent man like Constantine actually saw this as anything other than useful propaganda. Claudius was, anyway, not exactly of ancient patrician stock, being another successful soldier from Moesia who defeated the Goths but only reigned for two short years. Constantine's personal ambition, a sense of his own worth and superiority certainly played a part, but even the most cynical historian must allow for a degree of his wanting to stop the seemingly incessant civil wars and allow Europe to develop the economic potential he had witnessed. He certainly saw this as vital if he were to go on to defeat the Persians. Whatever his personal beliefs, he saw Christianity as the vehicle through which he could achieve his objectives. He would make it the religion of the army, of victory, the empire and a better life.[14]

Whatever his true motives in re-uniting the empire, what is absolutely clear is that he realized he needed to build an army that would allow him to do so. Various attempts had been made to reform the Roman army after Valerian's catastrophic defeat. Gallienus (260–268) had created a separate cavalry corps which Aurelian (270–275) had commanded with distinction, but the army that Diocletian inherited in 284 would have been familiar to Julius Caesar and Augustus.[15] It was still structured around legions of heavy infantry organized and equipped much as they had been for the last 300 years. Diocletian, himself a successful field commander, began the process of modernization, but it was Constantine who consolidated the reforms of the past decades to produce an army that was capable of furthering his ambition for the empire and which would never lose a battle during his reign.

A key issue for Constantine was how to improve the army's deployability. Legions tended to be based for a very long time in the same place, as we have seen in Britain, which meant that they lost their 'edge', becoming part of the everyday life of the communities served by their garrisons. The administration of provinces was the responsibility of governors who traditionally doubled up as military commanders, so that the civil administration became inextricably linked to the army. Legions were not just fighting troops but used by governors as police forces, as a pool of labour and for any other tasks that needed performing by an organized force with a hierarchical structure that answered to the central authority. By 314 Constantine had restructured the provinces themselves, dividing the empire into approximately 100 provinces, which were in turn divided into 12 dioceses each under an official called a *vicarius* or a *vices agens praefectorum praetorio*, a deputy to the praetorian prefect. There were then four praetorian prefectures: Gaul, Italy, Illyricum (modern Greece and the Balkans) and the East. Praetorian prefects now had no military responsibility.[16] This may have been because the business of civil administration was becoming too burdensome for one person to combine both functions. It was also because it removed any danger of a praetorian using the army to seize power and set themselves up as a rival emperor, although this became increasingly less plausible as Constantine tightened his central control. However, the main reason was to create a mobile command structure for the army easily separable from the civilian administration.

Each province now also had a *dux*, responsible for military matters, although it was common for one *dux* to command several provinces together. There were, for example, two *duces* (plural) in Britain but 12 along the Rhine and the Danube where the border was more threatened.[17]

Constantine's next move was to divide the army into two distinct parts: garrison troops who guarded the border and performed internal security duties under the *dux*, who were termed the *limitanei* or *ripenses* – literally guarding the limits/borders and the banks, given that the most contentious border was along the great European rivers. These units, which gradually became heavily reliant on cavalry to cover the distances involved in their patrolling, took the older, less fit soldiers. They were still broadly organized into legions, but their unit size was more flexible, depending on the local situation. Fitter, and, given the physical norms of the 4th century, younger, men were recruited into the field army – the *comitatus* – and known as *comitatenses*. Instead of a legion being required both to perform garrison duties and police the borders, this division meant that the field army could be trained and equipped to deploy and fight. The *comitatenses* enjoyed better terms of service than the *limitanei*, were paid more, had better equipment, and could expect to spend their lives on campaign. This meant that it was more difficult for them to marry; they were compensated by being allowed to serve for shorter periods and given generous resettlement grants when they did finally leave.

Constantine also addressed the issue of field command – long something of a problem for an army that had combined political and military responsibility in the same appointment, and which had led to a succession of tactically challenged patricians failing on the battlefield. Since the mid-3rd century, the practice had been for the army to supersede the old system by appointing its own most effective officers to high command; the majority of senior commanders and emperors between 260 and 306 had been professional officers, many of humble origin, and mostly from Moesia, Pannonia and the provinces that now form the Balkans. What Constantine did was to formalize the system, structuring the army to give a career path for able men to rise to the top. He created two senior posts – *magister equitum*, inspector of cavalry, and *magister peditum*, inspector of infantry – and a number of senior officers held the post of *magister militum*, who were entrusted with active command of armies when the emperor was not present. Under them were a whole range of ranks, mostly inherited from the old Roman army, from a junior soldier, or *munifex*, to a centurion, and the centurions in a legion were ranked according to their cohort, to a *praefectus* who commanded a legion. Typically by the time of Constantine's re-organization they had risen through the ranks, as opposed to being appointed due to family influence.[18]

There is considerable debate about the size of Constantine's legions. The traditional legion numbered approximately 5,000 when fully manned, which they rarely were because no military unit is ever at full strength, given such factors as sickness, absence or leave. Diocletian had originally split the legions into *seniores* and *iuniores*, literally senior and junior, which facilitated creating the new formations. It is very difficult to build a new army unit like a legion from scratch, as it needs experienced officers and older soldiers to train and develop recruits. By dividing an existing legion into those more suitable for garrison duty, the *seniores*, as opposed to those fitted for the field army, the *iuniores*, Diocletian and Constantine found a practical way both to structure the new units and for them to retain some legion esprit. Legions were fiercely proud of their history and traditions, so retaining the name and association was important – much as they always have been with regiments of all armies. A modern equivalent would be the way British infantry regiments are organized into battalions. Yet it is highly unlikely that both parts of the legion could be maintained at 5,000, and Constantine also saw the value in smaller units, which were easier to administer logistically but which, with improved weapons and training, could still have a similar impact on the battlefield. So while soldiers still 'belonged' to their parent legion, they found themselves increasingly being deployed in much smaller units, often referred to as *vexillationes*, or detachments, as the tactical situation demanded; these were probably around 1,000 men strong. Since Constantine, that has remained roughly the size of the infantry unit judged tactically most efficient, with contemporary infantry battalions ranging from roughly 600 to 1,100.

Constantine's next major reform was to the cavalry. Cavalry, organized in *alae*, or wings, had traditionally been an auxiliary force to the legions, which had remained the main strike force of the army. Gallienus had started to remodel the cavalry, something Diocletian continued, but it was Constantine who had seen how the Persians fought effectively mounted and who developed and institutionalized them as heavy and light cavalry. Traditionally Roman cavalry had been lightly armed and were used to act as flank guards, for skirmishing, on scouting and reconnaissance tasks and for liaison rather than as a strike force in their own right. During the 3rd century regiments of *lanciari*, who fought with light lances or javelins, were established, some of which were mounted wearing padded coats to provide some protection.

Constantine developed the *lanciari*, but he now gave both soldiers and horses armour for protection and equipped them with lances so that they could actually fight mounted. Known as *cataphracti*, but also widely referred to simply as *equites*, these regiments were revolutionary when deployed during the march into Italy in AD 312. When Constantine's regiments first appeared in front of the city of Segusio:

> what a spectacle that is said to have been, how dreadful to behold, how terrible, horses and men alike enclosed in a covering of iron! The men are covered with mail in the upper part, a corselet which extends down to the horses' chests and hangs to their forelegs protects them from the injury of a wound without impeding their gait.[19]

They were the forebears of the European knights in armour who would dominate the battlefield for the next millennium.

Cavalry regiments were typically 500 strong, the optimum number tactically which was also logistically supportable and which again remained the model size for cavalry regiments until they were disbanded in the First World War. Cavalry and infantry now trained and operated together as *comes*, or what today would be a brigade, often being permanently paired. Cavalry officers also started to assume high rank, which had previously been the preserve of the legion infantry. One critical reform was the introduction of a new cavalry saddle. Stirrups were not then used, making it more difficult for a rider to sit securely in his saddle and to absorb the shock of charging with a lance. Constantine's saddle had four corners, which kept the rider as secure as he could be without stirrups, although considerable skill and training was still required for recruits to achieve the necessary grip. He also brought together the various types of catapults and siege machinery to form specialist artillery regiments.

Within the cavalry Constantine created elite units whose role was to guard him and the staff of the imperial administrative offices who accompanied him. The Tetrarchs had each continued the tradition of the Praetorian Guard, originally created by Augustus as his personal bodyguard and intelligence service, and who had become rather a despised institution over the centuries. While the main praetorian base was in Rome, the Tetrarchs had copied their model in their own capitals. Organized as infantry, they also had a cavalry wing, the *equites singulares*. Constantine set up his own bodyguard, which was primarily cavalry, and when he took Rome in AD 312 he abolished the Praetorian Guard altogether. His concept was to create a series of regiments, called the *scholae palatinae*. He eventually created five of these, from which he drew an elite group of approximately 50 *candidati*, who were a combination of close personal bodyguards, advisers and companions. Many of his senior commanders came from the ranks of the *candidati*, which doubled up as a sort of higher command training school: men like Gaiso, who became governor in Spain; Flavius Salia, who would become *magister equitum*; Junius Bassus, who would be a praetorian prefect; Flavius Ablabius, who would tutor Constantius II, Constantine's son with Fausta; Bonitus, the first Frank to become a *magister militum*; Arcadius Proculus, who would also become a praetorian prefect; and many more.

Another innovation Constantine made was to integrate 'barbarian' units more fully into the army. The term 'barbarian' is confusing, being used for anyone who wasn't Roman but also for the tribes north and east of the great European rivers who regularly threatened the empire and would eventually overthrow it. Constantine was used to the concept of non-Roman units performing key functions – something which both made use of their specific skills, especially mounted units, and also helped swell numbers when recruiting was challenging. His father's personal bodyguard in Gaul and Britain had consisted of Gallic horsemen commanded by a splendid Gallic chieftain called Crocus, from the Alamanni tribe. He had originally been a strong opponent of Rome, leading a bloody revolt against Gallienus. Captured and sentenced to death, before his planned execution he was taken on a tour of Gaul to see the destruction his revolt had caused. He was then by comparison shown the delights of the Roman cities that he could have enjoyed, whereupon he repented and it proved politic to spare him. Devoted to Constantius, he assembled a unit of Alamanni warriors as his bodyguard. Constantine's policy had wider implications. He had seen during his visit in 303 that Rome had become irrelevant to the government of the empire. His world was what we would now regard as European as opposed to Roman, and he saw nothing threatening and illogical in including non-Romans more closely. Barbarian units, although often trained and led by Roman officers especially in the early part of his reign, became a key part of his army; by his death approximately 20 per cent of the officers were of non-Roman origin, including about 20 per cent of his closest companions, the *scholae palatinae*.

The size of Constantine's army varied considerably during his reign and obviously increased as he consolidated power, subsuming the armies of his rivals; by the 320s it may have reached 400,000. This required a constant flow of recruits to keep it up to strength, probably about 40,000 annually; over the centuries a 10 per cent turnover in armies has remained fairly consistent outside major wars. There were various ways in which young men could join the army. Many, probably most, were volunteers from within the empire. Given that everyday life was tough, the army offered regular pay and food and also the prospect of escaping from the drabness of tending animals or winding cloth, in much the same way that recruits have been attracted to serve for centuries. The sons of soldiers were also required to serve and were directed to join the same units as their fathers, which played to the idea of the legion as family although it was seen by some as a form of conscription.[20] Men from outside the empire could also volunteer, as we have seen, and many did, mostly from the tribes beyond the Rhine and the Danube but a few from Persia, Armenia and North Africa.[21] Another common form of recruitment were levies imposed on specific areas, especially those recently conquered, although there was an exemption system that allowed payment in lieu. A third method, and one applied increasingly as rival armies were defeated, was simply to enlist prisoners of war. The normal practice after a victory was to separate out a number of the fitter prisoners to be sold as gladiators, consign others to be executed in the various amphitheatres around the empire to satisfy the public's seemingly endless appetite for violent entertainment, but simply to recruit the majority into the imperial army.

And their terms of service were good. A legionary in that army received basic pay of 1,800 denarii, or 2,100 if he was a cavalryman, given that the cavalry had extra expenses for their horses. In addition, they received rations including oil and salt. However, the most important part of their pay was *donativi*, donatives or bonuses paid regularly either on special occasions, such as the emperor's birthday, or to celebrate some success. Typically about eight donatives were paid annually, which meant that a legionary's pay would be around 10,000 denarii each year.[22] Given that the average labourer's wage was around 40 denarii per day, which was just about a subsistence wage, a legionary was adequately but not well paid.[23] In AD 313, the best box in the theatre in Trier cost 60,000 denarii and a quality horse 40,000, considerably more than a male slave at about 5,000 denarii.[24] Pay rates escalated quickly with rank so that centurions received approximately 15–30 times what a young legionary got, depending on his appointment; a senior centurion could earn 300,000 denarii, which meant he could live very well. There was also a sophisticated saving scheme within the legion whereby soldiers were encouraged to invest half their donatives in a retirement fund. On joining, recruits were given a new identity, receiving the extra name 'Flavius', for Constantine's Flavian dynasty, and swearing an oath to the emperor. They were required to learn enough Latin to understand commands and were issued with their standard uniform and 'dog tags', discs worn around the neck so they could be identified.[25] Units had their own doctors and priests, although it is not clear at what stage these became Christian.

Constantine also reviewed and improved the terms under which a soldier served. A soldier in the *comitatus* now signed for 20 years, as opposed to the *limitanei*, who served for 24, reflecting the fact that they enjoyed relatively settled lives. On retirement soldiers were given generous discharge bonuses and exempted from the hated *munera*, or civic duties and taxes, and so were their immediate families while they were actually serving. Worried that if this was not actively policed veterans might slip into poverty, Constantine issued several laws to ensure that they did not. 'The framers of the revenue, also, shall not interfere with veterans who, after their long service, shall forever enjoy tranquillity,' he decreed, and another law allowed soldiers to leave their property to whomever they wished, unlike civilians who were bound by strict rules on inheritance. A special edict was also issued to ensure that veterans were 'given farms, money for equipment, a yoke of oxen and seed grain and tax exemptions'.[26] In 326 he issued a further law stating that veterans 'shall receive vacant lands and they shall hold them tax exempt in perpetuity'.[27] This is the first comprehensive law documented that was designed specifically to care for veterans.

Considerable effort went into ensuring that the army was well equipped and supplied. Arms factories were established across the empire, *fabricae*, another initiative begun under Diocletian but which Constantine developed. By the end of his reign there were 20 in the West and 15 in the East making weapons and armour.[28] The old plate armour, so familiar from images of the traditional legions, was slowly being replaced by chain mail, again something imported from Persia, which was easier and more flexible to wear on a horse as witnessed before Segusio.

The infantry now carried two javelins as well as their traditional short swords, the *gladius*, and were also issued with new weapons, such as weighted clubs, to use against cavalry, and lead-weighted darts. The old rectangular shield was replaced with a round one that was easier to handle, and helmets became lighter and less cumbersome without side and back plates. Again the new equipment went to the *comitatus* and it would take several years before the *limitanei* were similarly equipped.[29] Although some cavalry officers rode their own horses, the vast majority were issued from the wide network of stud farms that Constantine started across the empire. Horses had always been vital for transport, but the cavalry-orientated force now also needed the right stamp of war horse. Constantine was very horse-minded, being particularly interested in horse welfare and issuing specific laws to safeguard horses' well-being; one specified that horses could only be 'urged on not with clubs or sticks but only with whips'.[30] Horse care in the army, which had been wanting and compared unfavourably with the Persians, improved dramatically, meaning that the army could move faster and further. Constantine also pioneered a new circular design for cavalry stables which could be erected quickly while on campaign. It was based on a round thatched hut with a central pole. Each hut held about ten to 12 horses who were tethered with their heads facing inwards, thus reducing the danger of kicking and making it easier to feed and water them. These circular stables could either be easily made permanent with brick walls and tiled rooves once a garrison became permanent.

All this came at a substantial cost. Paying the army's wages alone has been estimated at 33,000 pounds of gold per annum.[31] In the early years of Constantine's reign, this was funded by a variety of specific taxes such as the *equorum collatio*, designed to pay for the cavalry's horses, and the *vestis militaris*, which was meant to pay for uniforms, while the *anona* was a grain levy that paid the army in kind so they could bake their bread. Gradually these somewhat clumsy levies were abolished in favour of paying the army in coin, helped considerably by Constantine's introduction of new gold coinage, based on the *solidus*, from 310. The new gold coins, coming relatively soon after Diocletian's disastrous Edict on Maximum Prices in 301, quickly gained peoples' confidence and became the standard currency throughout the empire, which now was effectively a gold-based economy.

Taxes were also paid in gold, which increased in supply as successive conquests made pagan temple gold available. The gradual improvement in trade as the empire became settled also meant that, despite the high cost of the army by the end of his reign, the state books were balanced and the currency stable.

These reforms did not all happen at once – some were not completed until the 320s – but they were well under way in the first decade of Constantine's reign. The army he slowly built up on the Rhine, and which he led into Italy in 312, was probably about 150,000. Of these, 100,000 were *limitanei* and stayed behind to guard the frontiers, while the field army numbered around 40,000, but they were the best trained and equipped force in the empire – restructured, experienced from raiding across the Rhine and confident. A majority probably came from Gaul, Britain and what today is the Balkans, a northern army as opposed to Maxentius' army drawn from southern Italy and his father's North African veterans. Constantine's army had specialist training officers, the *campidoctores*, generally the third most senior centurion in a legion, so carrying considerable authority. Their role, which Constantine appears to have formalized, was to ensure that the soldiers were all fully competent and to conduct field manoeuvres.[32] This training in warfare was to prove critical to their success. As important as the training were the expeditions mounted against the barbarian tribes across the Rhine, specifically the Alamanni and the Bructeri. One of these raids against the Bructeri in September 307 sheds an interesting light on Constantine's attitude. The tribe had been harassing Roman settlements along the Rhine and had taken advantage of Constantius' absence in Britain to raid into Gaul. As part of their punishment, two of their captured chieftains, Merogaisus and Ascaric, were taken back to Trier where they were sentenced to be eaten by wild beasts in the arena. They were not alone as, so the panegyrist tells us, 'the adults who were captured, whose untrustworthiness made them unfit for military service and whose ferocity for slavery, were given over to the amphitheatre for punishment and their great numbers wore out the raging beasts'.[33] This episode alone suggests that at this stage Constantine was unlikely to be Christian.

Constantine's strategy was first to secure control of the West, where his position was threatened less by Galerius, after his setbacks in trying to take Italy, but rather by Maxentius. He, Maxentius, had been declared emperor in Rome by the Praetorian Guard shortly after Constantine's accession in York and, having defeated Severus, then assumed the title of Augustus, again with no reference to Galerius who, in the curiously complex world of the Tetrarchy, was also his father-in-law. Despite Constantine now hosting his estranged father, Maximian, and being married to his sister, Fausta, Maxentius declared Constantine was a false emperor and a bastard. Maxentius appears to have been a competent politician and general who was backed by the formidable army of North Africa, 100,000 soldiers recently commanded so successfully by his father. He also enjoyed the authority of being in Rome with the senate and the Praetorian behind him. Despite severe food shortages the city remained supportive, not least because he was the one emperor of the five still then in office who would retain it as the capital. The few images we have of him, including one rather striking one on a coin, shows a boyish and thoughtful man devoid of laurels and with a distinctly un-imperial aspect.

Before Constantine could move against him, he had to deal with an unexpected problem in Gaul. In 310, while he was campaigning east of the Rhine, Maximian, his father-in-law, to whom he was extending protection, tried once more to seize power. He attempted to start a rebellion by subverting some of the troops Constantine had left behind. The soldiers remained loyal to Constantine, and Maximian fled to Marseilles. Constantine showed how decisively he could act, marched back across the Rhine, besieged Maximian in Marseilles and forced him to surrender. The story was that Maximian apologized and agreed to behave himself. Constantine accepted his apology, but that night Maximian crept into Constantine's chamber and tried to stab him as he slept. Forewarned, Constantine had substituted an unfortunate slave, who was duly murdered. Maximian was then told he had the option of execution or suicide and, being a proud Roman, chose the latter. Constantine then pronounced that peculiarly Roman sentence of *damnatio memoriae* (damnation of memory) on him, which meant that his name and memory were to be erased from all monuments and statues so that he should vanish as though he had never been. Fortunately, we have the works of Lactantius and Eusebius and his image on coins to tell us what he was like.

Galerius died in May the next year, AD 311. Lactantius could not resist pouring invective on the man he regarded as the worst of the persecutors as he lay dying. 'A malignant ulcer formed itself low down in his secret parts and spread by degrees' until, he reported gleefully, 'a gangrene seized all the neighbouring parts ... the distemper attacked his intestines, and worms were generated in his body. The stench was so foul as to pervade not only the palace but the whole city and his body with intolerable anguish was dissolved into one mass of corruption.'[34] In December he was followed to the grave by Diocletian, by then almost irrelevant. Licinius now became Augustus in the East, where he immediately faced a revolt from 'that half-barbarian' Daia who had allied himself to Maxentius. Constantine, realizing that he needed to protect his flank when he moved south, offered an alliance to Licinius, who gratefully accepted it. Constantine was now clear to move against Maxentius, crossing the Alps in the summer of 312.

His subsequent campaign stands out as being not only one of the most efficiently executed in history but also one which, possibly, had the greatest consequences for Europe. The first engagement was Segusio, now Susa, as the army disgorged from the Alps. Although Segusio shut its gates, Constantine's men managed to gain a foothold on one of them, forced them open and took the city, but there was no slaughter and the troops behaved well. Word now spread of his advance, and as he approached Turin he faced an army Maxentius had sent north under Ruricius Pompeianus, a competent general with experience in Africa. Constantine had placed his army on a rise. Pompeianus' cavalry appeared to have charged straight up the hill into Constantine's centre where his own heavy cavalry were positioned. They fell back and Pompeianus' horsemen were engaged by Constantine's club-wielding infantry. Panicked, they withdrew and Constantine then swept up Pompeianus' infantry with his *cataphracti*. It was a decisive victory. Both Augusta Taurinorum (Turin), and Mediolanum (Milan) then opened their gates without a fight.

Three rather sad tombstones were found near the Turin battlefield for members of one of Constantine's *scholae* who may have fallen guarding him as Pompeianus' horsemen charged. They were all part of a specialist Dalmatian sub-unit, the *Numerus Dalmatarium Divitensium*, two *exarchs* and a centurion who were *contubernalis*, which means they messed (shared their food) together – a sad reminder of the human cost of war.[35] Milan had an active Christian population by 312, and, to judge by the various contemporary inscriptions, a thriving Mithraic community as well. Neither Maximian nor Maxentius appear to have been much liked in northern Italy. Maximian, so Lactantius tells us, had behaved very badly while Milan was his capital, bringing false charges against rich citizens so he could seize their wealth, raping both boys and women, and 'delighting in blood and over-flowed with ill-gotten wealth'.[36] It would seem as if Constantine's reputation had gone before him, which, together with the good behaviour of his army, begins to add some colour to the concept of this being a campaign with a moral purpose.

Pompeianus made another stand at Verona but was again defeated, and he was killed. The road to Rome was now open and Constantine followed the route of the Via Flaminia south over the Apennines. He must have expected to be ambushed at various points along the way; there were several classic positions as the road passed through the mountains from which Maxentius' troops could have tried to halt his march. It's possible that he had to fight a skirmish at Spoletum, modern-day Spoleto. There is a gravestone there for Florius Baudio, a veteran almost certainly from Germany. He had 25 years' service and was 40 when he died, so he must have signed up at 15. He was an officer, a *vir ducenarius protector*, so a rank above a senior centurion and possibly commanding a detachment. Lactantius also mentions Maxentius having several successes over Constantine's army, which might support the notion that the passage of the army was not uncontested.[37]

Constantine approached Rome in mid-October. His army was estimated still to have been about 40,000 strong, while Maxentius had a far larger force. There was a rebellion in North Africa, not an uncommon experience at the time, and Maxentius had to leave a sizeable force there under his Praetorian Prefect Rufius Volusianus to ensure Rome's vital supply of corn was not interrupted; even allowing for that he probably faced Constantine with about 60,000–70,000 men. He also had the city of Rome to provision him and the Praetorian Guard, with the Imperial Household Cavalry, the *equites singulares Augusti*, to give his army authority. Rome was well defended, with its walls in good repair, so rather strangely he decided to leave the safety of the city and confront Constantine just north of the Tiber where the Via Flaminia drops from an escarpment and bends west towards the Milvian Bridge. It may have been a decision influenced by his having consulted the sacred *Sibylline Books*, a collection of prophecies by a sybil allegedly purchased by Lucius Tarquinius, the last king of Rome, and consulted in times of dire emergency, but regardless, he does not appear to have been particularly confident. Before he handed over control of the city to a prefect called Anullinus, he hid the symbols of his authority – sceptre, orbs and spears wrapped in linen – in a wooden box under the Palatine where they remained until they were discovered in 2006. He also moved his wife and surviving son away from the Palatine and into a house in the suburbs.[38] His army deployed with his most trusted troops, his household troops and the Praetorian, on his right in front of the river, with his less reliable troops in the hills on his left.

What is clear about Constantine's campaign is that he had an efficient intelligence service, almost certainly run through the *scholae*, although annoyingly we know little about how this operated. He had warning of Maxentius' move, something Maxentius had anyway made fairly obvious by building a bridge of boats just upstream of the Milvian Bridge to ferry his army across what was then a fast-flowing river. Constantine probably set up his headquarters at a place called Saxa Rubra, the red rocks, just north of Rome on the Via Flaminia. There is a farmhouse there with an arch that dates from Diocletian's time, which is popularly supposed to have been where he camped, but there is no hard evidence. It is also possible that his advance guard skirmished with Maxentius' men nearby, which may have forced a halt.

Constantine committed on 28 October, AD 312, advancing towards Rome and quite possibly hoping, despite what his intelligence was indicating, that the city might surrender as had Turin and Milan, but as the Via Flaminia neared the Tiber his scouts brought back reports that Maxentius' army had taken up battle positions. Constantine therefore drew his army up in his traditional two lines, with the majority of his cavalry on the left alongside the river, but, as the river bent, they also had the disadvantage of having it behind them. We are told that the night before the battle Constantine had a dream in which the 'Highest God' appeared and showed him the Chi Rho, the Christian symbol of a cross surmounted by a 'P' and told him, 'in this sign, conquer'. Constantine is then meant to have had his army paint the divinely revealed symbol on his soldiers' shields, no mean feat on the morning of a battle as they were manoeuvring into position and which would have tested even Constantine's efficient supply system. Using easily identifiable signs was a common practice when opposing armies were often dressed and equipped the same, and it may well be that the army had already adopted some sort of emblem so they could identify

Constantine's campaign in Italy

Constantine's army

Alternative routes to Mediolanum

N

50 mile
50km

Brigantium
Mt. Genèvre pass
Segusio
Augusta Praetoria
Eporedia
Augusta Taurinorum (Turin)
Vercellae
Ticinum
Dertona
Genua
Placentia
Cremona
VIA AEMILIA
Bergomum
Mediolanum (Milan)
Brixia
Tridentum
Verona
Hostilia
Mutina
Bononia
Ravenna
VIA POPILIA
Concordia
Aquileia
Ariminum
Fanum Fortunae
Furlo Pass
Scheggia Pass
VIA FLAMINIA
Forum Flaminii
Spoletium
Interamna
Narnia
Ocriculum
Saxa Rubra
Rome
Pons Mulvius

Battle of the Milvian Bridge: Opening Stages

River Tiber

Constantine's Army
Maxentius' Army
Cavalry
Infantry

Bridge of Boats
Milvian Bridge
Tor di Quinto
VIA FLAMINIA
VIA CASSIA
VIA TIBERINA CLODIA

friend and foe. What matters, however, is the mythology that grew up around Constantine's dream; it came to be seen as the defining moment in both his conversion and that of the empire, and in later years he was possibly not amiss to elaborating on it.[39] What is also clear is that the idea of Christianity, of the 'Highest God' being a God who was not only on Constantine's side but who favoured an ordered, hierarchical society where community was valued, became the dominant force in the Western Empire as it would soon also become in the East.

The battlefield – a narrow plain north of the Tiber surrounded by wooded hills, which you can still discern amongst the suburbs of the modern city – was a restricted space, in which over 100,000 men were crammed so tightly that there was little room to manoeuvre. Constantine's army had the physical and psychological advantage of space and could redeploy troops behind their lines, a move impossible for Maxentius' army, whose men were jammed between their enemy and the river. Maxentius himself appears to have stayed in the city until the last possible minute, only riding out to join his army as Constantine attacked. Constantine fought in the van but no doubt so closely surrounded by his *scholae* as to be almost impregnable. His army advanced; Maxentius' appears to have withstood the onslaught of the legions for a time but was slowly pushed back against the river, while Constantine's heavy and well-armoured cavalry pushed into his retreating infantry from Constantine's left, hacking into them as they struggled back towards the bridge. At some point panic appears to have set in amongst Maxentius' men, their retreat being restricted by the narrowness of the bridge of boats, which collapsed; hundreds of them were swept away by the Tiber, including

Maxentius himself, who 'went down into the depths like a stone, when he fled before the power of God which was with Constantine', Eusebius recounted with great glee.[40] On Constantine's right his cavalry moved forward to cut off those trying to flee over the Milvian Bridge itself, which seems to have already been damaged. Maxentius' troops on this flank appear to have been weaker – maybe recent recruits from North Africa and the local area, who may have not particularly cared who was to be their future emperor. Those who couldn't flee, surrendered.

Later Christian propaganda, and a lack of more objective sources, makes it difficult to determine exactly what gave Constantine such a complete victory, one of two which would give him ultimate control of the late Roman Empire. Leaving aside God's possible assistance, a more prosaic answer is that his army was far superior. We have seen how carefully he had trained and equipped it, and his men were now relatively experienced fighting Maxentius' legions after the north Italian battles. Again we don't know much about Maxentius' army, but we do know that it had spent time fighting an insurgency in North Africa. Bitter as some of the fighting there probably was, it would not have been comparable to facing a cohesive, combat-ready army like Constantine's, fielding the latest technology and fully prepared for warfighting. There must also be some doubt as to just how motivated Maxentius' troops were. The Praetorian and the household troops were almost certainly loyal, having much to lose, as maybe were his father's veterans. The loyalty of the North African and local Italian recruits, and those who had surrendered with Galerius and who were posted on the left, is more open to question. Even if we cannot accept the Chi-Rho story at face value, morale in Constantine's army was high and he was now a proven battlefield commander.

The next day Constantine made a ceremonial entry into Rome but, to the dismay of the city elders, omitted to offer a sacrifice to Capitoline Jupiter. He behaved much as he had in northern Italy, seeking no revenge, confirming Maxentius' city officials in post and simply assimilating what was left of his army into his own. He did, however, insist on the restitution of any confiscated church property, and he also, to their horror and disbelief, disbanded the Praetorians, posting them to distant parts of the empire. Their barracks was razed and became the site of the church of St John Lateran; you can still see its foundations in the crypt. There is something rather satisfactory in thinking of some arrogant, overweight Praetorian, so used to dictating affairs in Rome and parading in his splendid uniform, being sent to join a *ripenses* unit on some far-flung outpost on the Danube. It is also likely that Helena would soon make her home in Rome, which can only have helped further establish its credentials as the capital of Christendom – although her son's new city would soon cause that claim to be questioned. For good measure Constantine also issued a *damnatio memoriae* on Maxentius, as he had for his father Maximian.

Constantine didn't stay long in Rome, much to the agony of a city which slowly began to realize that the centre of the empire was now in the east and North Africa, although Helena appears to have spent some considerable time there. Rome, however, worked a cunning revenge on Constantine, constructing an abomination of a victory arch to him which would be unveiled at his *decannalia*, the celebration of the tenth anniversary of his accession, in 316. Probably initially started for Maxentius, it was intentionally crude, oblique in its references to God, and with much of its decoration plundered from other monuments. It was, and remains to this day, the most Roman of insults. It also has interesting inscriptions. It makes no direct reference to the Roman gods but neither does it acknowledge the part apparently played in Constantine's victory by the Christian God. Instead it says that Constantine won 'by the inspiration of divinity and the greatness of his own mind'. That would be significant, as Constantine later tried to work out whether he was really some sort of god himself. It also has graphic scenes of Constantine's army forcing Maxentius' men into the river and contains some interesting historical details such as trumpeters blowing battlefield calls, an indication of the growing sophistication of the army's organisation.

From Rome Constantine moved to meet Licinius in Milan, where they would together issue the famous Edict of Milan in 313. This allowed freedom of worship to Christians across the empire but did not, despite what later Christian writers would have us believe, make Christianity the state religion. Eusebius, who can be justly accused of being the most persistent of Constantine's eulogizers, actually writes that the two emperors proclaimed that they were 'resolved, that is, to grant to the Christians and to all men freedom to follow the religion which they choose, that whatever heavenly divinity exists may be propitious to us and to all that live under our government'.[41] It was a remarkably tolerant pronouncement, the wisdom of which would sadly escape future rulers. There remains much controversy over whether it really was an edict at all, but as with the dream before the Milvian Bridge, it would subsequently be used to strengthen Constantine's legacy. Licinius married Constantine's sister, Constantia, and the two emperors agreed an equitable split of the empire between East and West, with Licinius governing from Nicomedia and Constantine from Trier and Milan.

Later in 313 Licinius defeated the half-barbarian Daia and there followed a period of relative peace. It was around 314 that the empire was officially split into 12 dioceses each under its own *vicarius*. Constantine's Western Empire comprised Britannia, Galliae, Viennensis, Italia, Hispaniae and Africa; while Licinius, still technically the senior Augustus although at that stage no match militarily for Constantine, took Oriens, Pontica, Asiana, Thracia, Moesia and Pannonia.[42] The future links between the Christian church and the Roman state were becoming clear, lending weight to the view that Constantine saw the value of Christianity as a model for stable, hierarchical civilian government. Between 312 and 316 he busied himself establishing the Western Empire on a secure footing, probably visiting Britain again, being drawn into a series of tiresome Christian theological quarrels which tried his patience, and securing the Rhine against the persistent attacks by the Alamanni. But from 316 the relationship between the two emperors began to break down. The reasons are unclear. In 315 Licinius and Constantia had a son, followed by Constantine and Fausta the following year, their first child after nine years of marriage. Constantine already had Crispus with Minervina, who was now growing up, but he was possibly seen as being born outside the imperial circle. There were also various machinations around creating new Caesars, junior emperors, the details of which are irrelevant to this story but suggest that part of the reason for Licinius and Constantine falling out may have been dynastic. In 316 they clashed at Cibalis near Sirmium in modern-day Serbia and not far from Constantine's birthplace at Naissus. It was an overwhelming victory for Constantine, which he followed up the following year at Mardia in Thracia, modern-day Bulgaria. Licinius' army proved more effective than it had at Cibalis and, although still outclassed, the battle cost Constantine heavy casualties. The war was ended by a treaty negotiated at Serdica in March 317, by which Constantine gained significant territory from Licinius in what today we call the Western Balkans, although still left Licinius in control of Thracia and the dioceses to its east.

Constantine's two motivating forces – the ambition to unite the empire and to establish a unifying system of governance which Christianity offered – together with his dislike of Rome now drew him to the East. He may still have seen the Bosphorus as offering a more definitive border between him and Licinius; more probably, given his early life and possibly influenced by his adored Minervina being from Antioch, he saw the empire as a whole over which he sought sole authority. In 324 he again pursued Licinius, defeating him first at Adrianople, again in Thracia in July, and finally at Chrysopolis, just on the Asian side of the Bosphorus, in September. Interestingly, the Chi-Rho story makes a reappearance here, the labarum on which it was displayed apparently causing Licinius' troops to melt away. Licinius was captured and his life temporarily spared although he was later executed.

Constantine was now free to turn his attention to other matters. In 325 he enacted a whole series of military reforms which both unified what was left of the Eastern army into a single force with his own Western army, and consolidated the terms of service of the various component parts, *comitatenses* and *limitanei* and the benefits they received. He still had years of fighting before him as he campaigned along the Danube to control the Alamanni and the Gothic tribes that threatened Thracia and Moesia. In 325 he was preparing for a campaign against the Persians. He remained ever conscious that the army was his power base.

In 326 he moved his capital to Constantinople, founding what would become one of the world's greatest cities and the capital not only of the later Roman and Byzantine empires but also of the Eastern Christian Church. By the time he died in 337 he had also adjudicated on the divinity of Christ. The Council of Nicaea, over which he presided in 325 in the town just south of Byzantium, would become one of the most important of the round of tortuous theological arguments to which the Christian church would subject itself. The resulting Nicene Creed, articulated by Constantine, makes him certainly the most quoted Roman emperor and possibly one of history's most quoted men, ever. The task of the council was to determine whether Jesus Christ was actually the son of God, so consubstantial with the Father, or a human who had been chosen by God for his special purpose, the so-called Arian heresy after Arius, the North African bishop who proposed it. There were, as with all such debates, pressing political issues which affected the outcome. Constantine himself was consumed with rage with Crispus. It is not clear what Crispus had done but Constantine had him executed that year along with Fausta, whom he had suffocated in her steam bath, which possibly distracted his attention from heavy theological debate. Those who opposed Arius were led by a clique of bishops from Alexandria. They threatened to cut off the grain supply to the empire – which remained largely dependent on the North African harvest – if they did not get their way.

Constantine is thought to have favoured Arius' position; he knew that he, as emperor, was worshipped as a god in several parts of the empire, much as previous emperors had been. He was, after all, possessed of supreme, godlike powers and had actually designed a niche for his statue alongside that of Jesus Christ in the Church of the Apostles he was building. In the event, practical politics won through, and Arius' position was declared heretical which, given the subsequent effect of his pronouncement, must be regarded as something of a tragedy.

It is a fascinating story, as is the building of Constantine's great city which bore his name until it became Istanbul after the First World War, but one that sadly is not relevant to the point of this book. That is rather to demonstrate that by thinking through exactly what an army should be, completely restructuring it, uniting civilian and military power, building a proper defence industry, looking after its soldiers, ensuring it was affordable and endowing it with a moral purpose, Constantine created one of history's most successful armies and one that would, despite some serious interruptions, still be a formidable force 1,100 years later. It succeeded because it was an army prepared for warfighting, for high-intensity combat forged from Constantine's experiences in Persia, while Maxentius' army had been busy conducting counter-insurgency in North Africa.

The *Panegyric of Nazarius*, delivered in Rome in 317, and admittedly more a work of flattery than objective commentary, says, 'For there was also your army, flourishing and firm, full of strength, full of spirit, delighting in arms and performing its military duties out of eagerness rather than necessity, since its years of service are fewer than its battles', which Nazarius quickly corrects: 'by battles I mean victories and besides as fond of you as you are of them'.[43] Certainly flattery, but flattery with more than a grain of truth. A modern 21st-century soldier standing in Constantine's battle line would have recognized many of the features of the army that surrounded him. Yet he might have felt even more at home had he stood in the ranks of another army, over 1,100 years later, as it prepared to destroy the last vestige of the empire that Constantine had created.

Chapter Three

The Ottoman Army of Mehmet the Conqueror, 1453

'Verily they will conquer Constantinople. Truly their commander will be an excellent one. Truly that army will be an excellent one!'

Hadith attributed to the
Prophet Mohammed

On the morning of 11 April 1453 the army of Sultan Mehmet II stood in front of the great walls of Constantine's city, capital of the Eastern or Byzantine Empire for over 1,100 years. Rebuilt by the Emperor Theodosius in the 5th century, the 100-foot walls had never been breached. Around the sultan were encamped the 80,000 soldiers of his army, including 10,000 janissaries and 70 cannon. Nicolo Barbaro, a Venetian who wrote a detailed account of the events that were about to unfold and who was perched high on the walls, counted 145 galleys as Mehmet's fleet moved slowly towards the city through the calm blue waters of the Bosphorus. As the sun rose, the largest cannon, a giant of 27 feet named Basilica, manufactured and commanded by a Hungarian called Orban, fired the first of its 800-pound stone balls at the walls. The siege of Constantinople had begun.

What astounded many observers was that the sultan was able to field such a formidable army at all. The Ottomans were one of the Turcoman tribes who had emerged from central Asia and settled in Anatolia and the country east of the Black Sea since the 8th century. Successive waves of Mongols from central Asia pushed them further and further west so that they began to bite into Byzantine territory. The Seljuk Turks emerged as the principal Turcoman dynasty at some time during the 13th century and, under their charismatic leader Alparslan, inflicted a major defeat on the Byzantines at Manzikert in 1071. This cleared their path to what is now western Turkey and effectively isolated Constantinople from the south. During the next 300 years there was a gradual power shift as the Seljuks were themselves defeated by a subsequent Mongol invasion and lost influence to another Turcoman tribal group, the Osmanli or Ottoman Turks.

Their first known leader was Ertugrul, but it was his son, Osman, who became their sultan in 1299, who is held to be the real founder of the dynasty. Osman was famous because of a dream that entered Ottoman folklore. He saw a tree sprouting from his navel whose shade encompassed the world. Taken as a sign of God's intention that he would found an imperial dynasty, Osman's dream became a guiding force in his descendants' rise. In 1301 he inflicted a decisive defeat on the Byzantine emperor at Bapheus, effectively giving the Ottomans control of Bithynia or the area immediately south of Constantinople. He died in 1323, leaving a legacy of conquest so that by the mid-14th century the Ottomans had established control over not only Anatolia and Bithynia to the south and west but also the area north-east of Constantinople, pushing west into what is now Bulgaria. In 1346 Osman's son, Orhan, took the important Byzantine city of Bursa which controlled access to the Dardanelles, the narrows where the Sea of Marmara joins the Aegean, crossed into Europe and began to expand north and west into the Balkans. In June 1389 an Ottoman army led by Sultan Murad fought and defeated an army drawn from Central and Eastern Europe commanded by Prince Lazar of Serbia in Kosovo. Although it was, narrowly, an Ottoman victory, it was an expensive one, with both Murad and Lazar amongst the dead alongside tens of thousands of their soldiers. Marked by terrible atrocities, with the Ottomans systematically executing those prisoners they couldn't sell into slavery, it has entered Serbian legend as the battle of Kosovo Polje, the Field of the Blackbirds, the battle that defines the Serbian nation. Serbia became an Ottoman vassal state. Murad was succeeded by his son Beyazit, who is thought to have murdered his brother Yakub, thereby establishing a grisly Ottoman precedent, and who pushed further north into Hungary. In 1396 he decisively defeated an ill-prepared and badly led crusader army at Nicopolis on the Danube. With Constantinople now surrounded by Ottoman lands, it looked as if its fall must be imminent, and in 1397 Beyazit blockaded it. The Byzantine Emperor Manuel managed to slip out and spent three fruitless years attempting to raise military support from the West.

Ironically, it was another Mongol invasion that spared Manuel and Constantine's city. In 1402 Tamerlane, claiming spiritual and possible blood descent from Genghis Khan, and fresh from subduing Persia, moved into Anatolia. There followed an increasingly bizarre stand-off between Tamerlane and Beyazit involving the exchange of some extraordinary insults, but on 28 July 1402 their armies clashed near Ankara.

They fought all day with neither obtaining a decisive advantage, despite Tamerlane using both war elephants and an early version of a chemical weapon – an incendiary substance which later became known as Greek Fire. Eventually Tamerlane's reserves surrounded Beyazit's men, who began to desert, and both he and his son Murad were taken prisoner. Three of his other sons fled, but by that evening the Ottoman Empire was reduced to what it had been in 1390, with Tamerlane in turn pushing west to Smyrna, modern-day Izmir, where, true to form, he decapitated the population. Beyazit's supposed fate would entertain chroniclers and playwrights for years, the most popular rumour being that Tamerlane kept him in a silver cage. Whatever became of him, he was dead the next year.

The Mongols were reluctant colonists, preferring to destroy and plunder rather than settle, and then to move on. Tamerlane duly left Anatolia to invade China, leaving Beyazit's three surviving sons to fight for what was left of the empire. Eventually in 1413 Mehmet I emerged victorious, being succeeded by his son Murad in 1421, by which time, with Tamerlane now long-since departed and no Western powers coming to the Byzantine emperor's assistance, the Ottoman lands were almost back to where they had been prior to the disaster of 1402. Constantinople was an increasingly isolated vestige of what had once been the mighty Roman Empire. Murad ruled until 1451, either alone or in partnership with his son Mehmet II, who now stood before the Theodosian Walls.

However, both Mehmet I and Murad realized that their army, although successful against the chaotic crusader force at Nicopolis, had failed them at Ankara and that if Osman's dream was to be realized then it needed to be completely reformed. The traditional Ottoman method of warfare was to employ waves of fast-moving and lightly armoured mounted archers to provoke and entice the more heavily armoured Byzantine and European troops to break from their positions to pursue them. When they did so the Ottomans then turned, surrounded and slaughtered them. This was much as the Turcoman and tribes from the Asian steppes had waged war for millennia, a tactic that was said to trace its roots to the great Arab conquests of the 7th and 8th centuries. It was remarkably repetitive, and what surprised the Ottoman commanders was that their Western opponents never seemed to appreciate that. It was probably as well for them that they had not, because the make-up of the 14th-century Ottoman armies did not lend itself to more flexible tactics. The core of the army was found from landowners, *timaris*, who held *timars*, or fiefs, in return for which they were liable for military service together with a number of soldiers. Known as the *timariot* system, it operated very much like the feudal system in Western Europe. The problem was that when everything was going well, with land and slaves being acquired, the *timariot* system worked effectively, but when it came to a hard-fought battle like Ankara, a large part of Beyazit's army had deserted; the western Anatolian tribes and the Tartars were blamed in particular. Over time the *timar* holders had also become too involved in administering their estates, losing their military edge and developing power blocs which threatened the cohesion of the empire. When they did deploy they tended to act as individual war lords rather than as part of an overall command structure, and their cavalrymen, their *sipahis*, were liable to become more interested in looting than fighting.

There was also a lack of professional infantry, with foot soldiers being conscripted by the *timaris* but lacking any consistent training. There was no full-time core which could be trained to develop the new ways of fighting that were becoming apparent from the European campaigns. Above all, the sultans did not have direct control of their armies, something which contradicted the highly centralized system of government on which the Ottoman state was based. Attempts had been made to solve this problem by employing slave soldiers, an ancient Arab practice originally used by the great Islamic Abbasid caliphs. In the late 14th century the Ottomans established a slave-based system where they selected fit prisoners of war and men from conquered territories and subjected them to intensive training in a school at Gallipoli, the *Acemi Ocağı* or the 'Hearth of the Inexperienced'. There they spent two years being trained as infantrymen but were also employed as naval construction workers and galley slaves for the fleet. Conditions were primitive and harsh. Unsurprisingly, this experiment was only a limited success, ex-prisoners and captives not necessarily being the most enthusiastic members of the army which had defeated them. There was also the dreadful lesson of the Mamelukes, the slave soldiers who had got rid of their masters, the Ayyubid dynasty in Egypt, and established their own government and empire in its place, which now sat menacingly on the Ottomans' southern frontier. Clearly there were advantages to a slave army but it needed radical reform if it was to be kept under control.

Neither Mehmet I, whose short reign ended in 1421 when he was thrown from his horse, nor Murad II had the luxury of rebuilding their army at peace. Succession wars lingered on into the 1420s, with a combination of impostors and relations jostling for the throne, while both Hungary and Venice used the resulting instability to combat Ottoman expansion in the Balkans. Meanwhile the Marcher Lords, the great landholders in Anatolia, hedged between support for Shah-Rukh, Tamerlane's heir, who threatened from afar, and the Ottomans. The Emirate of Karaman continued to resist Murad's forces, as did the rulers of Aydin, Mentese and Germiyan. This need to maintain forces capable of both facing the Western powers in the Balkans while maintaining peace in Anatolia and the east of the empire was to become one of the key drivers of Ottoman policy in general and of their military policy in particular, much as it had preoccupied their Roman and Byzantine predecessors who had ruled between Europe and Asia.

The unrest lent urgency to the army reforms and especially to the creation of the *Kapıkulu*, or full-time professional troops directly under the sultan, of which the major and most celebrated corps were the *Yeniçeri Ocağı*, the new soldiers or janissaries. The Ottoman reaction to the failure of their original slave soldier scheme was pragmatic. If the existing soldiers were unenthusiastic and disloyal, then the system must be revised to create one capable of correcting these faults. That meant recruiting at a much younger age to allow soldiers to become properly educated – or perhaps more accurately, indoctrinated – in both Islam and the Ottoman way. The result was the *devşirme*, the forced enslavement of boys on a quota system. Boys from conquered territories were taken, although when there were not enough the quota was applied to provinces across the empire.

Konstantin Mihailović, a Serbian janissary, wrote:

Whenever the Turks invade foreign lands and capture the people, an imperial scribe follows immediately behind them, and whatever boys there are, he takes them all into the Janissaries. If, however, the number of them from enemy peoples does not suffice, then he takes them from the Christians in every village in his land who have boys, having established what it is that every village can give so that the quota will always be full.[1]

The quota was set as one boy in 40, and boys taken through the *devşirme* were known as *chilik*, meaning 'one of 40' in Persian, while those taken as war booty were called *pendik*. The difference appears to have been jealously observed, with the *chilik* boys allowed to leave their property to their families on their deaths while the *pendik* boys' property reverted to the sultan. The elite were those recruited via the *devşirme*.

The burden fell most heavily on the Christian provinces in the Balkans, the Slavs being thought to make the best soldiers and to be more physically robust. Sometimes the quota was applied across the Anatolian provinces, both by the sultan and the local rulers, but Turkish boys and Muslims were excluded, except in Bosnia. Jews and gypsies were not taken, as they were thought to be unsuitable, while Russians and Persians were thought too undisciplined, so the burden fell largely on the Ottoman European lands. The idea was that by taking boys young they were more impressionable and amenable and could also be trained physically to the tough standards required, especially drawing bows. The age bracket was wide, with the youngest around eight and the eldest up to 18, although the target was 13- to 14-year-olds. They were taken to Istanbul, where they were processed and suffered the pain and indignity of circumcision. They were then categorized according to ability and, inevitably, by looks. Those judged most suitable were sent on for further education in one of the palace schools, from which they would enter the personal service of the sultan; it was from this privileged group that so many future grand viziers would come. Slightly strangely, the more physically fit would become palace gardeners, which was also a route to high office. The majority, however, were destined to be janissaries and were sent out to live with Turkish farming families for a period that seems to have varied between four and eight years both to toughen them up and so they could learn Turkish customs and manners and become good Muslims. If they tried to escape, they were liable to be sold on as ordinary slaves. They then returned to the *Acemi Ocağı*, which Mehmet later moved to Istanbul, where they completed their training.

The *devşirme* probably started in the 1390s but was not enforced during the civil war, so it was not until the 1420s that it was actively prosecuted. It drew predictable outrage from Western commentators, who objected not so much to the enslavement but that the boys were forcibly converted. 'What would a man not suffer were he to see a child whom he had begotten and raised... carried off by the hands of foreigners, suddenly and by force, and compelled to change over to alien customs and become a vessel of barbaric garb, speech, impiety and other contaminations,' lamented the Metropolitan of Thessaloniki.[2] In 1438 a monk called Brother Bartholomew wrote a 'Letter on the barbarity of the Turks', in which he raged, inaccurately, that one in ten Christian boys was taken, whom the sultan made 'his special slaves and shield-bearers and, what is worse, Saracens'.[3] Yet the system may not have been quite as barbaric as it was portrayed. Certainly boys were enslaved and converted, but life in the sultan's service potentially offered considerably more opportunity than that as a peasant farmer in the Balkans. Although the boys were forcibly converted, they were paid and later allowed to marry. Many would rise to the highest ranks in the Ottoman system, a system that was based on slavery in a way that is difficult for modern commentators to understand.

Once they had completed their military training back in the *Acemi* the boys still had another phase to complete before becoming janissaries. They were initially allocated to one of 31 'dormitories', where they were given domestic duties in the palace or the dockyards or on construction projects. They were finally drafted into the janissaries as vacancies allowed, by which time they were thought to have been thoroughly indoctrinated and capable of being loyal soldiers, an assertion that was to prove largely correct. They were then trained in specific military skills, 'some as archers who shoot bows, some are gunners who shoot mortars, others muskets, and still others crossbows', but the majority were trained as infantrymen who would form the core of the *Kapıkulu*, the standing army on which the Ottomans came to rely.[4] Initially, as the system bedded in, they numbered around a thousand, but they grew rapidly so that by the mid-15th century there were 12,000 of them, costing the sultan's treasury 66 million *akça* – a fifth of the entire military budget.[5] By the middle of the 16th century their numbers had risen to 35,000.

Over the coming century the janissaries would develop their own idiosyncrasies, using their power as a permanent armed and organized force at the centre of government for their own ends. Although 'the loyalty of the corps to the Ottoman dynasty was never in doubt', thus demonstrating the effectiveness of Murad and Mehmet's re-working of their recruitment and training, 'this did not preclude disloyalty to individual sultans'.[6] They would force the abdication of Beyazit II in 1512 and later murder two other sultans. Various grand viziers would try to limit their numbers partly because of cost but also because of this disproportionate power they could wield, and janissary mutinies and power struggles would become commonplace in the story of the empire. However, what is sometimes overlooked is that possession of the corps gave the sultans a counterweight to the traditional land-based Turcoman aristocracy who now no longer enjoyed a monopoly of force. The strength of the corps was undoubtedly one of the main factors in allowing the sultans to exercise supreme power and which gave Mehmet the authority he needed to reform the *timariot* system.

As the size of the corps grew so its internal organization and structure matured, and what had been one unit was divided into regiments, the first use of such a system in Europe and one which pre-dated Western European armies by at least a century. It was much the same logic that had led Constantine to reduce the size of his legions, creating units of a size that could be efficiently employed on the battlefield or which could become the repository of a specialist military skill. The Ottoman system was decimal, with units being divided into groups of 10, 100 or 1,000, a system which is perpetuated in the contemporary Turkish army where a captain is called a *yüzbaşı*, or 'head of 100', while a major is a *binbaşı*, or 'head of 1,000', and a major general a *tümgeneral*, or 'head of 10,000'. A corporal was known as an *onbaşı*, so the head of ten.

The regiments soon became the focus of the soldiers' loyalty, a replacement family, a concept still prevalent almost universally amongst armies today. Each regiment quickly adopted their own unique identity and customs, their own standards (flags), often with horse tails affixed to their poles and topped by a crescent finial, and special symbols – images of which the young janissaries had tattooed on their shoulders. Uniform was common across the corps, with their distinctive high white bonnets denoting their royal links, and was issued by the government again well ahead of any Western army providing standardized equipment. Overcoats and red shoes were issued, although senior officers had yellow shoes and junior officers, black ones. Distinctive variations in dress were awarded, such as special turbans, for acts of especial valour. Bands were introduced both to add impetus to marches and to instil enthusiasm in battle, another tradition introduced long before it was common to European armies.[7] They were particularly keen on drums, which were used to signal – in much the same way as other armies would use trumpets – and also to accompany attacks, when they had the effect of both encouraging the janissaries and terrifying the enemy. Increasingly, bands became used in parades and ceremonial, accompanying the parading of regimental banners with their horse tails, again something that would be imitated in the West.

Of particular interest was the system of generating officers. They were not posted in from privileged families, as would later become common with other European royal guards, but were generated within the corps so that apart from the commander in chief, the *Yeniçeri Ağası*, the Aga of the Janissaries, who was appointed directly by the sultan, there was genuine promotion by a combination of length of service and merit. Were a senior janissary to be passed over for promotion then he would be compensated by being awarded a valuable *timar* or another military appointment. Officers were known by a bizarre series of ranks that related to cooking, although the origins of this rather strange focus on food are unknown. The most revered janissary symbol was the sacred cauldron, the *Kazan-i-Şerif*, with regimental commanders known as *Çorbası*, or Chief Soup Maker; quartermasters were *Aşibaşı*, or Chief Cook, and lieutenants were *Odabaşı*, or Head of the Mess. It was a system of strange customs and rituals that will be familiar to anyone with military service, the quirks and traditions that serve to bind men together when they must face the hazards of war but which also serve to give structure to their life in peacetime.

Whatever its traditions and idiosyncrasies, the creation of a permanent infantry force was to transform the military capability of the Ottoman army. Janissaries could now be trained in new weapons and tactics knowing that there would be a long-term return on that investment and that it would not all be forgotten as soon as a campaign was over. Consequently, the traditional Ottoman tactics, which had failed so spectacularly in Kosovo and at Ankara, could be replaced with new methods of fighting derived from the lessons of these campaigns. Janissary regiments specialized in new techniques, so that the 82nd Zenberekçi Regiment specialized in steel crossbows, while the 22nd and 92nd specialized in firearms. The traditional janissary weapons remained the bow and sword, but Mehmet was particularly interested in developing the use of muskets, so that by the early 15th century the janissaries had introduced volley fire by ranks – nine ranks, given the length of time it took to load a contemporary weapon using 'a kneeling or standing position without the need for additional support or rest'.[8] They used this technique to devastating effect at the battle of Mohács in 1526. Other regiments had slightly alternative roles reflecting their nature as personal troops, so that three regiments – the 64th, 68th and 71st – were dedicated to breeding hounds and organizing royal hunting parties, something that was as important to the sultans as it was to their royal counterparts across Europe.

Importantly, the janissary structure allowed the study and development of battlefield tactics to utilize these new weapons and skills. Rather than the traditional Turcoman feigned-retreat tactic, Mehmet introduced a totally different technique which maximized the advantage he now possessed in trained infantry and superior weapons. The army would instead be centred on a strong defensive position manned by the janissaries, created with trenches and palisades, sometimes with wagons lashed together, a tactic copied from the Hungarians – the so-called *wagenberg* – so that the enemy were drawn into attacking it. Light cannon, musket and bow fire would then fix the enemy in position. 'They shoot muskets, spears (arrows) in abundance and all sorts of other defensive things that are necessary stand in profusion', commented Mihailović. 'The shot from the bows is very heavy.'[9]

The job of luring the enemy into attacking this fortified position was that of the *azabs*, part-time infantry recruited from across the empire as a forced levy as and when they were needed. All able-bodied men who were of fighting age and who were not slaves were eligible for recruitment, which was conducted by local magistrates usually on the basis of one soldier per 20 households. Each of the 19 households exempted then had to contribute towards the selected man's costs and his equipment and had to provide a guarantee of his conduct. It is difficult not to judge the *azabs* as anything but cannon fodder, 'conscripts whose lives were expendable', an inferior body to the janissaries who, although some ended up in semi-permanent service such as manning fortresses, were there as a screening force.[10] With only basic training, they were not dissimilar to the men produced by levies across Western Europe. Numbers varied depending on the requirement, so that before Constantinople Mehmet had as many as 20,000 who would take the brunt of the Greeks' defensive fire as they attempted to storm the walls. Their presence was evidence of the ruthless efficiency of Mehmet's system.

Although the balance of the army was now weighted more to the infantry, the cavalry continued to play a key role. Alongside the janissaries, Murat and Mehmet created a Household Cavalry, a select force that originally numbered 1,500 but which rapidly grew to about 7,500. Their role was the intimate protection of the sultan both on campaign and in the palace. There were six regiments, referred to as the 'The people of the six regiments' or more commonly as the 'Cavalry of the Porte', literally the gate of the palace. Each had a specific role. The two most senior, the *silahdaran* and the *sipahiyah*, were the most prestigious and originally recruited from the sons of palace staff and the land-owning aristocracy, although Mehmet soon put a stop to this, preferring to recruit from the same pool as the janissaries. They were the largest, numbering over 5,000 each by 1500, were closest to the sultan, paid better than the janissaries and thus were offered considerable opportunity for advancement.[11] The remaining four regiments, which were raised later, were termed either 'salaried men' or 'poor strangers', both being more in keeping with the social strata Mehmet trusted. As a permanent salaried force, the six regiments were able to develop cavalry tactics and weapons in the same way the janissaries did for the infantry. This was, again, an innovation and, as with so much else from Mehmet's army, would establish a pattern in Europe for generations, being the model on which both Louis XIV's *Maison Militaire du Roi* and the British Household Cavalry were based.

Yet the bulk of the cavalry were still founded under the *timar* system, albeit a much reformed one. The basis of the system, whereby a *sipahi* held an estate in return for military service together with a prescribed number of men determined by the size of his landholding, remained the same. What changed was that Mehmet II removed many of the long-established aristocracy from their estates, replacing them with soldiers who had distinguished themselves on operations or who held palace office. The largest estates, those worth over 100,000 *akçe*, were reserved for senior commanders and governors, while the mid-size holdings were allocated to regimental commanders. Ordinary estates worth about 2,000 *akçe* were gifted to junior officers. The only way of achieving *timariot* status was therefore through distinguished military or government service, although inevitably the system was open to corruption. In newly conquered lands *timars* were granted to effective commanders who could mobilize and lead local manpower. Those who failed to produce their quota were immediately replaced and then disqualified from re-applying for a *timar* for seven years, a most effective way of getting rid of the well-established aristocracy who had grown fat off the land in the closing decades of the 14th century. The numbers produced by the *timar* system again varied according to need, but they were still numerically the most important part of the army; in the campaigns of the 1470s there were 40,000 from Rumeli, or Europe, and 24,000 from Anatolia, although this balance would gradually alter so that by 1500 there were similar numbers from each. In the field they occupied the wings; those from Anatolia were placed on the right while those from Rumeli were on the left. Their role was to surround and destroy the enemy once they had been fixed by the janissaries in their well-defended static position, a tactic which seemed to work repeatedly as European armies failed to learn the lessons of previous battles.

Perhaps Mehmet's most successful innovation was in his organization and use of artillery. Cannon development has been seen as a largely European affair, but it was Mehmet who saw the potential of using artillery both in sieges and to support the army actually on the battlefield – what came to be termed field artillery. Gunpowder, a mixture of saltpetre (potassium nitrate), sulphur and charcoal, seems to have emerged from China in the 8th century and, as with so many ideas and inventions, to have travelled slowly to Europe via Ottoman lands. The Ottomans had experimented with firearms in the late 14th century, but it was Mehmet who saw their real value and whose adoption of the new technology would revolutionize the battlefield. The industry he nurtured was multi-faceted. Although well known for the production of large siege cannon used for battering the walls of cities and which were manufactured to fire a ball in as straight a line as possible, Ottoman engineers also produced mortars and what were later referred to as howitzers – guns that fire a projectile or explosive in a parabolic curve. They also produced lighter, more portable guns which came to be known as culverins and which could be fitted to ships.

Importantly, the industry also started to produce muskets – individual firearms that fired a ball and that could be carried and operated by a single soldier. The development of the musket would be as fundamental to warfare as the advent of cannon, leading to the infantry gradually becoming dominant on the battlefield over the armoured cavalry, which had traditionally been regarded as the battle-winning arm. Mehmet therefore faced the inevitable resistance to innovation from his cavalry, the *sipahi*, who could not see the advantage of heavier weapons to an army that had traditionally prided itself on its mobility and its archery. The development of the janissaries and the musket were to some extent complementary, the full utility of the new weapons only being exploitable with a regular trained professional corps who would train and learn the necessary tactics.

Musketry would, however, take longer to perfect, and the priority in 1452 was to develop siege artillery sufficient to break Constantinople's previously impregnable walls. Mehmet cast his net wide, recruiting the leading European artillerymen, who appear to have been quite happy to take the sultan's money to bombard fellow Christians. The artillery corps, the *Topçu Ocağı*, together with the accompanying foundry, was initially established in Edirne, the Ottoman capital, although it would later be moved to Istanbul. It was divided into the actual units who operated and fired the guns and the foundries that produced them, which were remarkably mobile, accompanying the army and casting guns on site, although eventually there were 18 permanent cannon foundries. The empire was also fortunate to have the raw materials required for manufacturing powder. An initial facility was established near the Hippodrome in Istanbul but sensibly soon moved down to the Sea of Marmara, the first of what would become 25 such manufactories across the empire. By the 16th century the empire was producing 1,000 tons annually, more than adequate for their own needs and allowing a surplus for export. Supporting the artillery were a corps of *cebecis*, or armourers, who also looked after the janissaries' firearms. The cannon were made of bronze, iron casting only being introduced later, and they fired balls of stone. In fact, the Ottomans' preference for bronze guns would last well into the 17th century, the Ottomans having a good supply of bronze which was considered a safer material than iron, although the smaller guns were generally made of iron.

By 1453 Mehmet had recruited 250 artillerymen, and they would play a celebrated role in the siege of Constantinople, as we will shortly see. Most of these were initially employed serving the giant cannon used to batter the walls, and casting large cannon for sieges remained a favoured tactic for the next century. A Venetian commentator remarked that at the siege of Jajce in Bosnia in 1464 the army fielded five cannon, 'each seventeen feet long' which they threw into the River Vrbas as, having been cast on site, they were presumably too difficult to transport.[12] However, increasingly, as lighter guns were procured which could be used within the *wagenberg* on the battlefield, the artillerymen became part of the field army and were recruited from the *devşirme* and the palace schools. By 1527 there were over 2,000 of them, and by 1670 over 8,000.[13] By 1513 the Istanbul foundry was producing 188 cannon a year, and four years later it produced 700. It is no wonder that the visitor to Istanbul today sees so many of them decorating the palaces and the streets. Alongside the *Topçu Ocağı*, Mehmet also founded the *Lağımcı Ocağı*, literally 'the Hearth of the Miners', those specialist engineers who were essential to prosecuting the endless sieges.[14]

Lastly, Mehmet overhauled the logistic troops he needed to support what was rapidly becoming both a large and increasingly complex force. Traditionally, these support functions had been performed by two groups, the *Yayas* and the *Müsellem*, whose membership was hereditary. Both corps were about 20,000 strong and were unpaid but received tax exemptions. Their role was to provide transport, build roads and perform what today would be called 'rear area' tasks. However, by the 1420s both organizations were not functioning as they had been when they were established, so that Mehmet also overhauled them, rehabilitating the

Derbendi corps, also auxiliaries recruited from a local population in return for tax breaks but with responsibility delegated to village leaders so that there was a communal liability, a concept originally used by the Seljuks. Beyond that, the Ottomans had a pragmatic genius for recruiting and organizing local tribes in areas they conquered to provide the support that the army needed. What was crucial was that they paid so much attention to logistic support, in order to free up their combat troops for fighting.

Closely associated with the army was one more group, the *Akıncı*, or raiders, meaning 'those who flow' because, so Mihailović tells us, they 'are like torrential rain that falls from the clouds'.[15] The *Akıncı* approach was fundamental to the Ottoman way of war. They were rather like the privateers of Elizabethan England, freebooters who raided and pillaged across borders under license from the sultan. Their chief interest was plunder and slaves, but they also performed useful military functions both in terms of reconnaissance and in destabilizing the border areas, so that they became an important precursor to main operations. Mehmet's aim was that they should operate under license and within guidelines laid down by the government, although in practice it was difficult to exercise control and they were not paid, living off their spoils. The regional *voivode*, the senior local Ottoman official, would declare a raid and put out a notice inviting the *Akıncı* to gather at a certain point, 'and, having struck a drum which is called the *talambas*, so he releases them, and such a great tumult is raised by them as they jostle ahead of each other, each wanting to be in front... and so they ride away who knows where burning and killing, plundering and committing every evil thing'.[16] Their chief booty was slaves; boys had to be handed over to the sultan, but the older men, women and girls ended up in the slave markets of the East.

The army found them difficult to work with, undisciplined and violent, and their constant raids encouraged European countries to reinforce their border defences. Estimates of their numbers vary, but by 1453 there were at least 10,000 and maybe a lot more.[17] They operated mostly on the Rumeli, the European front, where they caused considerable terror and hardship to border communities; in the East, on the Anatolian front, Crimean Tartars came to offer the sultan a similar and equally violent service. There is one satisfactory afternote to the *Akıncı* story which falls outside our immediate period but which is worth recalling. In 1595 they were operating with an Ottoman army in Wallachia, which was pursuing a rebellious *voivode* called Michael. The *Akıncı* force got separated from the main army and found itself trapped against the River Danube. Michael's army found them and charged, either cutting them down or forcing them into the fast-flowing river where they drowned. Decimated, it was the *Akinci*'s last foray into Europe and at least some historic justice for those poor Hungarian girls whose lives were spent in Eastern harems.

Two forces bound this seemingly disparate army together. The first was the Ottoman concept of benefit and reward. The empire was based on constant movement – constant expansion with the accompanying benefit of newly conquered lands to be settled. 'Turkish or heathen expansion is like the sea… it never has peace but always rolls,' wrote Mihailović.[18] By linking the bestowal of *timars* on those who had distinguished themselves militarily, the sultans could look after their soldiers, reward success and save themselves money. 'The Sultan,' wrote the Venetian diplomat Alvise Contarini, 'could put into the field an army of 200,000 horsemen without spending a penny of the treasury's money', and although he exaggerated the numbers, 'it remained a fiscal principle for the Ottomans to maximize their participation on campaigns'.[19] Similarly, through their links to the various irregular bodies who could be rewarded through tax exemptions and permission to raid, the cost of the army was reduced while the power of the sultan was enhanced. Social and military prestige and advancement became inextricably linked, but both depended on continuing conquest.

There was also a system of very direct rewards on the battlefield, where sultans employed special officers, *chavushes*, whose job was to circulate and note acts of especial bravery, which would be reported back and publicly rewarded. Battlefield promotion was frequent and effective. A large part of the role of the *serdar*, the commander to whom the sultans delegated operational authority, was to be a cross between a modern paymaster and personnel officer. His role was to ensure that 'no soldier suffered from feelings of exclusion'.[20] He balanced the distribution of prizes and the ceremonial bestowal of *ihsan*, the regular cash bonuses paid across the army. The close-knit regimental system which developed, with its emphasis on units of ten, also meant that it was difficult for a soldier to be overlooked, a structure still in use across almost every modern army, albeit with differing sized sub-units. Sultans and grand viziers also made periodic bonus payments to reward success and were careful to look after older soldiers who felt they had been bypassed for promotion by the award of a *timar*. Compensation payments for injured soldiers were generous, and although the *timars* were not paid a salary, they were generously compensated for any loss, especially of horses, on which both their civilian lives and usefulness as soldiers rested.

However successful the system of payment through *timariot* holding and plunder, the standing army still had to be paid for. A rough look at those who stood in front of the Theodosian Walls that April shows they numbered around 10,000 janissaries; 2,000 Household Cavalry; 4,000 other *Kapıkulu* troops; 40,000 *timaris* and 15,000 *azabs*, with 8,000 support troops. Across the wider empire were a further 10,000 *Akıncı* and 10,000 fortress troops. Paying those who were salaried and the expenses of those mobilized still amounted to a considerable sum. It was certainly the largest part of the sultan's expenditure and reckoned to be approximately one-fifth of his overall budget, being roughly 12 per cent for the regular troops and 8 per cent for the other costs. At this stage in its story, the Ottoman Empire was solvent, and the army enabled expansion and new revenues, the sultan taking one-fifth of all war booty as well as all the captured boys.[21] Only in later centuries, without the surplus of conquest, would the army prove unaffordable. The overall genius of Mehmet's achievement was to make every soldier in his army feel part of and to have a share in a great endeavour, initially to take Constantinople but then to push on both east and west, for the glory of the regime and also because it brought them personal gain.

The second unifying force was Islam, although it remains unclear just how strong a motivating force it was for the army. There is no doubt that Mehmet saw himself as conquering in the name of Islam. He was deeply religious and demanded strict adherence amongst his followers. Yet an enduring image of the Ottoman army as heir to the great Arab conquests of the 7th century, sweeping all before it as it converted Anatolia and the Balkans, is false. Constantinople had still not fallen 750 years after the time of the Prophet, and what inroads Islam had made in Europe by Mehmet's time, mostly in the Iberian Peninsula, were soon to be quashed. Mehmet was not the caliph, which title remained in Egypt until 1517. The more difficult question to answer is whether his soldiers saw themselves as *gazis*, holy warriors, or whether, devout Muslims as they were certainly expected to be, religion was not necessarily a major factor for them, not least perhaps because so many of them had been forcibly converted. Mihailović, writing about his comrades in the janissaries, makes the point that some 'heathenized Christians are much worse than true-born heathens'. Equally, he tells us:

> the Turkish emperor is very insecure and the Turks greatly fear that Christendom might rise up and invade their lands more valiantly. For if the Christians who are under them saw this, they would revolt against him and would be in accord with Christendom. And this I have heard from them many times, for which I ceaselessly pray God that it happen.

And he finishes his account by exhorting the 'Lord God Almighty' to 'help faithful Christians against the ignoble heathens, to wipe them out'.[22] Amongst the *timariot* and the *Akıncı*, Islam probably was inevitably a stronger force not least because it gave them justification, at least in their eyes, for their raiding. Mehmet's success, despite Mihailović's reservations above, was rather to create an Islamic army that was loyal to the Ottoman state rather than an army that was motivated by *jihad*, not least because over the coming decades it would be employed fighting fellow Muslims as well as Christians.

Mehmet was not the originator of many of the reforms that his army now embodied but, like Constantine, his skill was to consolidate and formalize the improvements that had been initiated by his grandfather, then tested and developed by his father. In 1444 Murad's army had won a great but very costly victory at Varna over the combined Christian forces of King Ladislas of Poland and John Hunyadi of Hungary. It had nearly been a disaster but the Ottoman army was saved, as so often, by the mistakes of the crusaders. Riding across the field strewn with Christian corpses that evening, Murad remarked to one of his companions, Azab Bey, 'is it not amazing, that they are all young men, not a single greybeard among them?' to which Azab Bey replied, 'If there had been a greybeard among them they would not have embarked on so rash an undertaking.'[23] The day had been saved by the janissaries, a lesson that Mehmet would remember despite the janissaries mutinying early in his reign. Varna was 'one of the most decisive events not only of Ottoman but also of Western history'.[24] It was seen as the effective end of trying to prevent Turkish encroachment into Europe and as sealing the fate of Constantinople, which was now surrounded by Ottoman lands and cut off from the West; even Mehmet I had said to the Byzantine Emperor Manuel, 'Close the gates of your city and rule within it as I own everything outside the walls.'[25]

After Varna, Sultan Murad abdicated, an unusual step for a sultan much as it had been for Diocletian a millennium earlier, handing over power to Mehmet. It was a mistake. Mehmet was too young; the Ottoman establishment lacked confidence in him, so the grand vizier, Halil Pasha, and the janissaries petitioned Murad to return, which he duly did in 1446, only handing over finally to a chastened and bitter Mehmet in 1451.

Mehmet II was 21 when he inherited. He was well educated, an accomplished linguist, bisexual and culturally astute. He had Gentile Bellini brought from Venice twice to paint his portrait. He was less self-indulgent than his father, who had drunk liberally and was rumoured to have employed 2,000 huntsmen and 2,000 hawkers; Mehmet gave the hawkers the choice of joining the army or dismissal. He was, above all, ambitious, focused and seized with that same drive that Constantine must have possessed, a drive to expand his empire. He was also cruel and bloodthirsty. When Bellini and he were arguing over what a decapitated man's head looked like, Mehmet is alleged to have summoned a slave and cut off his head with his sword to prove his point. The appalled Bellini fled back to Venice. Mehmet is also reputed to have slit open the stomachs of 14 of his pages so he could discover which one had stolen a melon. It was also Mehmet who formally instituted the unattractive if effective Ottoman habit of murdering any other claimants to the throne when he inherited, having a seven-year-old brother strangled.

Yet he was also an efficient and meticulous organizer and an inspirational field commander whose immediate focus on assuming power was to take Constantinople, a city which to his mind was a vestige of a now-vanished empire and an insult to Ottoman power. It was the natural capital for his Islamic empire, which he was determined would rule the known world much as Rome had once done. 'The project would bring him glory and, equally important, the city was located in the middle of the territory of the Turks but was then not his possession,' wrote Pope Pius II. He continued, 'accordingly, the conquest of the city would surpass the glories of his own forefathers who had incurred shame when they had failed to succeed in this undertaking.'[26] Mehmet's father had also besieged the city but was unable to take it because the Byzantine forces were reinforced by sea.

Now Mehmet spent two years preparing to succeed where previous sultans had failed. Sieges were an important and unavoidable operation for contemporary armies, and although Murad and Mehmet had arguably designed their forces more for fighting battles, their revised structure meant that they could be adapted to the costly and time-consuming business of besieging a city. However, Constantinople, with the advantages of its natural position and mighty walls, offered a quite considerable challenge. Aware that he must first prevent the city being reinforced by sea, Mehmet started by building the impressive fortress of Rumeli Hissar on the European shore of the Bosphorus so that he could control all sea traffic into the city from the east as well as the west. It was approached in typical Mehmet fashion, being completed in record time between April and August 1452. Mehmet laid the first stone himself and decreed that all ships must stop. Soon after its promulgation, three Venetian ships carrying grain attempted to ignore this rule. The first two managed to sail through but the third was hit by a cannon ball and sunk. Its crew were rescued and taken to Edirne, where they were beheaded. The unfortunate captain was impaled, a particularly unpleasant form of execution favoured by the Ottomans which involved slowly driving a sharpened stake through a man's anus until it emerged behind his shoulder. The stake was then dug upright into the ground and the victim left to die. If the stake had punctured his vital organs he might be lucky and die quickly; otherwise he could be left in agony for days.

The Byzantine Emperor Constantine XI Palaeologus had inherited the throne from his brother in 1448. His focus was to save his city, all that was left of Constantine the Great's empire. By 1453 the entire population was just 60,000 souls, many of whom were monks. The once thriving city had been reduced to a series of villages within the Theodosian Walls, but the walls themselves had been well maintained and had never been breached. True, Constantinople had fallen to the Western European barons of the Fourth Crusade in 1204, but they had taken and then comprehensively sacked the city by treachery rather than storm; even now, in its enfeebled state and with but few troops to defend them, the walls still represented a formidable obstacle. Constantine XI Palaeologus had tried since his accession to reach an agreement with the Pope and the Western European powers to send support, but his argument had foundered on the theological divide between his Greek Orthodox Church, of which he was the Basileus – something approaching Christ's representative on earth – and the Western Church led by the Pope in Rome. So bitter was the divide that there were many of his more important subjects who declared that they would prefer to live under the Turks than the Pope. Realizing that he must find a compromise if he was to receive any Western support, in November 1452 he welcomed Cardinal Isidore, the Pope's ambassador, and in a service in the great Cathedral of St Sophia proclaimed a union of the churches. It was too little and too late, and although Isidore had brought Italian mercenaries with him, the resentment caused by the union, which saw the Latin rite chanted in the holiest of Greek churches and celebrated with a solemn *Te Deum*, caused more problems than it solved.

He also had to contend with the Genoese and the Venetians who had carved out colonies for themselves in his diminishing dominions. The Genoese colony was in Pera, immediately across Constantinople's natural harbour, the Golden Horn, from where they treated freely with the Ottomans, and the Venetians put trade before loyalty to Christianity, whatever form it took. The truth was that, protest as he might, the Pope was unable and possibly unwilling to intervene to save a city which, however much he would come to mourn its loss, was as foreign to him as Mehmet's capital at Edirne.

As the winter of 1453 turned towards spring, with Rumeli Hissar effectively closing the straits and with no sign of any more help arriving from the West, Constantine, who had monitored Mehmet's military reforms and preparations with increasing alarm, faced the inevitable. The story of Constantinople's fall is one of the most poignant, as that great city, rich with a millennium of Christian tradition and treasure, founded as the known world became Christian, finally fell over a thousand years after Constantine had laid the first stone. Although the crusaders had helped themselves to much of Constantinople's treasure in 1204 – such as the lions which once graced the Hippodrome which were stolen by the Venetians and still stand outside San Marco – the city's churches and monasteries, its libraries and palaces still held immense wealth. They also held the accumulated relics of many saints and the most sacred icons of the Eastern Church. The Cathedral of St Sophia, the Church of Holy Wisdom, built by Justinian in the 6th century, was the largest church in the world and its dome a marvel of architectural achievement. Rising high above the Bosphorus, it was visible for miles, the embodiment in stone of the might of the Greek Church, of the Byzantine Empire and of Constantine's legacy. Even more splendid was its interior decoration, its altars and the glory of its services. Yet it was but one of nearly 300 churches in the city together with 60 monasteries, many as rich in their frescoes and gold, their paintings, their vestments and their plate. Depopulated and now but a shadow of its former glory when it had been the largest city in the world, Constantinople still exercised its mystique across Europe, a mystique which Mehmet was determined to harness to Islam and the house of Osman.

Constantine XI had very few troops on which he could call to defend the city, and, however formidable the great walls remained, they were of little use unless they were manned. He had but few sources to consider. Many of his reduced population clung to the optimistic belief that God and the Icon of the Virgin and Child, believed to have been painted by St Luke, would be their strongest defence; others argued that Constantine had brought the siege on himself by his union with the Latin Church.

Those who opposed the compromise held a meeting in St Sophia, drawing up a list of 25 errors of the Latin Church, which they helpfully despatched to Pope Pius in Rome who was, belatedly, attempting to persuade both the Venetians and the Hungarians to send forces to Constantine's aid. Venice, infuriated by the way Mehmet had treated its ships, did promise to send troops and started to assemble a force, but there was little reaction from elsewhere in Europe. Hungary was weakened by their defeat at Varna, and their charismatic commander, John Hunyadi, thought that 'Christianity will always be damned until the Greeks are destroyed. When the Turks take Constantinople the Christians will be able to have victories again.'[27] The Genoese, safely, or so they thought, ensconced across the Golden Horn in Pera, continued to scheme so that they might benefit from the city's fall, although one Genoese, acting independently, did come to Constantine's aid. A *condotierro* called Giovanni Giustiniani arrived off the Golden Horn on 29 January

1453 with 700 soldiers whom he had personally recruited. A grateful Constantine promised him the island of Lesbos, one of the few territories still under Byzantine control, as a reward. For the next two months they worked to strengthen the walls, train what citizens Constantine could persuade to fight, and float a massive boom across the entrance to the Golden Horn, the natural harbour that separated the old city from the new settlements of Pera and Galata, to stop any Turkish assault from that side of the city. By late March, as word reached them that Mehmet was on the move south from Edirne, Constantine could muster about 9,000 men to defend the 14 miles of wall that ran from the Golden Horn in the north to the Sea of Marmara in the south, with many of his subjects still refusing to fight. A group of monks were handed 70,000 gold florins to fund work on the defences. Instead they buried the money which was, ironically, found by the Ottomans after the siege.[28]

By early April Mehmet had surrounded Constantinople from the west and north, thus blocking off all access from the land while his fleet denied the Bosphorus. With him came his siege train, including Orban and his Hungarian gunners and the massive Basilica. The sultan pitched his own tent directly opposite the Romanus Gate, the main city gate to the west. Grouped around him were his artillery and the janissaries. On 11 April Basilica fired its first 800-pound stone ball at the Romanus Gate, causing little damage as the gunners found it hard to calculate the correct elevation. After firing a few rounds the gun blew up, killing Orban and its crew. Orban was a loss but Mehmet had several other similarly large cannon, and once the Ottomans had established the range they started a concentrated fire. For a week they battered the gate and the walls either side; then, on the balmy night of the

18 April, Giustiniani and his defenders heard the ominous sound of drums and cymbals followed by cries as wave after wave of Turkish troops rushed forward. There was panic on the walls as the Greeks massed their force to react and the population rushed to the churches to pray for deliverance. In fact, Mehmet was only testing the defences and the troops he employed were unfortunate *azabs*, expendable infantry who left more than 200 of their comrades dead in the ditch in front of the gate when they were recalled after four hours.

The defenders were further cheered when on 20 April four Genoese ships managed to sail into the Bosphorus, where they were attacked by the whole Ottoman fleet. Superior seamanship and ship design meant that the Ottomans completely failed to stop them so that they were able to get through the boom and into the safety of the Golden Horn. In a fury, Mehmet had his admiral, Suleiman Baltoglu, flogged and stripped of his rank and all his possessions. The grand vizier suggested that after these reverses they should come to a deal with Constantine and lift the siege – but Mehmet's reformed army remained confident, and four Genoese galleys were not a relief force. Although their success may have lifted the city's spirits, there was still no word of the anticipated Venetian fleet. Mehmet did, however, send emissaries offering Constantine the Peloponnese, which was under Ottoman control, if he would surrender the city, but they were predictably rebuffed.

Mehmet now decided on a bold and novel tactic. If his ships could not gain access to the Golden Horn from the sea, he would make them do so by land. Accordingly he put preparations in hand to haul between 30 and 80 boats – sources differ as to exactly how many – overland from the Bosphorus, bypassing the Genoese in Pera, and re-launch

The Ottoman Empire c. 1453

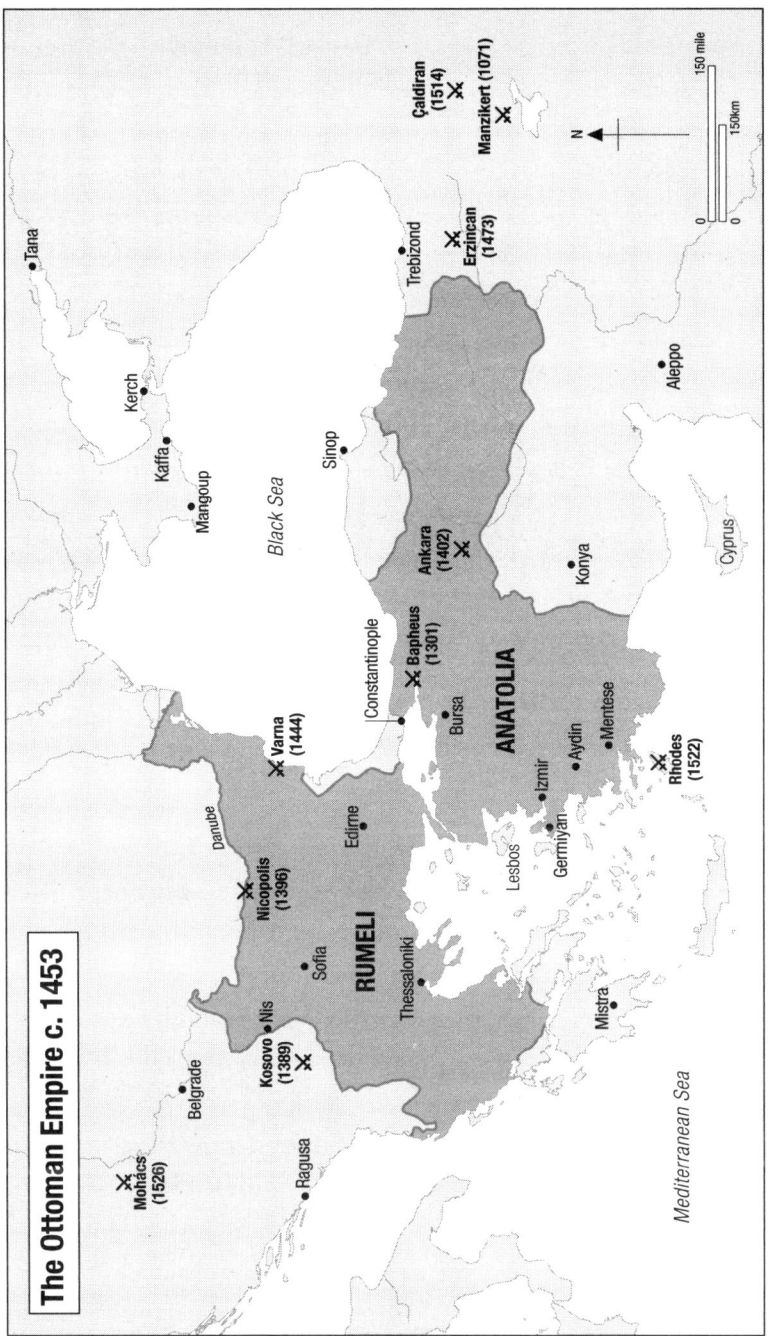

Mohács
(1526)

Belgrade

Ragusa

Nis

Kosovo
(1389)

Nicopolis
(1396)

Danube

Sofia

RUMELI

Thessaloniki

Edirne

Varna
(1444)

Mistra

Lesbos

Germiyan

Aydin

Mentese

Izmir

Bursa

Constantinople

Bapheus
(1301)

ANATOLIA

Konya

Rhodes
(1522)

Sinop

Ankara
(1402)

Black Sea

Mediterranean Sea

Cyprus

Aleppo

Trebizond

Erzincan
(1473)

Manzikert (1071)

Caldiran
(1514)

Tana

Kerch

Kaffa

Mangoup

N

150 mile
150km

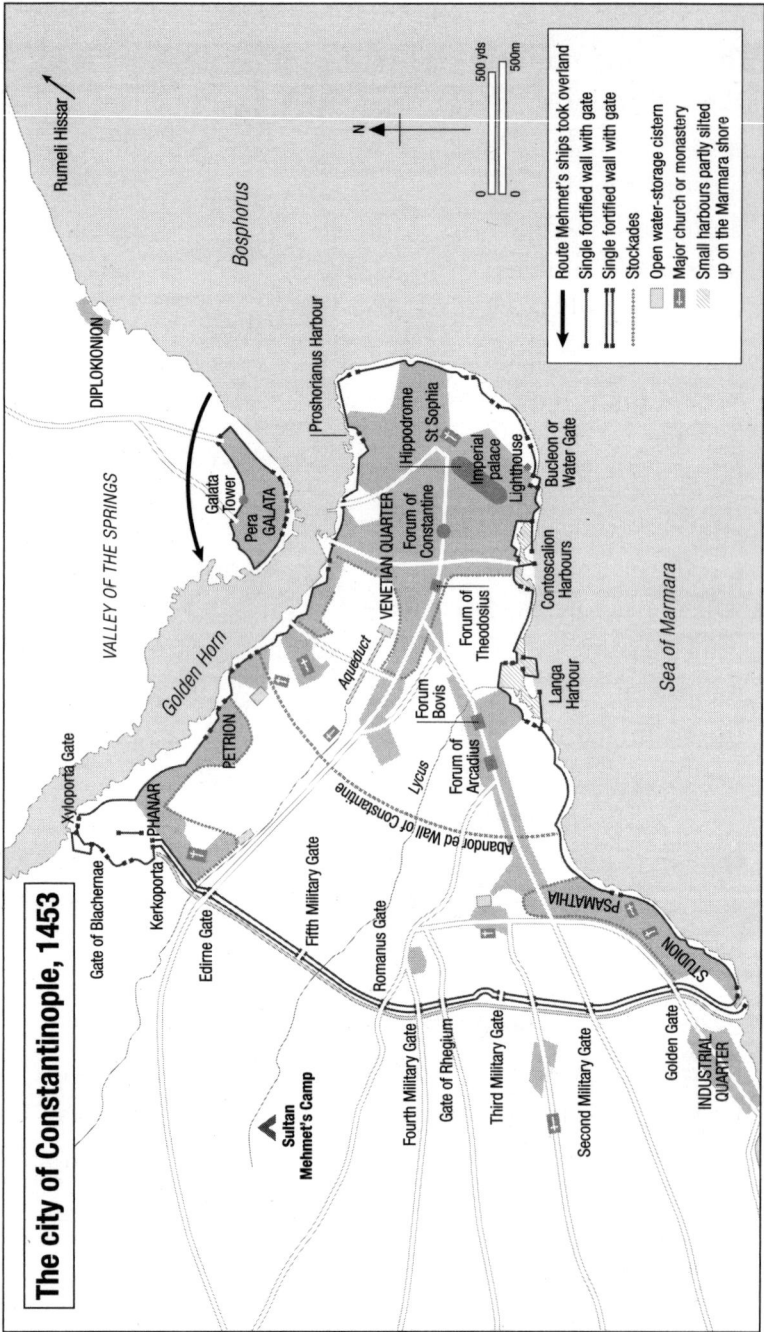

The city of Constantinople, 1453

Rumeli Hissar

Bosphorus

DIPLOKIONION

VALLEY OF THE SPRINGS

Galata Tower
Pera
GALATA

Proshorianus Harbour

Golden Horn

Xyloporta Gate

Gate of Blachernae

Kerkoporta
PHANAR

PETRION

Aqueduct

VENETIAN QUARTER

Hippodrome
St Sophia

Imperial palace

Lighthouse

Bucleon or Water Gate

Forum of Constantine

Contoscalion Harbours

Forum of Theodosius

Langa Harbour

Forum Bovis

Lycus

Forum of Arcadius

Edirne Gate

Fifth Military Gate

Abandoned Wall of Constantine

Sultan Mehmet's Camp

Romanus Gate

Fourth Military Gate

Gate of Rhegium

Third Military Gate

Second Military Gate

PSAMATHIA

STUDION

Golden Gate

INDUSTRIAL QUARTER

Sea of Marmara

N

500 yds
500m

Route Mehmet's ships took overland
Single fortified wall with gate
Single fortified wall with gate
Stockades
Open water-storage cistern
Major church or monastery
Small harbours partly silted up on the Marmara shore

them at the northern end of the Golden Horn. He would achieve this by pulling them on greased rollers along a specially prepared path. It was an enormous undertaking but one that his army was confident could be achieved. By doing so he would stretch the Greeks even more thinly, as they would now have to guard a far longer stretch of walls and he could position artillery batteries on Pera Hill. All the time this operation was progressing, the cannonade against the Romanus Gate progressed and was doing serious damage to the walls, which was becoming too extensive for the defenders to keep repairing. On 22 April they also awoke to see the Golden Horn full of Ottoman ships. An attack on these by their own ships, using fireships, failed, and the sailors captured were lined up and decapitated on the Pera shore in full view of those watching from the city. In retaliation, the Greeks pulled 280 Ottoman prisoners from their dungeons and hanged them over the walls opposite Mehmet's camp.

On 8 May Mehmet assaulted the Romanus Gate again, this time in earnest and using the janissaries. Fighting was fierce and Giustiniani was nearly killed by a janissary. Ottoman losses were severe. Mehmet now started to bombard the northern part of the walls around the Blachernae Palace as well, and managed to penetrate a force inside the walls but it was beaten back. On 18 May, to the amazement of the Greeks, the Ottomans built a siege tower overnight. This was pushed against the wall by the Romanus Gate and nearly succeeded in overwhelming the defenders until it was set on fire and collapsed. At the same time Mehmet's miners were working to lay mines along the walls, frustrated by a German counter-miner fighting for Constantine who managed to intercept and destroy them.

Despite these successes, the defenders were slowly weakening. Casualties were high, food was short, the walls were becoming badly damaged and there was still no word of any relief. On 23 May Mehmet sent Ismail Hamza to offer Constantine one last chance to surrender. The terms were the same as before but this time contained the threat that if the city continued to resist it would be sacked and no quarter offered to its citizens. Constantine must have realized that the end could not be long in coming but still he refused. 'To surrender the city is not in my power,' he told Hamza, 'nor in the power of anyone here. We are all prepared to die and shall do so without regret.'[29] The priests now – unhelpfully – started to see signs that the city was about to fall. The Statue of the Virgin had slipped and fallen while being paraded around the streets; a strange red crescent-shaped light had been seen shining on Hagia Sophia, and there were violent storms and fog which should not have happened in May.

The atmosphere in the condemned city, already poisoned by the divisions within the defenders' ranks, and recriminations between the Venetians and the Genoese, was made even worse when, on the night of 28 May, Giustiniani was wounded by a musket ball; bleeding profusely, and despite the pleas of Constantine, he was carried to one of the Genoese ships in the harbour. On the morning of Tuesday 29 May Mehmet launched his main attack on the Romanus Gate, again led by *azabs* who were killed by janissaries if they retreated, but this time backed up by the full janissary corps. To the north, where Mehmet had developed a secondary axis, a group of janissaries skirting under the walls found a small gate by the Blachernae Palace, the *kerkoporta*, which was usually bricked up but which had been opened to be used for a sortie and not properly barricaded afterwards. Charging through, they overwhelmed the Greek troops stationed there under Lucas Notaras – Constantine's Grand Admiral and one of the wealthiest men in the city – and fought outwards inside the walls to link up with the janissaries storming the Romanus Gate. There was an old Byzantine legend that the city would fall by the enemy entering through this postern gate so the oversight in failing to close it properly was a serious one. Later, rumours would circulate that it had been left open on purpose which, given the possible treachery of many in the city, was not unbelievable.[30]

Constantine must have realized that it was now finished. He was last seen charging into the mass of Ottoman troops inside the gate and only later identified by his purple boots. All that morning Mehmet's troops massacred the remaining defenders who had not managed to flee to the ships in the harbour, and then gave themselves over to sacking Constantinople's churches and houses, its palaces and shops. After Constantine's last rebuttal of his terms, Mehmet had authorized three days of pillage for his soldiers. 'All its wealth, its silver, gold, silk cloth and women will be yours; only the walls and the buildings will be mine,' he is alleged to have promised them, and they now took full advantage of their license. 'Suddenly the city had fallen; all those who dared offer resistance were slain; and the troops turned to plunder,' lamented Pope Pius, who had done precious little to save it. He went on to say:

Infinite was the number of victors who began to look for their pleasure: their cruelty could not be checked by anyone's dignity, age or sex. Orgies mixed with slaughter, slaughter mixed with orgies. In jest did they drag away both old men who were at death's threshold and common women as their booty. Anyone could snatch up wealth or heavy dedications of the churches.[31]

The treatment of St Sophia, where so many fugitives had sought sanctuary, provoked the most outrage in Europe. Having smashed down its great bronze doors, the victors showed no mercy to those trapped within:

> Turks entered the church and dragged the fugitives off to slavery. Two by two the men were tied together with cords, the women with belts, without consideration for age or status. Scenes of indescribable horror ensued. The statues of the saints were shorn of their jewels and smashed... Topped with a Janissary's cap, the crucifix was paraded in mockery and they used the altars as tables; when they had finished eating on them they used them as beds on which to assault boys and girls.[32]

Mehmet himself entered the city around midday, riding through the Edirne Gate escorted by his Household Cavalry. He rode directly to St Sophia, where he gave thanks to God, had the Muslim Creed proclaimed from the pulpit, half-killed one of his soldiers who was engaged in hacking away at a mosaic, repeating that the buildings belonged to him, and had Justinian's great church converted to a mosque. He then set about re-establishing order, stopping the looting on the third day. Many of the prominent citizens were beheaded, although those Venetians and Genoese who could afford it were allowed to offer a ransom. Lucas Notaras had survived and was brought before him. Mehmet asked why the city had defied him for so long, to which Notaras replied that they had been receiving messages from the Ottoman camp that the siege was about to be lifted, thus confirming the sultan's long-held suspicion of Halil Pasha, his grand vizier. Notaras was sent home but the next day, the Chief Black Eunuch, the sultan's executioner, was sent to his house demanding that Notaras surrender his handsome 14-year-old son to the sultan's harem. Notaras refused, saying he would rather be beheaded than hand his son over to such a dishonourable fate. He was then taken in front of the sultan with both of his sons where he had to see both boys beheaded before he himself was executed. Otherwise Mehmet spared those who would be useful, such as architects, builders and others who would now help him make the fallen capital of the Roman and Greek empires into the capital of the Ottoman Empire. It would remain so until 1923 and then briefly become the capital of Turkey until that was transferred to Ankara by Mustafa Kemal, better known as Ataturk.

Constantinople was only the beginning and was one of the severest tests faced by Mehmet's reformed army. Over the next 28 years he would fight a further 17 campaigns. The most challenging were in the East, where Uzun Hasan, the ruler of what is today Iraq and much of Iran, threatened the security of Karaman, that part of Anatolia which remained outwith Ottoman control. Mehmet faced him on the Upper Euphrates in eastern Anatolia in August 1473. Their first encounter ended in stalemate, but a week later Mehmet trapped him at Bashkent, near Erzincan, where his cannon and the janissaries' firearms enabled a decisive victory, after which the troublesome state of Karaman, what is today south-east Turkey, was finally annexed. By 1478 Mehmet's forces had also annexed the northern Black Sea littoral, including the Crimea. Yet their eastern borders remained a problem for the empire, being rugged and distant and difficult to police.

It would not be until 1514, when Sultan Selim I decisively defeated the Shi'ite Safavids, heirs to Uzun Hasan, at Çaldıran, that there was some degree of permanence. Suleiman I – the Magnificent – subsequently took Baghdad in 1534.

The year after he took Constantinople, Mehmet launched another campaign in the West against the Serbs, and although his siege of Belgrade in 1456 ended in failure, by 1459 Serbia was fully integrated into the empire. By 1460 he had completed the conquest of the Peloponnese, and by 1463 Bosnia and Herzegovina were annexed. War with Venice that same year saw Mehmet defeat Venice's client state of Albania, which was occupied, and to push into Italy, with Otranto falling to him in 1480. The same year the Ottomans besieged Rhodes, the island fortress of the Knights Hospitaller after they had been expelled from Jerusalem, although they failed to take it; Rhodes, long seen as an impudent Latin outpost in what was rapidly becoming an Ottoman-dominated eastern Mediterranean, would eventually fall in 1522. Then, in August 1526 Suleiman the Magnificent decisively routed Louis II of Hungary and Bohemia in a two-hour battle at Mohács in southern Hungary, killing him and taking his capital at Buda, although it would not be permanently occupied until 1541. It was at Mohács that the janissaries first used their tactic of firing volleys in nine ranks, which proved devastating. Hungarian casualties were estimated at over 20,000, while the Ottoman army lost fewer than 2,000. The effect of Mohács was profound. The Hungarian Jagiellonian dynasty ended with Louis' death so that control of Hungarian and Bohemian lands passed to the Hapsburgs. For nearly a century the Hungarians had been the defenders of Europe and of Christianity, and their valiant efforts, often overlooked by historians, came at enormous cost.

As the Ottomans' ambitions pushed them further north into Europe they would come into direct conflict with the Holy Roman Empire.

These victories, enabled by the army that Mehmet and his father had built, were just the beginning of a series of Ottoman conquests which would see the empire expand so that, by the end of the 17th century, it controlled the North African littoral from Algiers to Egypt; the Red Sea coast, including the Hijaz and the Holy Cities; Yemen; what is today Iraq, Syria and Palestine; Greece, the Aegean and the Balkans; the Black Sea and the Sea of Azov; Hungary and Romania as well, of course, as Turkey and what is today Bulgaria. In 1683 they failed for the second time, narrowly, to take Vienna. It was a substantial fulfilment of Osman's dream.

More than that, it enabled both the development of a trading network originally around the Mediterranean and the Black Sea but which would extend far wider and which brought with it wealth and prosperity for millions. It enabled the spread of Islam, with the sultans becoming caliphs, at least in name, after their defeat of the Mamluks in 1517, which also gave them custody of Mecca and Medina. Although part of the success of Ottoman colonization was that they tolerated existing religions, the spread of Islam remained core to their vision. It allowed the rebuilding of Constantinople, renamed Istanbul, and its rebirth as capital of a second empire. Although the conversion of churches into mosques would be deeply unpopular, as it remains to this day, the building programmes sponsored by the sultans not just in that city but across the expanse of their empire have given us some of the world's most incomparable buildings.

Yet these were manifestations of the idea, of Osman's dream. It was a dream that could not have been achieved without an army, as it was the army that allowed the dynasty and its state to exist – to conquer, to expand, to annex, to reward, to harness the state to the dynasty. In an empire that depended on expansion, on movement, the army and the state became indivisible; the one was what made the other function. The army was the state and the state was the army, and both were of course served by the same system of recruiting. Once this method of recruiting was corrupted, the state would begin to lose cohesion.

Decline would, of course, eventually come, and it is usually dated from the failure of the second attempt to take Vienna, when in 1683 Western Europe finally managed to create an alliance to defeat an army led by Kara Mustafa Pasha, Grand Vizier for Sultan Mehmet IV. This marked the high point of Ottoman expansion into Europe. Many Turkish commentators would cite the decline of the army and the recruitment of Muslims into the janissary corps as the reason for their failure. The *devşirme* started to break down in the late 16th century so that the traditional source of manpower became corrupted. Such was the prestige and opportunity offered by membership of the janissaries that palace officials and army officers started to bribe the recruiters to accept their sons, 'persuading the clerks who registered them, to enter their parents' names as senseless names in infidel languages' and to 'bribe the surgeons who carried out the circumcisions'. By 1630 a contemporary writer complained the janissaries were taking 'city boys of unknown religion, Turks, Gypsies, Tats, Kurds, outsiders, Lazes, Turcomans, muleteers and camel drivers, porters and confectioners, highwaymen and pickpockets and other people of various sorts'.[33] By around 1700 the old system had died out. The change was not, however, entirely due to opportunistic place seekers. The size of the corps increased rapidly in the 17th century – by 1609 it numbered 40,000 – as the requirement for infantry trained in the use of firearms expanded; the *devşirme* was simply unable to produce the numbers required. Gradually the old slave-based system gave way to an army of free men, although slavery would remain part of Ottoman society until the 19th century; the Istanbul slave market only closed in 1846. The *timar* system would prove more durable, at least as far as providing manpower was concerned, still producing over 40,000 well into the 17th century.[34]

Yet although 1683 may have marked the end of Ottoman expansion into Europe, and the next century would see territorial losses and internal disorder, the empire was to remain a formidable force. Despite being defeated by Prince Eugene at Petrovaradin on the Danube in 1716 and outside Belgrade the next year, by 1739 they had recovered sufficiently to re-take Belgrade and remain a serious threat to Europe until the end of the century. By the 1780s they were also coming up against an expansionist Russia under Catherine the Great that was pushing aggressively west along the Black Sea and had annexed the Crimea in 1783. The Hapsburgs intervened in 1788 as allies of Russia, fighting a lacklustre campaign which failed to re-take Serbia and saw the Ottomans successfully penetrate across the Danube. Austrian military preparedness was poor and they lost more soldiers to malaria than from fighting, but the war of 1788 to 1791 was effectively the last major clash between the empires. The effort had, however, weakened the Ottomans in the Mediterranean as they withdrew troops to reinforce their armies in Europe, leading to their losing control of Egypt in 1791, which established itself as an independent state. The beginning of the empire's final decline can fairly be dated from this period and it was Russia rather than Austria who continued to threaten Ottoman territory throughout the 19th century. Ironically, given the long history of Ottoman–Hapsburg confrontation, in the First World War the empire allied itself with the Central Powers, with Austria and Germany, fighting Russia.

It was not until 1922 that the sultanate was abolished and what was left of the empire created by Mehmet's army was divided away in the wake of that war.

The principles on which Mehmet constructed his army were the same as those followed by Constantine – creating, training and equipping a professional combat force that was flexible and could adapt; harnessing new technology; ensuring that the army and the state were in harmony; making soldiers respected in Ottoman society and ensuring that they were well cared for – admittedly a cause the janissaries would on occasion take into their own hands – and creating an industrial and logistic system that was under government control and which was sustainable. He also made his army affordable by adopting novel methods of financing and tax relief.

The Ottoman army was certainly not invincible. It suffered tactical defeats. That reluctant janissary Mihailović pointed out, correctly, that the Ottomans always fought in the same way, and that if only the Western powers would take note then they could be defeated. He cited the Tartars as being quicker to learn so that they 'have several times won victories over the Turks but the Christians never, and especially in pitched battle, most of all because they let the Turks encircle them and approach from the flank'. He also cites the Christian armies' old-fashioned habit of weighing themselves down with 'cumbersome armour and heavy cavalry lances', whereas the Turks had mastered the art of manoeuvre, of moving quickly and using new weapons.[35]

What Constantine's and Mehmet's armies did was to enable them both to realize their ambition of empire and to establish respectively Christianity and Islam within it; indeed religion, or the social order it encompassed, was the force that inspired them. They also enjoyed absolute power and would come to exercise a monopoly of force across their domains. Consequently, the political system in which their armies operated was, in a sense, straightforward as they both held supreme political and military authority. The next three armies we will look at had to develop within a much more nuanced political environment and to follow similar principles but without being able to draw on the same advantages.

Chapter Four

The New Model Army, 1645

'Necessity hath no law.'
Oliver Cromwell, 1654

The civil wars in the British Isles were fought as the Thirty Years' War – which had caused such misery and destruction in Europe from its outbreak in 1618 and which involved all the major European powers – was staggering to its miserable end at the Treaty of Westphalia in 1648. One of the main lessons European rulers had learnt by then was that they could not control the mercenary armies that had dominated that conflict in the 1620s and 1630s and which had become their own arbiters of power. After Westphalia the demand was for armies that were answerable not just to themselves but to the authority of the state. The following decades would see the Hapsburg army rebuilt as it now faced south against the Ottomans, while the Russian, French and Prussian armies would undergo similar transformations. Yet the nation which rebuilt its army first was England, and those who led that military revolution acted from the necessity of saving their lives.

The civil wars between the forces of King Charles I and those of the English Parliament, more commonly but inaccurately referred to as the English Civil War, exposed the islands to a similar bloodletting – if perhaps not quite so much agricultural and commercial devastation – as central Europe had suffered in the previous decades. They were approximately twice as bloody in terms of both military and civilian casualties as the First World War. Figures remain inexact, but it is estimated that in the decade following their outbreak in 1642, England lost 4.5 per cent of its population, so about 200,000 souls. Scotland lost 6 per cent, or 60,000, while Ireland suffered a massive 20 per cent loss from fighting, massacre, famine, plague and forced exile, in which thousands were sold as indentured labourers to the West Indies.

By 1644 the war had raged for two years but neither side had achieved a decisive operational advantage. England had no standing army when the king had raised his standard in Nottingham in August 1642. In the first months of the war both sides had attempted to raise armies from the Trained Bands, the county-based organizations that had formed a somewhat unreliable home defence structure since the days of Elizabeth I. It was not a great success. Sir Edmund Verney, one of the king's commanders, wrote that 'there was never so raw, so unskilful, and so unwilling an army, brought to fight'. 'Out of 2,000 there were not 200 that could fire a musket,' added Lord Hamilton.[1] The Parliamentary recruiters shared a similar experience from the Trained Bands in the counties they controlled. They found them 'effeminate in courage and incapable of discipline' and the noted Parliamentary commander Sir William Waller said that 'They are so mutinous and uncommandable that there is no hope of their stay. Yesterday they were like to have killed the Major

General, and they hurt him in the face. Such men are only fit for a gallows here and a hell hereafter.'[2]

Consequently, the early engagements of the war had been indecisive. The armies had clashed at Edgehill in October 1642 as the king attempted to move south. Parliament's forces failed to halt him, but he was turned back at Turnham Green on the outskirts of London that November by the London Trained Bands under the command of one of the few professional soldiers then serving, Sir Philip Skippon, who had extensive experience fighting in Europe. These were the only really effective group in the kingdom, numbering nearly 18,000 men organized into regiments by ward. They also contained the best trained artillerymen. Thereafter neither side had managed to achieve a decisive victory during 1643. Parliament's forces were grouped into four armies which acted semi-independently, while the king's forces were similarly split, one army with the king himself and one with his nephew, Prince Rupert of the Rhineland Palatinate, and numerous local forces which were equally uncoordinated. The king had an unfortunate habit of allowing his supporters to raise new regiments rather than filling up the gaps caused by casualties and desertion in his existing units, so that 'after a few months fighting the Royalist army was full of colonels whose regiments were no stronger than a troop or a company.'[3] Although volunteers flocked to both sides that winter, numbers remained insufficient so that both resorted to impressment, which was understandably highly unpopular and produced ineffective troops.

In September 1643 Parliament did, however, manage to effect an alliance with the Scots – the Solemn League and Covenant – which promised military support to help Parliament rid the British Isles of Roman Catholicism and 'popery', and to protect the Scottish church. In July 1644 a Scottish army had linked up with the Parliamentary armies of the Earl of Manchester and Sir Thomas Fairfax outside York, and on 2 July they staged a surprise attack on the Royalists' northern army under Prince Rupert at Marston Moor. Although the Royalists were outnumbered, they gained an early advantage and it looked as if they would prevail until late in the evening, when an action by the Parliamentary horse of the Eastern Association under Oliver Cromwell routed them. Prince Rupert's army lost 5,500 men and all their guns while Parliamentary casualties were just 300. It was a decisive tactical victory which led to the Royalist loss of the north and the destruction of one of their main field armies. It also made a reputation for Cromwell, at that stage an inexperienced commander, who wrote that the Royalists were 'as stubble to our swords'.[4] It should have resulted in an opportunity to get the king to pause the war and to discuss terms, but instead, in the last week of August and the first week of September, Charles I routed the Parliamentary army in the south-west under the Earl of Essex at Lostwithiel. Parliament's losses were estimated at 6,000, many dying as they attempted to reach safety in Southampton. By the autumn the war seemed to be as inconclusive as it had been the previous year and, as the Parliamentary commander the Earl of Manchester said, 'if we beat the King ninety-nine times he would be king still and his posterity; and we subjects still. But if he beat us once we should be hanged and our posterity undone.'[5]

The mood in the Parliament that winter was correspondingly bleak, not helped by recent missed opportunities against the Royalists at Newbury and Donnington Castle. The management of the war was the responsibility of the Committee of the Two Kingdoms who now cast about for a scapegoat. The ensuing argument, which would come to polarize the Parliamentary faction for the coming decade, was between those like Manchester and Essex who were thought, with some justification, to favour a negotiated peace, versus the more radical elements, championed by Cromwell, who would hold with no compromise. There is a view that Cromwell and his supporters were actually pursuing a social revolution and that they saw the outcome of the war as involving a restructured and democratic society. This is far from the truth. Cromwell was a religious extremist but not a social one, and he and his supporters in the mid-1640s came from the landowning gentry; their opposition to the monarchy was partly due to the king's attempt to exercise arbitrary power and partly due to his interference in their Puritan beliefs. Later, the army we are about to see come into being would certainly exhibit strong revolutionary traits but these had not yet developed; if they had, then the House of Commons, made up of members with similar backgrounds to Cromwell, would not have supported them. The men who took to the field against the king were, in the words of John Milton, 'men of better conditions of life, of families not disgraced if not ennobled, of fortunes either ample or moderate... prepared, not only to debate but to fight; not only to argue in the senate, but to engage the enemy in the field'.[6]

Throughout December 1644 and January 1645, the argument was, however, played out between the two houses of Parliament. The issue came down to perceived Parliamentary interference in the leadership of the army, which was, correctly, thought to have allowed the proliferation of individual commands and profiteering. In December the Commons passed a self-denying ordinance designed to prevent such practices and which legislated that 'during this time of war, no member of either house shall have or execute any office or command, military or civil'.[7] This was rejected by the Lords, who feared an army that they would be unable to control; in particular they wanted to retain the power to nominate for military appointments. By January the issue had been reduced to stalemate so that the Commons, finding their plans to combine the three existing armies of Manchester, Essex and Waller frustrated, now resolved to create their own army. This would be a 'new' army, to which all taxation would be directed, thus leaving the existing armies without funding. It was a drastic step, so drastic that the Lords had no option but to accept it and, with negotiations with the king breaking down, this New Model Army was created on 28 January 1645. Arguments continued over whether the officers should be appointed by Parliament or the commander in chief, eventually being settled as a compromise whereby the commander in chief would nominate officers but their names would then be passed to Parliament for approval.

The whole idea of building a New Model Army was in itself revolutionary, another example of having the vision and courage to meet a military challenge with an entirely new concept. The army they now started to build was to prove one of the most efficient in Europe at the time and the most important in British history. Much of it is still evident in the British Army today, and although some historians will contend that the modern British Army can only trace its roots to the Restoration of the monarchy in 1660, that Restoration army was only ever a continuation of the New Model. What Parliament's generals now did was to follow the principle established by Constantine and Mehmet – to maximize their military effort into a well-trained, well-equipped and well-supplied deployable field army.

The new army would be created with a speed and an energy it would retain when it took the field. It was largely based on the army of the Eastern Association, which provided half the colonels appointed to regimental command, but Manchester's place as commander in chief was taken instead by the able and well-respected general Sir Thomas Fairfax. Fairfax was a close ally of Cromwell and believed in outright victory. Although a Puritan, he remained a social conservative and was considered a safe choice by both the Lords and Commons. He was to have two subordinates. Based on his political agitation and his distinguished performance at Marston Moor, Cromwell would command the horse as a lieutenant general. One of Parliament's most experienced officers, who had long service with the Dutch Army in the Thirty Years' War, Philip Skippon, who had been in command at Turnham Green, would have charge of the infantry in the same rank. Skippon was more the professional soldier and a good trainer of men rather than a radical, and he would, like Fairfax, later distance himself from Cromwell's more extreme policies.

Several factors would weigh heavily on the trio of Fairfax, Cromwell and Skippon as they recruited, organized, equipped and drilled their soldiers. First, they were working under the shadow of the hangman's noose. Manchester's warning was not in vain, and should this new army not be able to defeat the Royalists quickly then its senior officers would be rebels who could expect little mercy. There was therefore a certain urgency to their work. Second, they were building a force at a time when much of Europe had suffered nearly 30 years of war, during which considerable advances had been made in tactics and procedures. Although men like Skippon had wide experience, the Royalist army had officers with much more. Sir Jacob Astley, who commanded the king's infantry, had fought under the Swedish King Gustavus Adolphus, considered one of the most effective European commanders. Sir Ralph Hopton, who commanded the Royalist western army, had fought in Bohemia, and both George Goring, who would command the king's cavalry at Naseby, and Henry Gage, who would be appointed Governor of Oxford, were highly experienced veterans. The New Model Army had some officers with European experience, such as Skippon himself, and their Scottish allies had several senior officers who had also served under Gustavus Adolphus, but the New Model Army certainly did not have a monopoly of tactical wisdom. They had to consolidate what they had learned so far, decide on formation and equipment, and build accordingly.

They did though have two significant advantages. First, they were well funded. On 13 January 1645 Parliament had agreed a monthly levy amounting to £53,436 from the 17 counties they controlled in the south, east and Midlands. They could also draw on the financial resources of the City of London, who advanced a loan of £80,000 to allow mobilization.[8] The king's army, by contrast, was permanently broke and often unable to pay its men. Second, the New Model Army could draw on the inspiration of Puritanism although, as with Mehmet's army, it is possible that the importance of religion to the rank and file has been overstated. The officers were all required to sign the Solemn League and Covenant but, somewhat strangely, those who refused were still allowed to serve. Cromwell and many of the colonels were strong Puritans; in fact, Puritanism can be said to have been the strongest force governing their participation. Cromwell's speeches and those of his senior commanders make constant reference to God, who must have become a little tired of having His name used so liberally, especially when associated in the coming decade with some of the New Model's worst excesses. There is something ironic in an army purportedly raised to protect freedom of conscience presiding over the most intolerant period in British history. However, there is some truth in the image of God-fearing, psalm-singing regiments fighting in the self-righteous belief that their religious practice offered the only hope of salvation.

Recruitment was a challenge. The size of the army was initially to be 22,000 men, composed of 11 regiments of horse each of 600 and 12 regiments of foot each of 1,200, as well as a regiment of 1,000 dragoons under Colonel John Okey. Later, as the army's tasks increased, so did its size, but it was difficult enough to find the manpower for even this relatively modest force that spring. Although Parliament had a total of about 60,000 men in its various armies, many of these were scattered in disparate garrisons and even taking the bulk of both the Eastern Association and Essex's armies, there was still a shortfall. This would gradually be made up, although it was not until July 1647 that Fairfax assumed command of all Parliament's forces across the British Isles. In the meantime, the gaps, which were primarily in the infantry, had to be filled by impressment, with a quota fixed for each county so that by May it is estimated that half the infantrymen were pressed men, many of whom were distinctly reluctant to serve. Even with impressment, when the army first took to the field it was about 4,000 below strength.[9] Desertions were common, and it is much to Fairfax's credit that he instilled sufficient morale and discipline to produce the force he did.

The next issue was how to equip and train the new regiments. At the start of the war the ad hoc forces assembled by both sides represented a strange mixture of equipment and weapons, from commanders like Sir Arthur Haselrig, who produced a troop of fully armoured men looking like medieval knights and laughingly referred to as 'Haselrig's lobsters', even prompting a rare joke from the king who remarked that 'if Sir Arthur had been victualled as well as fortified, he might have stood a siege', to men armed with little more than pitchforks.[10] The lesson from the great battles of the Thirty Years' War was that improved firepower from muskets had led armies to reduce armour, so improving agility and movement. There was no one particular army to imitate, there being examples of best practice not just from the Swedes but also the Dutch and the French. France had recently won its victory over Spain at Rocroi, routing the fabled Spanish infantry, previously considered the best in Europe. As the devastation of the wars came slowly to an end, the mercenary forces that had dominated its early years were giving way to state forces, but countries like Prussia had yet to complete the transformation that would allow The Great Elector finally to expel the Swedes. This will be discussed in more detail in Chapter Five.

The decision on the horse appears to have been driven by Cromwell and to have been based on his own experience. The Royalist horse had proved more than a match for Parliament, even at Marston Moor, and he knew that radical reform was needed. He correctly rejected the idea of heavily armoured horsemen carrying lances, still used in some European armies such as the Poles', as he did the idea of 'harquebusiers', or firing a shortened musket, a carbine, from a horse. Armour was restricted to 'fronts and backs', effectively iron cuirass plates that left the arms free. Helmets with face guards, called pots, replaced elaborate hats worn over a metal skull cap, and leather buff coats gave some bodily protection. Armament was a sword and pistols. Carbines were carried but used mostly for guarding and patrolling rather than in battle. Considerable care was taken over horses. Troopers could either bring their own, which many did, or else the army would provide them by buying in bulk, paying the exorbitant price of £10, which the war had made the going rate for a good-quality heavyweight animal; work horses typically cost half that amount.

Cromwell saw the horse as the *arme blanche*, the battle-winning troops who would deliver victory by the power and weight of their charge once the infantry had fixed the enemy in place. His aim, despite the additional cost, was to have half as many horse in a formation as infantry, a higher proportion than was considered desirable before 1645. Training that spring centred on perfecting the charge, which was to be delivered in a very different manner from that of the early days of the war. Regiments would be formed in three ranks, copying Gustavus Adolphus' tactic, as opposed to the traditional six, with each trooper locking his right knee under the left knee of his neighbour, 'as close as they can well endure', to present a solid mass.[11] The charge would be delivered at a walk or a brisk trot so that the tightness of the ranks would be maintained. The notion of officers charging at the head of their troops was abolished – it had never really existed except in the imagination of romantics – with officers riding to the side or back of the line so they could keep control and also avoid being shot by their own men in a mêlée. Pistols would be fired at almost point-blank range so they had a chance of doing some damage; even with modern weapons it is almost impossible to fire a pistol accurately at any distance off the back of a moving horse. The ranks would then close with the enemy with swords, try to ride through them and then, in a novel tactic, immediately re-form, turn about and charge again before the enemy had a chance to recover. This was something the Royalist horse could never master, lacking the discipline to keep formation, so that once they were committed it was almost impossible to re-form them. Cromwell's tactic was always, when he could, to charge first so that he maintained the momentum in a battle and which meant that his troopers did not have to withstand the shock of receiving a charge which risked breaking their ranks.

As well as the regiments of horse – in other words, troopers who fought on horseback and who were equipped and trained for the shock action Cromwell so valued – the army also contained a large regiment of dragoons. A dragoon was a mounted infantryman who carried a musket and used his horse simply as a means of transport, including on the battlefield. Their horses were correspondingly cheaper – an allowance of only £5 was made per animal – as they were not required to charge or fight. Dragoons were used for supporting tasks such as camp or flank guards, something they would perform with distinction at Naseby, and thus carried muskets as opposed to pistols or carbines. The regiment was commanded by John Okey, a London ship chandler who held fairly extreme Puritan views and who would later be executed for signing the king's death warrant. The dragoons were important not just for their contribution in the field but because they were the forebears of a capability and tradition which would become increasingly important in the British cavalry and whose heirs still serve today.

The later battles of the Thirty Years' War had also seen a major revision of infantry tactics. There were two types of infantrymen in the mid-17th century, being pikemen and musketeers. The pike was gradually giving way to the musket as its technology improved, but pikemen would still form one-third of the New Model Army's infantry. The heavy armour they had traditionally carried was abandoned, as it was with the horse, but they still wore cuirasses and helmets. The pikes themselves were usually made of ash and about 16–18 feet long, with a fearsome head that was protected by metal plates along the shaft to prevent it being cut off. There was much debate about pike heads. The Scots had a 'broadhead which is the worst in the world', while the preferred pattern was a lozenge-shaped head, because they were 'sharp to enter, and when entered broad to wound with'.[12] The pikemen tended to be the taller and stronger recruits and saw themselves as an elite within the army, although they complained incessantly about being 'imprisoned within their armour' and having to carry their heavy pikes while on the march, while 'the musketeer marched free and open to the air, which is no small benefit and happiness to him upon such occasions'.[13] They also had a bad habit of cutting their pikes shorter to make them lighter to carry. All pikemen also carried a sword for use if their formation broke or was penetrated by repeated cavalry charges.

Musketeers wore no armour, although many commanders thought that they should. Originally, muskets had very long barrels, which meant that they had to be fired using a forked rest, but by 1645 these had given way to a shorter-barrelled weapon which could be fired without. They were still cumbersome but highly effective weapons which discharged a ball weighing well over an ounce that would penetrate armour and cause terrible wounds. Contemporaries claimed that the New Model Army's muskets were effective at 400 paces, although this seems to be exceptional, and ranges on the battlefield tended to be much shorter.[14] The issue with muskets was more the reliability of their firing mechanisms.

At the beginning of the war, the usual firing mechanism was a firelock, which meant that musketeers fired their weapons by applying a lighted match, a length of tow, to the priming pan, thus igniting the powder. This was inefficient – soldiers were unable to fire until their match was lit – and caused considerable problems of concealment and numerous accidents. Gradually the old firelocks were being replaced with the *snaphanse*, a German-invented flintlock or firelock mechanism which ignited the powder by creating a spark in the priming pan. An earlier version utilized a small mechanical wheel to do the same job. 'It is,' as Lord Orrery, author of *The Art of War*, said, 'exceedingly more ready, for with the firelock you only have to cock and you are ready to shoot but with the matchlock you have several motions, the least of which is as long as performing as but that one of the other.'[15] Yet even a firelock required the musketeer to carry two types of powder: a fine powder for priming and a coarser mix as propellant.

The firelock meant that musketeers could now fire more quickly so that infantry ranks could be reduced from ten deep to six. Each man carried 12 rounds, balls and cartridges, in a bandolier across their shoulder and all also carried a sword. The method of firing had originally been for each rank to fire then retire to the rear while the next rank fired in turn. However, the New Model Army tactic as they trained that spring was to fire, stand still while the second rank advanced through them, and so on, until the first rank had reloaded. Again, it was a Swedish tactic perfected by Gustavus Adolphus, and although it would take the recruits some months to master it, it would become Fairfax's preferred method of operating. Not all the regiments could be equipped with firelocks – matchlocks would continue in service for another 30 years – but gradually the core infantry were all so equipped, leaving the older weapons for garrisons.

Another innovation copied from the Swedes was the way the New Model Army used field artillery, something Gustavus Adolphus seems to have copied from the Ottomans. There is, irritatingly, no complete list of the artillery in the New Model Army that spring, although we know that by 1647 Fairfax had 56 field guns as well as a heavier siege train for battering the various houses and castles the Royalists still held. Many of these were presumably Royalist cannon taken at Marston Moor. Field artillery does not seem to have played a major role at Naseby, but it was used very effectively at Langport on 10 July 1645 and in subsequent battles where it was well integrated with the infantry.[16]

One of the Eastern Association regiments that was absorbed into the New Model Army in April was that commanded by Colonel John Pickering, and following its progress gives a very good idea of how the army formed. Pickering was a typical Parliamentary commander in that he was a Northamptonshire landowner and a devout Puritan. Educated at Cambridge and then qualifying as a lawyer at Gray's Inn, he had joined Manchester's Eastern Association early in the war, first on the staff before commanding a regiment of dragoons. In March 1644 those dragoons, who had not been particularly successful, were disbanded and Pickering took command of a regiment of foot. A close ally of Cromwell, he was considered to have extreme Puritan views by the House of Lords, who tried to exclude him from command in Fairfax's list; he was supported in the Commons, however, so that his regiment became the twelfth to be accepted. That April they moved to Abingdon where, being badly understrength, they were amalgamated with Colonel

Thomas Ayloffe's regiment, although this still left them short
of their establishment of 1,200. Regimental amalgamations
are always difficult and so this one proved. Pickering had to
manage the respective jealousies and rivalries while insisting
on a strict new training regime. It did not help that the
army's administrative system had not yet matured so that his
men remained unpaid for 42 days. Neither was he perhaps
at his most tactful when he preached a sermon condemning
Presbyterians, given that many of Ayloffe's men were of that
persuasion. That the doctrinal differences between Puritans
and Presbyterians, which may pass the general reader by,
were to be such a source of discord says much for the febrile
religious atmosphere of the time. However, the new regiment
seemed to come together, and observers noted his rigorous
training regime with approval.[17]

And the regiment needed it. From Abingdon they were
sent on 29 April to join Cromwell in his abortive siege of
Faringdon Castle, which resulted in Pickering losing Captain
Jenkins and 14 soldiers. Accepting failure, Cromwell moved
to join Fairfax in besieging Oxford, but on 29 May the
Royalist army under the king took Leicester, and on 5 June
Fairfax left a skeleton force around Oxford and marched
north. Pickering's regiment went with him. By 7 June they
were at Newport Pagnell. The Royalist army advanced south
from Leicester, then withdrew towards Market Harborough.
On 14 June the king, vacillating between waiting to be
joined by Goring's army marching north from the south-
west or moving to meet his northern army, took the advice
of his nephew Prince Rupert and decided to face Fairfax. He
marched south, the two armies running into each other on
Fenny Hill just north of the village of Naseby.

The Civil War in England

1. Edgehill (1642)
2. Turnham Green (1642)
3. Marston Moor (1644)
4. Lostwithiel (1644)
5. Newbury (1644)
6. Donnington Castle (1644)
7. Faringdon Castle (1645)
8. Naseby (1645)
9. Colchester (1648)
10. Worcester (1651)
11. Sedgemoor (1685)

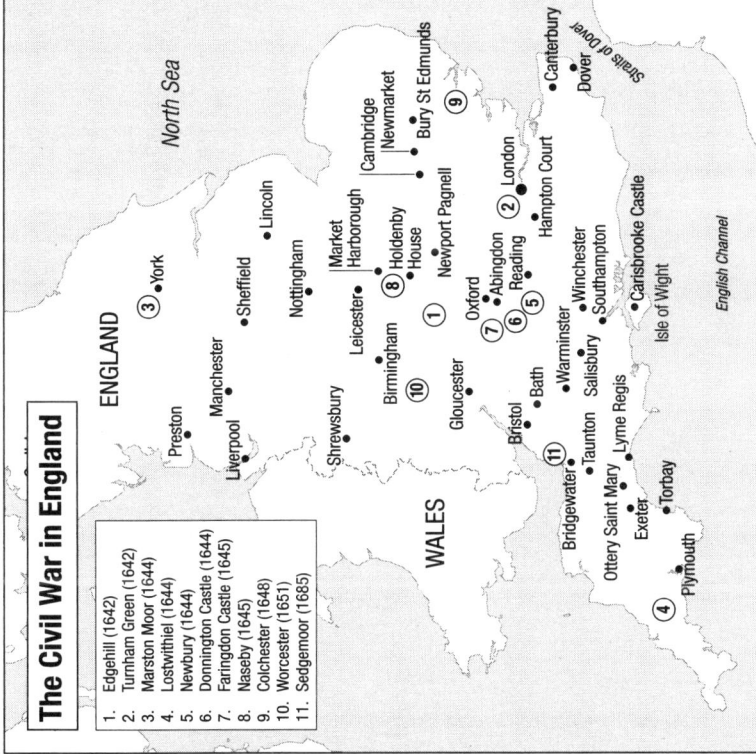

ENGLAND

WALES

North Sea

English Channel

Straits of Dover

Preston
Liverpool
Manchester
Shrewsbury
Birmingham (10)
Gloucester
Bristol
Bath
Taunton (11)
Bridgewater
Ottery Saint Mary
Exeter
Plymouth (4)
Torbay
Lyme Regis
Warminster
Salisbury
Winchester
Southampton
Isle of Wight
Carisbrooke Castle
Oxford (1)
Abingdon (7)
Reading (6) (5)
London (2)
Hampton Court
Newport Pagnell
Holdenby House (8)
Market Harborough
Leicester
Nottingham
Sheffield
Lincoln
York (3)
Cambridge
Newmarket
Bury St Edmunds (9)
Canterbury
Dover

The Battle of Naseby

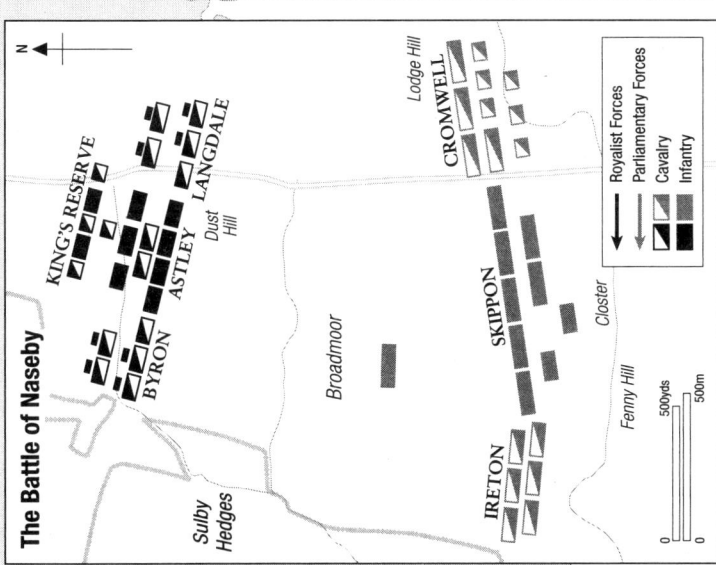

KING'S RESERVE

BYRON
ASTLEY
LANGDALE

Dust Hill

Broadmoor

Sulby Hedges

Closter

Fenny Hill

Lodge Hill

CROMWELL

SKIPPON

IRETON

Royalist Forces	Parliamentary Forces
Cavalry	
Infantry	

0   500yds
0   500m

Naseby is often taken to be the apogee of the New Model Army. In fact, it was the opposite. Decisive victory as it turned out to be, it was a battle fought more closely than later propaganda would have us believe. The Royalists were seriously outnumbered, fielding around 9,000 men against the New Model's 15,000, so Fairfax anyway enjoyed a significant advantage. Although his infantry regiments were short of men and training, his 11 regiments of horse, divided now into two 'wings' – one under Henry Ireton, Cromwell's son-in-law, and one under Cromwell himself – were at full strength and capable. Fairfax also chose his position well, using a crest to hide his infantry in the centre so the Royalists had to advance uphill. He placed Cromwell with six regiments of horse on his right flank and Ireton with five on his left. He concealed Okey's dragoons along a hedge to his and Ireton's left so they could fire into the Royalist flank as they advanced. Even so, the New Model infantry failed to hold their ground when the Royalist infantry under Astley attacked, urged on by Prince Rupert. The infantry were forced back, with Skippon being badly injured as he tried to rally them. At the same time, Prince Rupert's horse charged Ireton's regiments on the New Model's left, scattering them as they were distracted trying to help their infantry, and capturing Ireton. It looked very much as if the king would prevail. The day was saved by Cromwell using his new disciplined tactics to charge the Royalist horse under Sir Marmaduke Langdale, facing him on the New Model's right. His new tactics worked well so that he then regrouped and attacked the Royalist infantry on his left, stalling them and allowing Skippon to rally his men so that they returned to their previous positions, while Okey's dragoons were pouring fire into the Royalists' right from their hedge. Cromwell then crossed to rally Ireton's regiments, again hitting the Royalist right, while Fairfax attacked Langdale's men as they tried to regroup. Once stabilized, Fairfax caused the whole New Model to advance; what was left of the king's army was forced to flee. The New Model's casualties were very light, with only 150 killed, while the Royalists lost about 1,000. More significantly, the Royalist infantry were mostly taken prisoner; they lost all their artillery and 2,000 horses as well as their baggage train and the king's letter chest, publication of which would later do much to damage his image.

The New Model had passed its first test and, within a few short months of its creation, had justified its existence and the concept behind its inception. Naseby effectively ended the first stage of the civil wars, and although the regiments would go on almost immediately to fight Goring's western army, the Royalists no longer posed a realistic tactical threat. Pickering's regiment had lost a Welshman, Captain Tomkins, at Naseby and had 49 soldiers wounded, of whom only four would later die of their wounds, so they had escaped relatively lightly despite the New Model's infantry being in the centre of the fighting. It also says much for the New Model's fledgling medical services and the regimental 'chirugeons', or surgeons.

Sieges and battles continued throughout 1645, notably at Bridgewater and Bristol, but by February 1646 the last Royalist field army had surrendered at Oxford and the king had given himself up at Newark. Fairfax and Cromwell returned to Westminster, but poor Pickering died that winter at Ottery St Mary in Devon where his regiment were quartered. He was just 30 years old. He was not alone. The New Model lost hundreds of men that winter through 'plague', which was more likely to have been severe influenza. While the 'chirugeons' may have been skilled at dealing with wounds, they were less effective at controlling disease. Food was scarce and pay problems had re-emerged.

The story now becomes as much political as military, and as much one of sorting the New Model's administrative and logistic systems as it does of field tactics. Fairfax estimated that he lost about a third his infantry after Naseby, many of them pressed men who simply deserted.[18] Given the speed with which the New Model had been assembled, and the political poison surrounding its inception, this is not altogether surprising; what is more remarkable is that Fairfax, Cromwell, Ireton and Skippon could exercise such tactical skill to defeat an admittedly smaller but still capable and experienced Royalist force so decisively. The victories they had won, with the consequent pause in the fighting, now gave the army the opportunity to sort itself out. What emerged was the embryo of today's British Army. It is in the next few years that the New Model Army, Cromwell's army, or the British army, offers us the most valuable of lessons both in how an army can transform itself into what a nation needs to survive and how quickly it can fall. Within 13 years the heroes of Naseby were widely detested so that they faced almost total disbandment – *almost*, but not quite.

The army's administration would remain variable over the next 15 years of almost constant campaigning, but it was certainly a considerable improvement on what had gone before and was arguably superior to that of comparable European armies. It was helped by establishing a policy of fixed 'establishments', whereby each regiment or unit was structured the same. Previously, the size of regiments and the number of officers, non-commissioned officers and soldiers had been at the discretion of the colonel. Parliament had laid down the establishment tables in the spring of 1645 so, for example, each regiment of horse was to have six troops of 100 men. Each troop was to have four officers – a captain, a lieutenant, a cornet and a quartermaster – together with three non-commissioned officers, all corporals, although this was inadequate and their number would soon be increased. There were no sergeants in the horse, as the word 'sergeant' implied a servant, which rankled with the well-to-do troopers of the Eastern Association who would form the core of the new regiments. It is a tradition still practised by the British Household Cavalry today.

Infantry regiments were manned to a similar pattern, with each regiment having ten companies. Seven of these were 100 strong, while the senior company, the colonel's company, was established at 200, with his lieutenant colonel's company at 160 and the major's, the second in command of the regiment, at 140. The term 'lieutenant', which had been widely used for some time and which literally means 'in place of', was an official rank, meaning that the lieutenant colonel could act in place of his colonel while the colonel was about political or personal business. In addition, each regiment of both horse and foot had a 'regimental staff', or officers with specific functions, such as a surgeon, a chaplain, a provost-marshal responsible for discipline, as well as quartermasters and clerks.

Regiments of horse also had trumpeters who were heirs of the medieval heralds. They always rode grey horses so that they were distinguishable, and although their main job was to blow the calls to convey orders, they were also used as messengers. 'Trumpeters,' said Sir James Turner, 'because they are frequently sent to an enemy, ought to be witty and discreet, and must drink but little, so that they be rather apt to circumvent others, that be circumvented; they should be cunning, and wherever they are sent, they should be careful to observe warily.'[19]

Parliament had also laid down standard pay rates across the army, which was, again, a novel and welcome innovation. Pay was also generous. Officers were particularly well paid, with colonels earning 12 shillings per day and captains ten shillings in the cavalry and eight shillings in the infantry. It was also graded so that a trooper in a regiment of horse earned two shillings a day, considerably more than a dragoon at one shilling and sixpence and an infantryman who earned just eight pence. The discrimination was based on the fact that the cavalryman and the dragoon had to pay for their horses' forage, and the horses in the regiments of horse, being of a better quality than those of the humble dragoon, of course required better food! All soldiers were required to pay their food and lodging from their pay. It was probably a necessary distinction until foraging horses became centrally administered, but it led to a slightly unfortunate stratification of the British Army which would remain for centuries.

In the early days, the New Model soldiers were, generally, paid on time although not always, and when they weren't they could still go hungry. Rates were also subject to constant revision to take account of inflation and especially corn prices. They were increased in 1651, with the infantry receiving ten pence per day, although reduced again in 1655, after which they remained fairly static at two and three pence for the horse, one and eightpence for the dragoons, and ninepence for the foot until 1660.[20]

Another improvement was standardizing uniform and equipment. In the early years of the war, regiments had worn all manner of coloured coats, making battlefield identification almost impossible without some identifying sign; at Marston

Moor the Parliamentarians wore a white handkerchief and the Royalists orange scarves, but it wasn't a very satisfactory system. When Fairfax found himself surrounded by Royalists, he simply removed his white handkerchief and rode back to his own lines through the Royalist regiments who cheered him as one of their own commanders. A committee of six MPs had been selected by Parliament to oversee the New Model's procurement and, generally, they did a good job. It was decided to clothe the whole army in red coats, red being the cheapest dye available to colour white cloth. On the Royalist side, the Marquis of Newcastle's regiment famously wore white or undyed coats; some said that was because he wanted to spare the expense of dyeing them, while the more charitable ascribed it to his soldiers pleading with him to let them dye them in their enemy's blood. From the spring of 1645 all the New Model infantry regiments wore red, as did the dragoons. The horse wore leather buff coats which were expensive at £10 and highly prized – they were the first thing to be taken from prisoners – but practical for supporting 'fronts and backs'.[21] Weapons were also standardized so the whole army used the same firelocks, matchlocks and swords, although it would not be until the 1650s that they also supplied tents.

The army's logistics also started badly, the rapid march to Naseby proving too much for a system in its infancy. The popular notion was that the army acquired food and forage by 'living off the land', but that is a fanciful theory for 15,000 men and half as many horses moving through a few tiny villages in the month before the harvest had started. Almost certainly they were fed commercially, with merchants following up and running their own private ventures to source food from the major market towns. The quartermasters' job would have been to source rations, and accommodation, and then collect the money from soldiers' pay to cover it. Later, again, much work was done to source food and establish supply depots and magazines which were used for the later campaigns.[22]

By late 1646, as the final Royalist strongholds were taken and Fairfax felt able to return to a hero's welcome in London, he commanded an army that had achieved decisive success in the field, was increasingly well administered and supplied and which could, as its reputation and morale strengthened, also now recruit, although generous rates of pay and commercial disruption undoubtedly helped.

The crisis of 1644 had led to the formation of an army that was to prove the value of its concept. Not only had it convincingly won the war but it was now an efficient force which allowed its masters to exercise political power. A drastic political situation had called for a drastic military reform. Given how used we are to how modern armies operate, it can be difficult fully to appreciate just how extraordinary and revolutionary the New Model was. However much one may regret what happened in the civil wars, there can be no doubt as to the vision, effectiveness and single-mindedness of those who, in five years, had overthrown a dynasty and its established church and proclaimed a Commonwealth. They had done this with an army. The issue that army would now face was, who should those masters be?

The euphoria of late 1646 would, however, soon begin to disappear. With the king in their custody, Parliament came to represent the ultimate authority in what was still a kingdom. Having thanked the New Model for their service, although still owing them considerable back pay, on 18 February 1647 they moved to disband them, arguing that, now the war was won, they had no further use for them. This somewhat abrupt stance developed into a stand-off between Parliament and army, with Parliament, led by Denzil Holles and Philip Stapleton, demanding that the army submit to their will, while Fairfax and his soldiers refused to do so. The mood in the army was not helped by its arrears of pay nor by continuing efforts to recruit for service in Ireland. In April they presented Fairfax with a petition, 'The Apologie of the Common Souldiers'. The wording of this was surprisingly radical. Their enemies, by which they meant Members of Parliament, they complained, 'now lurked like foxes in their dens and cannot be dealt withal, though discovered, being protected by those who are entrusted with the government of the kingdom'. This was followed by a 'Second Apologie', which reminded Parliament that they had originally joined up to fight so that 'the meanest subject should fully enjoy his right, liberty and properties in all things'.[23] This was a departure from the standard military grievances. Here were soldiers who, through their successful service, had begun to come close to a power which previously had been totally foreign to them. Parliament's original concerns that the New Model was becoming socially extreme were beginning to prove correct. Holles scoffed that 'most of the colonels are tradesmen, brewers, tailors, goldsmiths, shoemakers and the like', which had not been the case in 1646, but, as those who had joined to fight from principle began to retire to civilian life, there was a perceptible change to a class of officer who saw service as a profession rather than an obligation.[24] As always the horse attracted the better-off recruits, with some of the regiments of foot becoming increasingly radicalized, combining extreme Puritanism with an agenda for political reform that went far beyond what either Parliament or their generals embraced.

At this stage Fairfax and Cromwell's position was to support their soldiers. The army's suspicions were heightened when correspondence emerged suggesting that the king, who was being held by Parliament near Oxford, was in league with 'the Presbyterians' as they referred to the Parliamentarians, to ally with the Scots and bring over a foreign army to destroy the New Model. With Cromwell's connivance, on 1 June an army detachment under Cornet Joyce rode to Holdenby House where the king was being detained and took him into their own custody. Parliament resolved to arrest Cromwell, whom they correctly blamed for this affrontery, but he remained outside London with the bulk of the army gathered at Newmarket. There they drew up a 'Solemn Engagement' – every declaration during this period was described as 'solemn' – declaring that the army would not disband until their grievances were addressed but, again, demanding guarantees of freedom for the English people.[25] Parliament was now becoming alarmed as the army demanded the impeachment of the 11 leading 'Presbyterians', including Holles and Stapleton, and they duly fled before they could be arrested. Holles went to Europe from where he would later return to be ennobled by Charles II. Parliament had an ally in the City of London with its own Trained Bands, but these too were overawed so that by late July the initiative was firmly with the army and thus with Fairfax and Cromwell.

Yet Fairfax and Cromwell were themselves becoming increasingly alarmed at the army's extremism and especially the influence of the Levellers, a movement dedicated to achieving social equality and an end to all discrimination on grounds of 'tenure, estate, charter, degree, birth or place'.[26] The Levellers' leader was a soldier called John Lilburne who had a long history of agitation but who had also served with distinction. In July 1646 he had been imprisoned for his trenchant criticism of Parliament, and Cromwell had intervened to try to have him released. In October 1647 the Levellers published *An Agreement of the People*, setting out their radical agenda which quickly circulated throughout the army.

The same month, Fairfax and Cromwell agreed to meet representatives from different regiments, known throughout the army as 'agitators', to hear the army's case. They met in St Mary's Church in Putney from which followed a series of extraordinary debates, with the army's legitimate concerns about its pay and its future being overtaken by some of its 'agitators' putting their extreme political views, inspired by the Levellers' *Agreement*. One of the most radical was Colonel Thomas Rainborowe, who entered into a lengthy argument with Ireton on universal suffrage, although he seems to have excluded various categories, such as anyone who had fought against Parliament, and women. Ireton countered that universal male suffrage would lead to anarchy. The arguments raged on into November, with the army commanders, now known by the army as the 'grandees', concluding that they must put a stop to a debate that was getting out of control. They closed the session on 11 November, sending the agitators back to their regiments.

The debates had also considered the position of the king, but on the day the debates ended news reached the grandees that he had escaped from the army's custody at Hampton Court. He had, in fact, only got as far as the Isle of Wight, where he was imprisoned again, this time in Carisbrooke Castle, but his political manoeuvrings that winter would lead to the Scottish invasion of England in May 1648, which encouraged sporadic Royalist uprisings across the country in what became known as the Second Civil War. The army's political agenda was temporarily set aside, to the relief of the grandees, as they mobilized once again, winning a series of small engagements and then decisively defeating the Scots at Preston in August. It was a dirty war, with atrocities committed by both sides, marked by the execution of Sir Charles Lucas and Sir George Lisle, the Royalist commanders at Colchester, after they had surrendered, in what became a notorious war crime.

By the time the army had finished mopping up pockets of Royalist resistance and returned south, it was in a rebellious mood. That November, at a meeting with Fairfax in St Albans, they issued a 'Remonstrance', which not only called for the execution of the king, who they held had directly caused the misery of the recent fighting, but was also equally critical of Parliament, which they wrote should be replaced with a supreme council elected frequently and 'with as much equality as may be'.[27] They were as good as their word. By early December they had replaced the king's gaolers to prevent a further escape attempt. On 6 December, persuaded just to 'purge' Parliament rather than disband it, Pride's and Rich's regiments forcibly ejected the London Trained Bands from their duties and assumed responsibility for security at Westminster. Forty-one MPs were arrested while many more stayed away in what became known as 'Pride's Purge'. With Cromwell now exercising control rather than Fairfax, he proceeded to put the king on trial followed by his execution in January 1649.

With the king dead and Parliament neutered, the triangular pillars of power now became the grandees, the army and what was left of Parliament – 'the Rump', as it came to be known. Parliament elected a Council of State, which became the sovereign power, abolishing the monarchy on 17 March and declaring England and Wales a Commonwealth in May. The army, however, remained restless, driven as much by an unwillingness to serve in Ireland – a deeply unpopular posting to which more regiments were being directed – as by Leveller sympathies. Despite their political demands being largely met, in April Colonel Edward Whalley's regiment mutinied, surprising in itself given that Whalley was held to be one of the more Puritan of the commanding officers. The mutiny was swiftly put down by Fairfax, but in May Colonel Adrian Scrope's regiment did the same thing in Oxfordshire, refusing to serve in Ireland. Leaving the unfortunate Scrope with a handful of men, they marched off to Bristol. Inevitably, they issued yet another pamphlet, a combination of demands for arrears and complaints about pay combined with Leveller calls for 'freedom, peace and happiness' and the adoption of 'An Agreement of the People'.[28] It was again rapidly suppressed by Fairfax and Cromwell, with the ringleaders executed, which had the desired effect of preventing further outbreaks. Cromwell was unrepentant. Had the Levellers succeeded, then 'England might soon have been overrun by an alliance of discontented persons, servants, reformadoes [and] beggars,' he wrote.[29]

What is of equal interest is that it was only a small proportion of the army who appeared to be so politically affected. Fairfax easily assembled a force to combat the mutineers; it is unlikely that more than 1,000 were deeply committed, which brings us back once more to the question of motivation. It is difficult to disentangle exactly what forces were at play. There can have been fewer deeply religious soldiers than Fairfax and many of his colonels, several of whom were semi-professional preachers like William Goffe, and all of whom would combine their military briefings with sermons about the need to do God's work. What is confusing, as it must have been to many then, was how this translated into the need for social reform. Reading the various pamphlets and tracts which had come to litter the London book-stands, one is struck as much by the demands for better pay and conditions as by the need to reform the franchise, and how the cost of stabling a horse overnight in an inn features as strongly as creating God's kingdom on earth.[30] Yet it is worth pausing to consider what an extraordinary position the British Isles now found themselves in. A professional army, unheard of just five years previously, held the balance of power, and far from discharging its duties to the legitimate government, had overthrown that government and was now apparently intent on forcing social change. It had moved very quickly from being a force that did what people wanted – or at least that part of the people who supported Parliament – to becoming a force that was, if not already at odds with the nation, dangerously close to being so. Still a highly professional and experienced military force, it would take one more step into the political abyss, one that arguably nearly brought about its destruction.

For the next three years much of the army was, ultimately, involved in Cromwell's war in Ireland, one of the most shameful and bloody episodes in the history of these islands and one which still defines Anglo-Irish relations to this day. It was followed by Cromwell's intervention in Scotland. Fairfax refused to command this campaign, launched in mid-1650, so that Cromwell was recalled from Ireland to take his place. Driven by the fear that the Scots, having formed an alliance with Charles II in exile, would once again invade England and cause another Royalist insurgency, Cromwell duly invaded in July, defeating the Scots decisively at Dunbar on 3 September.

He remained in Scotland with a significant force that winter, moving south to make short work of a Scottish army that had broken south with Charles II at Worcester, exactly one year later on 3 September 1651. Worcester effectively finished Scottish threats to England, but Cromwell left a sizeable army in Scotland to keep the peace, commanded by the reliable and efficient General George Monck. It was to prove a prophetic appointment.

Parliament, Rump as it was, remained determined that it should maintain power over the army. Events came to a head in mid-1652 as Parliament delayed and evaded passing bills that the army thought necessary to restore peace, moved to cut both their size and budget, and to frustrate Cromwell's plans for elections and a new Parliament that would be 'Godly'. Underestimating Cromwell's ambition once again, the Rump found itself ejected by force on 20 April. An attempt to elect another parliament that summer filled with men thought reliable by the army, nicknamed 'Barebones' after one of the members – the splendidly named Praise God Barebones – predictably failed, and in December Cromwell became Lord Protector.

The 'Protectorate' would last for five years. There were Protectorate parliaments, but they were ineffective until after Cromwell's death. Cromwell now found himself responsible for foreign policy as well as the more familiar domestic agenda which had previously consumed him. Here again his army served him well, also becoming a competent expeditionary army. From 1653 to 1659 they would fight loyally overseas, in Europe first against the Dutch, then Spain and latterly in Flanders in an attempt to take Dunkirk.[31] In 1654 Cromwell launched the Western Design, an expedition against Spain in the West Indies which resulted in the capture of Jamaica but failed to take Hispaniola. The troops who took part in this expedition were not from the New Model but were recruited separately, hence lacking training and organization. Overall that campaign was an abject failure that led to considerable loss of life, reinforcing the lessons of the need for sound training and administration.

Cromwell also came into power determined to reform an English society which he felt was morally weak and irreligious. Much as one may disagree with the self-righteousness of his Puritan zeal, it is difficult not to admire the single-mindedness with which he approached a solution. He had, by now and after his incessant arguments with a parliament whose class he still represented but who he felt were ineffective, lost faith in the local elites who dominated Parliament. He put his trust in the army to effect those social changes he thought vital but which the Parliamentary class would inevitably resent as undermining their local power base. Instead of reducing the army, which was a Parliamentary mantra, he argued that already 'the numbers were but few and the condition of the people such, as the major part, a great deal, are persons disaffected and engaged against us'. He feared another uprising and, he accused the MPs, 'instead of peace and settlement, instead of mercy and truth being brought together… weeds and nettles, briars and thorns have thriven under you, shadows, disettlement and division, discontent and dissatisfaction together with real dangers to the whole have been more multiplied'.[32] Instead of relying on the traditional English county establishments to effect the changes he wanted, he would instead appoint godly men from the army who would be able to run the shires according to the Puritan principles which he now regarded as being beyond question.

These officers, all senior men with considerable experience, were to be sent as a cross between lords lieutenant and regional governors, charged with bringing 'some proportion of serviceableness to the great works, designs and promises of God concerning the kingdom of his Son, our blessed Lord, and may be used as instruments in his hand for the continuance and increase of reformation and the security and settlement of these nations'.[33] By the end of 1655 England and Wales found themselves divided into 12 districts, each the responsibility of a major general charged with ensuring that his district came to be as godly as Cromwell envisaged. They were, in particular, required to 'keep all disaffected people under close surveillance' and to 'prevent any of them gathering together either in private houses or at horse race meetings, cock-fightings or bear-baitings', both because treason and rebellion were frequently hatched at such gatherings and also because 'much evil and wickednes commonly occurred at them'.[34]

Some of those selected came from the pre-war gentry in the areas to which they were assigned, like Cromwell's old friend Edward Whalley in the Midlands, who was not averse to profiteering from confiscated Royalist estates. Their reception was at best neutral. Others, like the ex-iron works clerk James Berry, in Wales, were thought to favour extremists and found it hard to become accepted. Berry was also colonel of one of the regiments of horse about which we will shortly be hearing a lot more. Similarly William Goffe, responsible for Berkshire, Hampshire and Sussex, constantly found himself 'so much tyred'. A Millenarian, who believed that the world would soon end, his excessively gloomy outlook did not fit in well with those trying to rebuild their lives. He considered himself 'so poore and inconsiderable a creature', an attitude which was hardly helpful when trying to run the home counties.[35] Many of those for whom he was responsible would have agreed with him.

It will not come as a surprise that these self-righteous prigs rapidly became both deeply unpopular and an object of scorn. England and Wales had now suffered war and its after-effects for 13 years. Many families had lost fathers, husbands or sons and had seen the destruction of their homes and villages. God-fearing as most probably were, they did not welcome this sanctimonious interference in the few pleasures they had left to them. What made the system even more unpopular was that anyone suspected of Royalist sympathies would have to pay for it through what became known as the Decimation Tax because it was levied on 10 per cent of income.

Unsurprisingly, the experiment failed. Apart from the fact that there were far too few major generals to make an impact, and that people disliked their interference with their traditional forms of local government and their tiresome determination that theirs was the only true interpretation of the scriptures, there was strong resistance to the fact that they were soldiers. By late 1657 the experiment was seen as a failure and a revitalized Parliament voted for its demise, a move encouraged by the increasing talk in London of a possible restoration of the monarchy, although initially the monarch was held to be Cromwell as opposed to Charles Stuart. The Rule of the Major Generals was the nadir of the New Model Army; an organization that had started with so much public support was now seen as an agent of repression and there mostly to maintain a regime which many thought illegitimate and found self-serving. How was the army to recover?

Cromwell died on 3 September 1658. He had held such extraordinary personal authority for the previous 13 years, and near absolute power for at least the last five, that there was no one of similar stature to replace him. His son Richard was briefly made Lord Protector in his place but the authority of the appointment had rested with Oliver Cromwell as an individual; there was no precedent for the post he had created and precious little support outside the army. For the next year England would suffer from a confusion of interests as different Parliamentary and military groups grappled for power. Richard Cromwell inherited a bankrupt exchequer and, under the electoral rules that his father had developed, in the autumn of 1658 he called a new Parliament. This was different to the old Rump and was seen as less uncompromising to the Royalist cause. It immediately aroused the suspicions of the army, not least because its members were slow to make good arrears of pay, moved that the size of the army be cut, and took action against army officers who they said had mistreated Royalist prisoners. The army, itself divided between a radical group of young officers and the grandees, demanded its dismissal. It was dissolved on 22 April, and the members of the old Rump returned once more. Richard Cromwell resigned that May. The Rump proved no more tractable and, in the summer of 1659, General John Lambert attempted a military coup, dissolving the Rump yet again and in August defeating a Royalist uprising in Cheshire led by George Booth.

But the mood in the country was now becoming strongly against the army. General Monck, commanding in Scotland, had remained outwith the chaotic struggles taking place in London, carefully controlling the radicals in Scotland and managing to find sufficient funds to keep his regiments well recruited, trained and paid. Monck had been a prominent and successful commander in the New Model and a close ally of Cromwell, but his roots were as a West Country squire and he had started the wars fighting for the Royalists. It is difficult to ascertain exactly what forces motivated him in 1659 but, despite loud and regular protestations to the contrary, he came to believe that the army must be subservient to the civil authority. He also believed that the popular mood was that the Stuarts should be restored. Monck would do very well personally out of the Restoration, but there must have been a genuine fear that, as a landowner and social conservative, the radicalism of some officers was now out of control. He also saw it as a threat to the army itself which he had done so much to create. Confident that his troops would defeat Lambert, he marched south. He was supported by the army commanders in Dublin, who had reached similar conclusions, and Fairfax, now living in retirement in Yorkshire, and whose support greatly enhanced the prestige of his cause. In the event Lambert's regiments fell apart and Lambert himself was arrested. Monck arrived in London in February 1660, started detailed negotiations with Charles II in exile in Holland and worked with him to agree terms for his restoration. The resulting Declaration of Breda was accepted by yet another Parliament, the so-called Convention Parliament, whose election Monck supported that spring and which was, allegedly, neither Royalist nor anti-monarchist, although in reality it was strongly supportive of the Restoration. On 25 May Charles II landed at Dover where Monck met him and escorted him to London.

The axis of power was therefore re-established between monarch and Parliament. It was hardly surprising that Parliament now set to work to disband the army which had caused them so much trouble, which they still held, correctly, to harbour strong Puritan sympathies and which was unaffordable. No sooner had Charles II landed than they voted money to pay off the whole force, which then stood at approximately 40,000 men. A rota of regiments for disbandment was determined by the Privy Council, with Monck intervening to ensure that his regiments were left until last.

But Charles II was acutely conscious that had his father had even the core of a professional army in 1642 then events might have played out very differently. He was also aware of the power that Louis XIV's *Maison Militaire du Roi* gave the French monarchy, a division of guards under the direct control of the king, a model that owed much to the Ottomans. Returning with Charles were those Royalists who had accompanied him in exile and who had formed troops of mounted guards, a Household Cavalry, to protect him and his brother James, Duke of York. There were also foot guards who had provided for his security in Holland. He was determined to keep these elements under his personal control.

Monck was also aware of the dangers of having an unguarded king at a time when many were still highly suspicious of the Stuarts. Given that Charles had no children and his heir was his brother, the Catholic James, Duke of York, any threat to the king's safety risked collapsing the delicate Restoration settlement. His fears were heightened, and the case for a permanent force of guards strengthened, by an obscure London wine cooper and Fifth Monarchist called Thomas Venner. Fifth Monarchists believed, rather unhelpfully so soon after the Restoration, that all earthly kings were evil and all earthly authority was 'Babylon'. They vowed not to sheathe their swords until they had established the universal monarchy of Christ on earth and 'until the kings of the earth should be bound in chains and the nobles in fetters of iron'.[36] On 6 January 1661 Venner and a group of his supporters broke into St Paul's and demanded of the unfortunate night watchman whether he was 'For the King'. He answered, logically enough, that he was for King Charles, whereupon Venner shot him through the head, declaring that he should only be for King Jesus. The Trained Bands were called from the Royal Exchange to evict them but they ran away. Next the Lord Mayor was called, who arrived with his own guards. They succeeded in driving the Fifth Monarchists to Highgate where they managed to barricade them in a house but were not inclined to do much more. Eventually it was Monck's Life Guard, together with the Duke of York and some of his companions, who managed to drive them out, the survivors taking refuge in a tavern in Wood Street, Cheapside. Colonel Corbet and the Life Guards then stormed the pub while the Trained Bands looked on and 'did a little desert him and retreated to the upper end of Cheape Side, calling out for foot, which does a little staine on their redd scarves'[37] – red scarves being then an officer's sign of office. Most of Venner's band were killed, but Venner himself survived, which was fortunate for the government as it allowed them to put him to a public traitor's death.

Monck, by now ennobled as the Duke of Albemarle, had in fact already drawn up plans as early as August to retain two regiments of horse and two of foot at an annual cost of £118,529 to form a royal guard force. The Convention Parliament had conveniently been dissolved that December, so that, with York and Albemarle demanding action, it was now open to the King's Council to adjudicate. York wrote to the Lord Chancellor saying that 'the King's Chief Counsellors, who had been eye witnesses [sic] to the insurrections and rebellions in the time of King Charles I, and what he suffered for the want of good guards, should now be so careless of the King's safety as not to have advised him to secure himself from such dangers for the future'.[38] It was a masterstroke of opportunism which led to the establishment of both English and Scottish standing armies, which Parliament would come to so deplore, and later the British Army. Had York and Albemarle moved a few weeks earlier, then Parliament would have been in session and would have insisted on the disbandment of the final regiments. Had the Venner riots occurred a few months later, then a more confident council may have seen them for the localized disturbance by a band of madmen that they were.

The process that would keep a core of the New Model in being is again best told by the story of one regiment. When Cromwell had invaded Scotland in 1650, he had asked Sir Arthur Haselrig, he of 'Haselrig's lobsters' fame, to raise a regiment of horse and one of foot from the northern counties. The horse were issued with blue coats, there being some blue cloth available, with a blue standard, and were predictably known as The Blues. They fought with distinction in Scotland. Haselrig remained in command, and after Manuel Dowsson, who commanded one of the troops, was taken prisoner and then murdered by the Scots, he replaced him with an experienced officer called Unton Croke. Croke came from the Oxfordshire gentry and was very much an old-school Parliamentary officer as opposed to being a Puritan. Fairfax had lived in the Crokes' agreeable country house at Marston when besieging Oxford. During the summer of 1651, Haselrig was replaced by James Berry, the extremist ex-clerk of that Shropshire ironworks who would later go on to be the major general in Wales. Berry tried to persuade his friend, the equally extreme preacher Richard Baxter, to come as The Blues' chaplain but, perhaps fortunately for the regiment, Baxter refused, as he said that Berry had once attended a Congregationalist service.

However extreme Berry may have been, he was undoubtedly a highly efficient operator. The Blues gained an excellent reputation, especially for horse care, and were moved south in 1653, where they were deployed in support of Cromwell's bid to become Lord Protector. In 1657 they returned to Scotland, where they came under Monck's command and, with Berry busy annoying the Welsh and also becoming a member of Cromwell's fledging 'upper house' – a sort of Puritan house of lords that gained but little traction – Unton Croke took over command as the lieutenant colonel. The regiment were still strongly Puritan and Monck found them riddled with Quakers. He wrote to Cromwell to complain that the Quakers were 'a very dangerous people, should they increase in your army, and be neither fit to command nor obey, but ready to make a distraction and to mutiny upon very slight occasion'.[39] Croke worked to eradicate them and by so doing seems to have gained Monck's confidence. Berry predictably joined in Lambert's revolt and was cashiered, thus leaving the way clear for Croke to assume full command. The regiment now made an extraordinary declaration – what became known as the Warminster declaration – in which, as well as declaring their unbounded support for 'liberty of conscience, as to spirituals, for all the Lord's people was a fundamental from which we will not swerve', they also added that 'we cannot willingly suffer our liberties, our estates nor persons to be disposed of by any but our just, legal and due representative in Parliament'.[40] They did go on to renounce Charles Stuart, which was the usual mantra for army declarations, but that was still a few months before the Restoration.

When Monck and Charles II debated how to keep the core of the New Model intact, The Blues, with the reliable and socially acceptable Unton Croke in command, whom Monck trusted, together with the regiment of foot raised alongside them, became obvious candidates. To preserve appearances, The Blues were put through a formal disbandment parade in Bath in December 1660 but then almost immediately re-instated as the Royal Regiment of Horse Guards on Tothill Fields in London on 6 February 1661 after the Venner riots. Charles II's guards became the 1st Foot Guards, while Haselrig's foot became the 2nd Foot Guards. Although the officers in The Blues were changed – reliable as Unton Croke was, he was still thought too associated with the Parliamentary cause to stay – the soldiers remained much the same. Here was one of what had been one of the most Puritan regiments in the New Model now fully transferred into royal service, which again must raise the question as to just how devoutly Puritan the Cromwellian army had actually been. Once Berry was released, he ended his days as a gardener, in which profession he was rumoured to have found complete satisfaction.

An even more interesting example was to be found in the Household Cavalry. Trotting behind the king's carriage as he was driven to London from Dover that May were those who had loyally served him in exile, but preceding the procession were Monck's own troop of Life Guards – in other words, trusted troopers who constituted his personal bodyguard. Many of these had been members of Cromwell's Life Guard, which Monck had inherited when he arrived in London, and they wore the same uniform, with standard

New Model fronts, backs and pots. The Life Guards, confusingly properly known as Horse Guards, would remain as three troops – one for the king, one for James, Duke of York and Monck's troop – and again be heavily involved in protecting the king from then on. By early 1661 there were therefore effectively four regiments of the New Model now under royal command and which would form the core of the British Army. All four regiments have been in service ever since.

The story of the next 25 years is one of the slow growth of the standing army. In the early years of Charles II's reign, the four regiments were used as both a royal guard force and for other government duties. In 1670, for example, The Blues had troops at Canterbury, Reading, Salisbury, Uxbridge, Islington and Farnham, where their role was to help keep the peace. They had a significant presence together with a detachment of foot guards in York, always regarded as strongly republican, in 1664, when 15 dissenters were executed. Troops escorted navy pay from London to the coast, accompanied the king when he travelled, and welcomed foreign dignitaries when they arrived in the Channel ports. They were also increasingly involved in controlling smuggling along the south coast, a task that would remain with the British Army well into the 19th century.

New parliaments remained as opposed to the 'guards', as they referred to them, as their forebears. In 1674 Parliament presented the king with a long 'Quest of Grievances', chief amongst which was a concern regarding the Life Guard:

[they had] never been settled by Act of parliament – nay; they have been so far from it, that whensoever they have been so much as mentioned in the House of Commons, they would never in the least take any favourable notice of them, always looking upon them as a number of men unlawfully assembled, and in no respect fit to be the least countenanced by the Parliament of England.

They went on to say that 'they were a vast charge to the kingdom' and 'a place of refuge for Papists'.[41] However, in 1670 Charles had negotiated his Secret Treaty of Dover with Louis XIV whereby he agreed to assist the French in the war with the Dutch in return for generous subsidies, and, when the time was right, to announce his conversion to Catholicism. This meant that he could pay for his 'guards' from his own pocket.

However, in 1672 Parliament did agree to raise nine new regiments for the Third Dutch War, and they deployed, along with a party of Life Guards, under Charles' illegitimate son, the Duke of Monmouth, where they fought bravely in one of the endless sieges of Maastricht. After the war was concluded by the 1674 Treaty of Westminster, most were disbanded but the concept of a regular core for expeditionary armies had been accepted.

There were also troops raised to garrison England's new colonies; after the Restoration, England slowly started on its path to empire. As early as 1661 a regiment of horse had been raised specifically for service in Tangier, part of Charles II's dowry when he married Catherine of Braganza, an arrangement to which, perhaps unsurprisingly, the local Moorish kings took exception. Parading for the first time on 21 October 1661 as The Tangier Horse, this new regiment was to all intents and purposes a regiment of New Model horse recruited from New Model veterans. After a difficult 23 years in North Africa, the regiment returned to England where, once again, it was disbanded and then immediately raised again as 'Our own Royall Regiment of Dragoons', modelled on Okey's regiment and with some of his veterans still serving, their links to the executed regicide to whose inspiration they owed their employment now conveniently occluded.[42]

The army also felt moderately well cared for. Pay was relatively generous. Troopers in the regiments of horse were paid four shillings a day, or £73 per annum, which was roughly equivalent to an 'eminent clergyman'; even lawyers were only averaging £154 per annum in 1660. Captains earned a sizeable £546 per annum. In the still struggling post-war economy, positions in the regiments were eagerly sought after and began to change hands for money – the origins of the 'purchase system', which would later become officially established. In 1682 the king commissioned Christopher Wren to build a 'hospital' as a home for veterans 'broken by age and war', The Royal Hospital Chelsea; a similar hospital was built at Kilmainham in Dublin. Regular pensions were introduced in 1685, with generous payments for those wounded on operations. Three soldiers in The Blues each received £30 8s., a substantial sum, and widows' pensions were also regulated.

Despite persistent criticism from Parliament, by the time Charles II died in 1685 the British Army numbered 7,500 men, with five regiments of horse and seven of foot. It was still small when compared with the 100,000 Louis XIV could claim, and even the combined Danish and Norwegian army boasted 32,000 men, but given that the New Model had supposedly been disbanded in 1660, it was still an impressive force. Age was not then regarded as so much of an issue as it later became, and it was an army that still contained many New Model veterans.

Charles having no legitimate children, when he died early in 1685 the throne passed to his Catholic brother James, Duke of York. Unpopular as this was, Parliament initially supported James, and when Charles' well-liked illegitimate but Protestant son, Monmouth, attempted a coup that summer, the army was despatched west to confront him. What was remarkable was that this professional army fought for a Catholic king against the Protestant pretender and did so very successfully. The battle of Sedgemoor was the first time the British Army had taken to the field as a coherent formation as opposed to actions fought by individual regiments.

Monmouth had landed at Lyme Regis on 11 June 1685. Both he and later William of Orange chose to land in the West Country partly because it avoided the Channel fleet and partly because it was home to many Protestants. Monmouth had raised a force from Dorset, Somerset and Devon, rather than an army, but it was an amateur affair, untrained and poorly armed. He had marched north from the coast, heading for Bristol, but had been outmanoeuvred by the king's army, the English Army, commanded by a timid Lord Feversham – whose only military qualification appears to have been that he was a nephew of the great French Marshal Turenne – but actually ably led in the field by John Churchill, later famous as the Duke of Marlborough. By early July Monmouth had become trapped in Bridgewater, a town surrounded by the Somerset wetlands, which offered him few options for escape. He attempted to break out overnight on Sunday 5 July, only to be decisively routed by Churchill. His poor army disintegrated, many being killed on the battlefield and many others being subject to the savage revenge of Judge Jeffreys, the ferocious Lord

Chancellor, whose 'bloody assizes' toured the west of England executing what survivors he could find.

Horrible battle as it was, the English Army had behaved professionally. Its tactics were sound, based on the lessons learned in the 1650s, and its behaviour reliable. It also numbered in its ranks men like Sir Francis Compton, one of the veterans of the civil wars still serving. He had been a Royalist, while many soldiers in his regiment, The Blues, had fought with Monck. The New Model Army may have been long gone, but its legacy lived on.

The army that had learned to fight in 1645, and which had come perilously close to self-destruction through interfering in government, had learned that armies must not just be well trained, well equipped and well cared for but that they must also work with the government as opposed to attempting to supplant it. The English and soon the British Army would never again threaten the established order. James II expanded the army after Sedgemoor so that by the time he was in turn ousted by William of Orange, ruling as William III alongside his wife, Mary, James' daughter, it had increased to 25,000 men and was costing nearly £1 million each year. There were no barracks, nor would there be for a century, so soldiers were either billeted on local families, which was generally unpopular, or lived under canvas, which was unsustainable over a prolonged period. James gathered his by now seemingly very large army together for annual manoeuvres on Hounslow Heath, threateningly close to London, and people naturally wondered why. A local gentleman, Sir John Reresby, thought it would be a great spectacle and took his wife and daughters to see a mock battle but then rather wished he hadn't, as all he found were 'tents full of lewd women'.[43]

Constantine in York, where he was proclaimed emperor. (Getty)

Constantine's supposed dream before the Milvian Bridge in which Christ urged him to conquer under the sign of the Cross. (Alamy)

How Christians saw the Milvian Bridge and possibly, in later years, how Constantine saw himself. (Alamy)

The Arch of Constantine was a less than subtle insult from the Romans for him not making their city his capital.(Getty)

We get the most realistic idea of what Roman emperors looked like from their coins. Shown here are Constantine and Diocletian. (Getty)

Maximian. (Getty)

Maxentius. (Getty)

Solid evidence that Constantine was not a Christian at Milvian Bridge. This coin from 318 shows Sol Invictus on the obverse. (Getty)

Sultan Mehmet portrayed by Gentile Bellini. (Getty)

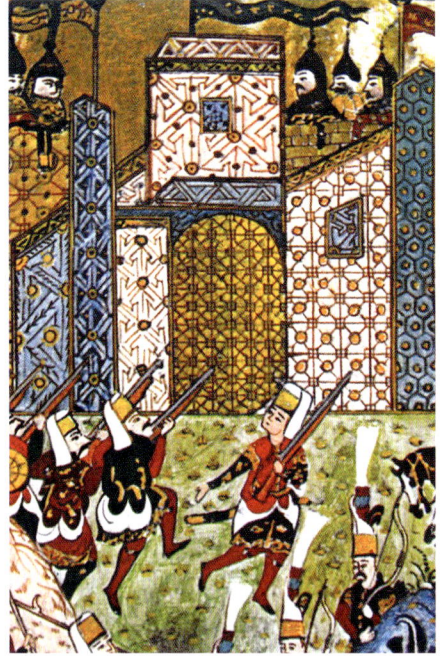
A stylised portrayal of Janissaries in action. (Getty)

The world on the last day. The final assault on Constantinople on Tuesday 29 May 1453. (Getty)

A stylised but accurate view of the siege. The fall of Constantinople stunned the Western world. (Getty)

Oliver Cromwell – an outstanding general and one of the founders of the modern British army. (Getty)

As effective as Cromwell was, much of the inspiration behind the New Model Army was Thomas Fairfax. (Alamy)

Cromwell's military genius resulted in his reorganisation of the cavalry which became the *arme blanche* of the New Model Army. (Getty)

Gerhard Johann von Scharnhorst – whose vision allowed the German enlightenment to take practical form. (Alamy)

Neidhardt von Gneisenau was one of the very first practitioners of the new Prussian staff system. (Alamy)

The Prussian *Landwehr*. The three-tier system proved to be one of the most effective models for a national army. (Getty)

George Marshall was responsible for taking the US Army from 19th in the world in 1941 to fielding 91 divisions within three years. (Getty)

George Patton was arguably the most effective of all the Allied commanders in the Second World War. (Getty)

The US Army was sent to war in 1942 with inadequate battle tanks. The M3 was totally outclassed by the German models it confronted in North Africa. (Getty)

It was rapidly replaced with the Sherman, which although equally outclassed, was produced in such numbers that eventually mass won over capability. (Getty)

While the Germans produced technically advanced tanks like the superlative Panther, they were never able to produce enough of them to give them battlefield superiority. (Getty)

The ultimate tank of the Second World War, and of the folly of the German production system, was the immensely capable but chronically unreliable Tiger. (Getty)

William of Orange landed at Torbay in November 1688 with a small Dutch army. In the event, the English army obeyed Parliament and not James, going over to William as he moved slowly eastwards, a decision by its commanders which is arguably as significant in the history of the British Army as Sedgemoor; the army which Parliament had feared might be used once again to promote absolutism was now obeying them as the legitimate authority, not the king. William, who never really trusted the English army after this, would nevertheless go on to make profligate use of them in his Nine Years' War against Louis XIV, an army now fighting against a Catholic monarch as opposed to with him. It was an army that had learned to obey the dictat of the legitimate government, however much they grumbled at the hardship and the danger. They fought loyally for William in the early engagements in the Nine Years' War. These were fought in Scotland and Ireland, as James II attempted to regain the throne by playing to that country's Catholicism and still burning resentment against England in the aftermath of Cromwell's rapacious behaviour. That campaign culminated in the Battle of the Boyne in July 1690 and subsequent fall of Limerick in 1691. Yet the main theatre of war was in the Low Countries, and large numbers – up to 56,000 – of English, Scottish and Irish soldiers served there from 1688 to 1697.

However, there were some regiments who, in 1689, remained loyal to James. When William prematurely ordered some troops to be shipped to the Low Countries, there was a local mutiny in Ipswich by a Scottish regiment who were awaiting transport to Flanders. Cromwell and Fairfax had dealt summarily with those who mutinied under the Protectorate, and there was no code of military law in place under which the current offending mutineers could be prosecuted. Parliament was at that time debating a Bill of Rights, part of which would have forbidden a 'standing army' in peacetime without their sanction. Their solution was to pass an annual Mutiny Act, establishing military law but only for a year at a time, thereby ensuring that they were able to maintain control of the army and that the king would have to call regular parliaments should he wish to go to war. The army created to vindicate Parliament in war was now the cause of its continuing existence in peace. From Parliament's perspective, the army should be raised for a campaign, with their authority and funding, but then disbanded once that campaign was finished, a principle to which they adhered during the Nine Years' War. From the monarch's and the army's perspective, while they accepted the need for the excess forces required for a war to be disbanded on completion, they sought to retain that professional core on which the crown had come to depend for security, and the generals as the professional basis on which to raise a future force. It was a debate that would influence British politics for many years.

An associated issue was how to handle what had started out in 1645 as being the rather un-Trained Bands. Irritated as they may have been by the notion of a standing army, Parliament did appreciate, particularly in the uncertain decades of the late 17th century, that they needed a force to maintain internal law and order both in the shires and in the expanding cities. The legacy of the civil wars meant that it was initially thought proper, as we have seen through the experiences of The Blues, to use the army to do so; much of the unrest was, after all, driven by similar passion and ambition. Yet once the country became more stable, this position would increasingly change, and instead Parliament, whose members had all lived through the civil wars, saw the danger in allowing the standing army which they deplored establishing a role in maintaining internal order. In 1662 Parliament passed a Militia Act, putting the discredited Trained Bands under their respective lords-lieutenant who were answerable directly to the king by whom they were appointed. Despite this direct link to the monarch, it was hoped that the militia would, by being controlled at a county level, act as a balance to the standing army, and prove to be a body who could be used locally to suppress trouble, thus preventing the need for royal troops. Yet the concept was confused from its inception, was inadequately funded and would never really work in England for the next century. It was the standing army who were called in to suppress the Jacobite risings of 1715, and 1745, arguably insurrections that would anyway have been far beyond the competence of the militia even if it had been effective. Militias were, however, raised successfully in English colonies such as the North American colonies to which, unlike Tangier, no regular regiments were sent. Colonists had to raise their own militia forces for their self-defence, creating a strong local focus, the origin of the American National Guard. History would show just how effective the system could be, not just when the colonies fought for independence, but in the future structure of the United States.

However, following the 1745 debacle, in 1757 the militia in England and Wales, together with Scotland and Ireland, was fundamentally overhauled. Each county was bound to sign up a certain number of 'citizen soldiers' who had to commit to annual training. Selection was by ballot so it was a form of conscription, with those who could afford it paying those less well-off to take their place – 'Militia Substitution'. When fear of French invasion in the late 18th century lent a new urgency to raising forces for home defence, militia regulations were again overhauled. Previously militiamen could not be deployed in their own county, for fear that local affiliation might affect their impartiality, or abroad. This was now changed, although many in Parliament objected, fearing that this would threaten security at home, with 10 per cent of each county regiment being allowed to serve overseas. During the Waterloo campaign in 1815, militiamen were again signed up as being at least partially trained recruits for infantry regiments, when, given the urgency, there was no time to amend legislation. Many fought in their militia uniforms, and even today archaeologists find many militia buttons scattered across the battlefield.

The militia also worked surprisingly well in Ireland, where the 1798 rebellion against British rule, Wolf Tone's rebellion, was primarily suppressed by the militia regiments, predominantly made up – 68.8 per cent – of Catholic soldiers but Protestant officers. Only in one county, Fermanagh, did the number of Protestants outweigh the Catholics by a significant ratio – 13 to 2. In the southern counties of Limerick and Tipperary the ratio was 14 and 19 Catholics respectively to every Protestant.[44] It was another instance of a militia policy being made to work.

Neither – given Parliament's consistent opposition to the size and cost of the army – did Britain develop a consistent policy on reserves. Why, ran the argument, do you need reserves for a temporary force which should only be raised for a single campaign and then disbanded? During the 19th century the British Army would wrestle with this issue, which was not finally settled until the Cardwell reforms of the 1870s allocated infantry regiments to counties with regular and reserve elements. Yet arguably the British Army has never fully resolved the issue of how it uses what is now referred to as a 'territorial' force nor whether that is a force in its own right or a reserve. Maybe it is now time, given the new threats faced by the United Kingdom, that this position changed. The next two armies we look at both had a much clearer policy, one which perhaps offers a better basis for the modern world.

Chapter Five

Prussia, 1806

'All inhabitants of the state are its born defenders.' [1]

Scharnhorst, 1807

Armies were a permanent feature in the Roman world as they were in the Ottoman Empire, but the idea of a standing army, as opposed to an army assembled for a particular war, only began to become normal in Western Europe in the second half of the 17th century. There had, of course, been exceptions, but from 1648 nations began to develop the machinery to support a permanent force, a standing army. In Britain the idea of a standing army was, as we have seen, inimical to a Parliament concerned both with its cost and the power it gave the monarchy. In France Louis XIV ignored such concerns, fielding armies of up to 400,000, but the nation which most enthusiastically embraced the idea of the army as a core part of society was Prussia.

The Prussian army that was created after that country's devastating defeat by Napoleon at the twin battles of Jena and Auerstadt in October 1806 offers us not only one of the most interesting concepts of how and what an army should be but is perhaps also the model of what modern armies may become. For those who still see German history through the prism of the First World War or Nazism, the reformation of the Prussian state and its army between 1808 and 1814 should make one realize that the period 1914 to 1945 was but an aberration – admittedly a terrible and dark aberration – in Germany's journey to nationhood. The path to Jena, and to Germany's 19th-century militarism, is a long one; to understand its evolution we need to take up the story from what was happening in Prussia as Cromwell was creating the New Model.

Of all the nations that suffered such terrible devastation during the Thirty Years' War, arguably the Electorate of Brandenburg, that sandy state on the north German plain, suffered the worst. In the first decade of the war it had escaped relatively lightly, but a brutal Swedish occupation in the 1630s turned it into a constant battleground. Berlin lost over half its population, and by 1648 there were only 600 habitable houses left. Brandenburg in general, and Berlin in particular, had, in the early decades of the 17th century, been developing from an insignificant state and city on the frontier of the empire, the Mark, into an increasingly important nation and capital. Now everything that they had strived for lay in ruins, as the poet Andreas Gryphius lamented:

> Now our devastation is complete.
> The brazen hordes of foreigners, the blaring bugles of war
> The blood saked sword, the thundering siege gun –
> They have consumed everything we worked so hard for.[2]

'For half a century,' wrote Frederick Schiller, the war 'smothered the glimmering sparks of civilisation in Germany and threw back the improving manners of the country into their pristine barbarity and wildness.'³ The bitterness was due largely to the war being seen as serving no purpose other than the enrichment of the mercenary armies who fought it. 'This whole war,' wrote Peter Thiele, a government official who lived in Beelitz, a small village near Berlin that had suffered particular depredation, 'has been a veritable robbers and thieves campaign. The generals and colonels have lined their pockets while princes and lords have been led by the nose. But whenever there has been talk of wanting to make peace they have always looked to their reputations. That is what the land and the people have been devastated for.'⁴ Writing 100 years later, King Frederick II of Prussia, better known as Frederick the Great, thought that 'the traces of war are to this day very discernible',⁵ and even in 1939 Berthold Brecht set his anti-war classic *Mother Courage and Her Children* in a Brandenburg ruined by the Thirty Years' War. The war created a sense of victimhood in Brandenburg-Prussia which, Schiller would come to believe, defined Prussia and later the German nation for centuries.

It would certainly and directly affect how Frederick William I, who succeeded his ineffective father as Elector of Brandenburg in 1640, built an army. The ruling house of Hohenzollern, who originated from Nuremberg in southern Germany and who had acquired the Mark of Brandenburg and their electoral title from the Holy Roman Emperor in 1411, had steadily consolidated their territories during the late 16th and early 17th centuries. They did this chiefly by marrying well, and a series of well-planned dynastic matches had made them, in 1618, dukes of Prussia as well as hereditary electors of Brandenburg. Prussia was not just the wild forests and marshes that stretched east towards Poland but included the duchies of Jülich-Cleves and the provinces of Berg, Mark and Ravensberg, valuable states on the Rhine which are today part of North-Rhine Westphalia and Gelderland. Assimilating these new territories was not easy, and Frederick William faced considerable local opposition as well as from the Grand Duchy of Poland, to whom Prussia technically owed allegiance. However, he negotiated skilfully at the Treaty of Westphalia and by 1648 found himself ruling the second largest German state after the Hapsburgs, albeit with much of it still under brutal Swedish occupation. He also found himself with a tiny military force of 2,000 which could hardly be dignified with the title of 'army' and which was anyway badly behaved. They had outraged the inhabitants of the town of Brandenburg as they 'tore out the lintels and beams, ripped up the floors, and burnt the timber' of their few remaining houses.[6] Having suffered from occupying forces for over a decade, the last thing anyone wanted in the Mark was yet more soldiers.

Yet Frederick William appreciated both that his expanding nation needed defending – not least to expel the Swedes – and that, having witnessed the inability of the German rulers to control the mercenary armies of men like the all-powerful imperial general Wallenstein, that era was at an end and in future any army of Brandenburg-Prussia must be directly answerable to the government – which meant, in effect, to him. Slowly, and with very little support from the Brandenburg parliament in Berlin and even less from his newly acquired Prussian lands, he built a new army, so that in 1655 he was able to defend the Mark against yet another Swedish invasion. Subsequently allying himself with the Swedish King Charles, in 1656 he felt strong enough to attack Poland. King John Casimir of Poland in turn attacked

Brandenburg, so that Berliners shivered as the renowned Polish cavalry approached the city. Ever flexible, Frederick William then changed allegiances once more, allying with John Casimir against Charles. In 1658 that resulted in no fewer than three Swedish armies approaching his capital. He responded by building the most remarkable defensive system around Berlin, still very much in evidence today and responsible for the rather un-Germanic twists and turns taken by the Berlin S-Bahn. In the event the attack was forestalled. Politically adroit, the Elector negotiated a settlement, and at the Peace of Olva in 1660 he was confirmed as Duke of Prussia, the same year Charles II was restored to the throne in London, although Sweden remained in occupation of much of his territory. By the 1670s he was confident enough in his army to attempt once more to expel the Swedes, defeating them decisively in June 1675 at the battle of Fehrbellin, a small town on the River Havel. Fehrbellin gave rise to two remarkable cultural achievements. The day had been won by a spirited charge by the Elector's cavalry, which had smashed the Swedish infantry. That inspired one of the very best of all military marches, *Der Fehrbelliner Reitermarsch*, arguably the most stirring in an extensive Prussian repertoire. It also gave the great early 19th-century Prussian author Heinrich von Kleist the material for his play *The Prince of Homburg*. In Kleist's play the prince leads the famous cavalry charge but he has done so without orders. Even though his actions win the day, he submits himself to court-martial for disobeying orders. Kleist identified a dichotomy in the Prussian military psyche to which we will shortly return.

Frederick William's other most celebrated military success was the Great Sleigh Ride, an operation of extraordinary imagination and courage, which saw him in 1679 commandeer all the sleighs he could find to rush an army in mid-winter deep into East Prussia to trap another Swedish army that had infiltrated south of Memel, now in Lithuania. It was an extraordinary move, taking the Swedes completely by surprise so that their force disintegrated, and few escaped back to Sweden. The Swedes would not threaten Prussia again for a century. The campaign would be used as a classic example of how the German army should fight and was studied by the then Major Heinz Guderian as he developed his theory of manoeuvre warfare, *Bewegungskrieg*, during the 1920s.

Frederick William's military success was equalled by the economic and social recovery he oversaw in Brandenburg after 1648. He saw the opportunity offered to Brandenburg-Prussia by the Hapsburgs' periodic expulsions of the Jews from their lands, offering them sanctuary and financial support, particularly in Berlin. He extended a similar welcome to the Huguenots, the French Protestants, mostly Calvinists, expelled from France by Louis XIV after the revocation of the Treaty of Nantes in 1685. Resettled, and with generous privileges, by the time he died in 1688 the population of Berlin was 2 per cent Jewish and about 15 per cent French. Most of the Huguenots were tradesmen but many were also soldiers, so that the Royal Guard could boast two whole companies of musketeers consisting entirely of Huguenots. Marshal Schomberg, one of Louis XIV's most successful generals, became the Elector's commander in chief, bringing with him over 600 officers. The Huguenot legacy is obvious in Berlin today, but the French influence on the army would be as important in the coming decades.

Frederick William was justifiably known as *Der Große Kurfürst*, The Great Elector. He was succeeded by his second son, Frederick, a monarch to whom history has possibly been too unkind and who, although no military man, left his legacy in the impressive palaces of Berlin and in that he succeeded in making the Hohenzollerns kings *of* Prussia after a rather untidy period when they had been known, due to Polish sensitivity, as kings *in* Prussia. He was succeeded in 1713 by his son, King Frederick William I (as opposed to Elector Frederick William I), who ranks as one of the strangest and most intolerant monarchs that the Hohenzollern dynasty produced. He was described as 'brusque, rude and distrustful in the extreme and given to violent rages and attacks of acute extreme melancholy'.[7] Yet he was also one of the most capable Hohenzollerns, and it was his military reforms that would create the army that his son, King Frederick II or Frederick the Great, would go on to use to such good effect. It was, however, the rigid adherence to the systems he laid down which would ultimately lead to the catastrophe of 1806.

Before discussing those reforms, it is worth quickly looking at the military situation in Europe as he ascended the throne. The Ottoman threat to southern Europe had been temporarily halted outside Vienna in 1683 when the Hapsburgs had managed to form an alliance capable of defeating them in the field. The Ottoman army, led by Grand Vizier Kara Mustafa Pasha, had been besieging Vienna for two months without success when it was attacked by a joint Hapsburg and Polish-Lithuanian force who routed them. The battle was famous for the charge of the Polish knights with feathers in their helmets so that they made a terrifying whistling noise as they bore down on the janissaries. The Ottoman army, weakened as we have seen in Chapter Three, broke, and Kara Mustafa was offered the traditional reward for failing the sultan of being strangled with a silken bowstring. Europe had since been consumed by the Nine Years' War between the Dutch and their English allies and Louis XIV's France, quickly followed by the Wars of the Spanish Succession, which pitted Hapsburgs and their allies, including the British, once more against France. Frederick I had contributed a force of 10,000 of his father's soldiers to the Hapsburg Emperor Leopold during these most recent wars, the price of being *of* as opposed to *in*, the subtleties of which may have passed by those who fought. The wars had come to an end at the Treaty of Utrecht in 1713, the same year Frederick William succeeded, only for the Hapsburgs to have to face south once again to contain a fresh Ottoman threat. Although that great Hapsburg general, Prince Eugene of Savoy, decisively defeated the Turks at Petrovaradin on the Danube in 1716 and again at Belgrade in 1717, the Ottomans remained a threat to the Holy Roman Empire and retook Belgrade in 1739.

Apart from the Hapsburgs wars, much of the rest of Europe was therefore enjoying a period of exhausted peace, which gave Frederick William an opportunity to build an army befitting a nation growing in importance and wealth. He disliked his father's grand Berlin palaces, preferring to rule from a modest manor house east of Berlin, Königs Wusterhausen, where much of his military legacy is still on display. The house and its contents portray a vivid picture of how this strange man saw Prussia as a state to serve its army even though that army would never actually fight a battle during his 27-year reign. Apart from reasons of prestige, it is not entirely clear why he should build the army he did. Prussia faced no immediate enemies, but Frederick William must have seen that it remained a disjointed country lacking geographical coherence and with different ethnic groups and religions. The army was a way of expressing national solidarity. Other nations also undoubtedly resented the *parvenu* nation which threatened the balance of power in northern Europe, and they were rebuilding their own forces so that 'armies were now an accepted part of society. Training, career structures, pensions and other arrangements became increasingly professional.'[8] Accepting those reasons, Frederick William's development of the Prussian army still bordered on the obsessive and, although it would allow Prussia to consolidate its position as a leading European power in the decades after his death, there was truth in the quip, variously attributed to Mirabeau or Voltaire, that whereas most states had an army, the Prussian army had a state.[9] Frederick William had inherited an army 35,000 strong, largely based on his grandfather's, The Great Elector's, regiments; when he died in 1740 it was at 80,000.

Since the 15th century the majority of German states had adopted a three-tier system for mobilizing armies when they needed them. The first tier comprised able-bodied men of military age, drawn by lots, who would form the deployable fighting force. Behind them was a second tier of older but still physically fit men who had some military experience and who would provide a reserve for the first tier. They were referred to as the *Landwehr*. Then the third tier, called the *Landsturm*, was made up of the old and infirm, typically also including women and boys, whose role was home defence. Different German states had used variations of the model for several centuries and it was this structure which Frederick William used as his starting point, albeit both he and his son, Frederick the Great, would prioritize the first tier, given the roles they envisaged and subsequently employed for their army. Later, as we will see, reformers would see the value of all three tiers.

The system Frederick William put in place was, however, efficient, logical and well administered, if harsh. It was based on the principle of universal service, laid down in a law in 1714, so that every male of military age was liable to be called up. However, the draft was now organized on a cantonal system so that each regiment was allocated an area of rural Prussia from where it was to find its soldiers. This had the advantage of preventing different regiments competing for recruits while also making it administratively easier for them. It also had the advantage of removing the recruiting burden from the towns, which had previously been the favoured hunting ground for young men given the obvious concentration they presented. Craftsmen, artisans, apprentices in a trade, officials and clergy were exempted, as were specific towns targeted for industrial development such as Berlin, Potsdam, Magdeburg and Brandenburg, although this policy was not evenly applied and was set aside by Frederick the Great when his wars started to consume recruits. A Berlin pastor, Pfarrer Lüdicke, noted sadly in his church records for 1762 that 609 more of his parishioners had been killed than had been born.[10] One of the few first-hand accounts we have of life as an artisan in mid-century Berlin was by a baker called Johann Friedrich Heyde, who had three sons in the army and who expressed relief when his eldest qualified as a master baker in 1761, as it saved him from further service.[11] However, altogether it is estimated that these exemptions amounted to nearly 2 million men of military age.[12] Once drafted, soldiers completed their basic training but were then sent back to their villages for up to ten months of the year so that they could continue as part of the agricultural workforce, reporting back annually for refresher training. They were not paid while at home but remained under military law and were required to wear uniform even when on furlough, although in practice a waistcoat was considered adequate. In peacetime the system was therefore not particularly arduous. It also had the advantage of providing a ready reserve, although there was no laid-down length of service so that young men could find themselves serving for most of their lives; in 1792 service was restricted to 25 years, but even that was excessive compared with other contemporary armies. However, in wartime, and there was to be a lot of wartime, it imposed a harsh regime on the poorer agricultural areas. Inevitably the system was liable to corruption, with richer families finding ways of making sure that their sons were not chosen, although again this became more difficult by mid-century as casualties mounted.

One of the strengths of the system was that it also applied to officers. Frederick William's view of society was almost feudal, the landowners and nobles, those whose families bore *Wappen*, or coats of arms, going to war leading their farm labourers. He started a cadet academy in Berlin which potential officers were expected to attend, and although many 'thought it a debasement to apply themselves to study and looked on ignorance as a title of merit and learning as ridiculous pedantry',[13] it served to create a flow of competent young officers whose fathers were pleased to find a way of providing a free education for their sons that their noble status demanded but which otherwise stretched them financially. Cadets learned French, history, geography, logic, engineering, fencing, military drawing and, strangely but in common with other contemporary military colleges, dancing. The officer system was certainly effective but it would come at some cost. The Wedel family from Pomerania would lose 72 young men in the coming decades, and the Belling family from Brandenburg 20 of 33 who served.[14]

Frederick William was less successful at developing a logistic system, possibly because his army was not actively engaged in large-scale war which would have demanded an efficient resupply system. Prussian logistics was based on garrisons and magazines, guarded by *Landwehr* troops so that the deployable army could be focused on fighting. Prussia had a strong linked fortress system, and as the conquests of the coming years expanded Prussian territory, so did the fortresses that allowed it to be controlled. Arguably this logistical approach was to hinder the army, which became tied to these fortresses for their resupply; the concept of more mobile logistics was still a century away, and this was to cause severe problems for Frederick the Great during the Seven Years' War.

Frederick William was equally focused on developing Prussian defence industry both to support the army and also because he realized its potential for the wider Prussian economy. In 1724 he banned the import of weapons, instead establishing two arms factories in Spandau and Potsdam. He also banned the import of foreign cloth while ordering that colonels should re-clothe their regiments every two years with locally produced textiles, resulting in a boom for the Brandenburg wool industry. Berlin wool production doubled between 1720 and 1730, with more than 5,000 weavers busy in the city. Weaving would remain the staple of the Brandenburg economy until the industrial revolution took hold a century later.

Frederick William was also a devout Pietist who not only believed that soldiers should have ready access to chaplains but that they should also be Pietists. There was history behind this decision. The Hohenzollerns had long been Calvinists, which had led them to clash with a strongly Lutheran population both in Brandenburg and East Prussia. Berlin would not, for example, boast a cathedral until the 1890s. Pietism was essentially a Lutheran movement but based on Calvinist principles. It emphasized that an individual's relationship with God should be direct and personal, with the chaplain's role more as helper and adviser than as officiator at elaborate services. It had become popular across Prussia in the early 18th century, with a famous school established at Halle, and its advent had done much to ease the tension between the contending reformist creeds. Its ethos of service and obedience also made it a natural choice for the army. Soldiers contemplating what might happen to them in battle generally prefer quiet reflection and spiritual guidance than tub-thumping sermons, and Pietism was to prove an enduring strength of the Prussian and later German army well into the 20th century. Its adoption also served to emphasize the individuality of each soldier and to engender respect. Although the Prussian military system demanded absolute obedience, with savage punishments meted out to those who went astray, Frederick William made service both a respected and an expected feature of Prussian society. The route to social advancement and in government service was to have held a commission and to wear a uniform in much the same way as it had been in the empires of Constantine and Mehmet.

By the time he died in 1740 Frederick William was 'not only half-barbaric but also strange', being 'exceptionally headstrong and bizarre'.[15] His eccentricities included forming a regiment of the tallest soldiers he could find, nicknamed the *Lange Kerls*, and other European monarchs would present him with exceptionally tall men as a present; what the men concerned thought of being so gifted is sadly unrecorded. He was also engaged in persecuting his son, Frederick, having his close friend and suspected lover, Hans Hermann von Katte executed under Frederick's window in the fortress of Küstrin where he was imprisoned. Yet it was Frederick who was to use the army his father had created to turn Prussia into the leading power in the German world. Frederick II, as he became when he inherited, or Frederick the Great as he is better known to posterity, was, as with many successful commanders, seemingly an unlikely general. Artistic, musical, almost certainly homosexual and socially liberal, he was also insistent on his absolute authority, dismissive of advice and intolerant of criticism. Undoubtedly one of the great commanders of the 18th century, and arguably the most celebrated monarch, he also brought Prussia close to disaster. His motto was 'The King of Prussia is the first servant of the state',[16] but it was the state as he determined it and, socially liberal as he certainly was – abolishing judicial torture, insisting on signing off every death sentence personally and encouraging both religious and sexual freedom so that his at least sometime friend Voltaire would quip that in Prussia one had the 'freedom of conscience and the cock' – he was driven by the same motive, as was The Great Elector, to establish Prussia as the dominant German nation. He did this by using the army so carefully constructed by his father in a series of wars of conquest. By so doing he proved the value of Frederick William's military revolution and, while accepting that later, many – such as the Poles – might question the desirability of Prussian hegemony, he eventually did so with outstanding success.

For the next 40 years Prussia would be engaged in a series of wars which both expanded and consolidated Prussian territory while exacting a high cost economically and in lives. In December 1740 Frederick invaded the Austrian province of Silesia, today in south-west Poland, north of the Sudeten mountains and astride the upper reaches of the Oder river system. Although he concocted a historical justification, there was no accepted reason for his actions other than that its ownership strengthening Prussia. His first battle, at Mollwitz on 10 April 1741, was very nearly a disaster, and Frederick fled the field before being called back by his general, Kurt Christoph von Schwerin, to be told that his infantry had saved the day. The grey horse he rode that day became known as the Mollwitz grey who lived to the great age of 40. It became celebrated throughout Prussia when Frederick subsequently rode in on parade, as it knew every Prussian march, snorting its appreciation of its favourites and acknowledging regimental colours as they passed. On 17 May 1742 Frederick won a decisive victory despite heavy casualties at Chotusitz in Bohemia, causing the Austrians to sue for peace. It was only to be temporary, and in 1744 the war started afresh, with Frederick invading Bohemia and taking Prague. Forced back by a combination of Austrian and Saxon forces, he took them by surprise at Hohenfriedeberg on 4 June 1745, again inflicting a major defeat and forcing their withdrawal. The subsequent Treaty of Dresden that December effectively surrendered Silesia to Prussia.

A decade of peace followed before Europe, and the wider world, again became engulfed in war. The Seven Years' War, from 1756 to 1763, which was fought both between European colonial powers in their newly acquired overseas territories and in central Europe, came close to destroying Prussia. The war started badly for Frederick, his army suffering a major defeat at Kolin in June 1757. He had left Berlin in August 1756 – he would not return to his capital for seven years – marching into Saxony and Bohemia and fighting a series of indecisive battles. However, on 18 June he attacked an

Austrian and Saxon force east of Prague. His troops failed to take the position and were forced to retreat, having suffered terrible casualties. Frederick had placed himself at the head of the Anhalt Regiment, famously roaring at its reluctant soldiers, 'Rogues, would you live forever!' to which an old grenadier allegedly shouted back, 'Listen, Fritz, I thought for thirteen Pfennigs pay we'd done enough.'[17] Despite decisive victories at Leuthen and Rossbach in 1757, the war dragged on, with Russia, ruled by the Empress Elizabeth, now engaged as an ally of Austria and Saxony. While Frederick was besieging Dresden in October 1760, a Russian force attacked and occupied Berlin. In the event it was not a particularly oppressive occupation, to the relief of Berliners who were already suffering the economic effects of a long war, and after three days they left, having caused more damage from the appalling habits of their soldiers than from bombardment. A worse effect was food prices temporarily multiplying six times.

Yet the presence of a Russian army in Prussia, together with the Austrians and Saxons totalling 130,000, meant that an exhausted Prussia was now vulnerable to destruction. Frederick thought he was finished but was saved by one of those remarkable accidents of history. In January 1762 Frederick's sworn enemy, the Empress Elizabeth of Russia, died and was succeeded by Czar Peter III, who, although he was not destined to last very long, regarded Frederick as a godlike figure and halted the Russian offensive. Peter was, as were so many of the Russian royal family, in fact a German prince from Schleswig-Holstein, who had long had a fascination for all things Prussian and habitually wore Prussian uniform, something which may have contributed to his early demise. The Peace of Hubertusburg in February 1763 saw Frederick's conquests formalized and was followed by a period of nearly 20 years' peace despite Prussia, Austria and Russia helping themselves to large parts of Poland in 1772; Frederick's share included West Prussia, thus enabling Brandenburg to be connected to East Prussia. The Poles were not strong enough to resist. Then, in 1778 Frederick mobilized 253,000 troops to prevent Austria from seizing the Bavarian throne from the Wittelsbachs. The Austrians mobilized a similar force, leading to stalemate, and there was little fighting.

Frederick's tactics were based on speed and energy in pressing an attack. He had met and been strongly influenced by the legendary Austrian commander, Prince Eugene, who had defeated the Ottomans so decisively. He was also influenced by two Prussian generals, Kurt Christoph von Schwerin, who would be killed at Prague in 1757, and Prince Leopold of Anhalt-Dessau, known as the 'Old Dessauer', both of whom had learnt much from Eugene. During his long campaigning career, Frederick would modernize and adapt certain aspects of the army he inherited, and he summarized his thoughts in his famous treatise *L'Art de la Guerre* published in 1751. He also wrote detailed *Instructions* to his generals after the Second Silesian War, although this was not published until later. Whereas his father had trained his cavalry, who were all regular full-time soldiers, to operate in much the same way as Cromwell's regiments – charging at the trot with troopers boot to boot – Frederick, with his dynamic cavalry commander Hans Joachim von Ziethen, experimented with charging at the gallop, unleashing the ranks 800 yards from the enemy. It was not a great success, and later he reverted to 150 yards although he still maintained that the shock of galloping unnerved the enemy and caused them to break. He was always critical of his cavalry, which was roughly half heavy cavalry wearing cuirasses and half light cavalry, thinking them less well trained than the infantry. He also instituted a reconnaissance force of hussars, which eventually totalled 7,000 men, whose job was gathering intelligence, guiding and screening, a tactic that was copied and perfected by Napoleon. He also comprehensively overhauled his artillery after the First Silesian War, placing light cannon in his infantry regiments to improve their firepower and introducing an early form of fast-moving horse artillery. At the same time he introduced the concept of brigade artillery, grouping batteries of ten heavier 12-pounder guns with every three to four infantry battalions. The Austrians had excellent artillery – always the strongest arm in the Hapsburg armies – and Frederick had to adapt to match their progress.

Yet his strongest arm was undoubtedly his infantry, which comprised approximately two-thirds of the army. Although they were well drilled in musketry, with a musket that was considered superior to the Austrian model because it had a conical touchhole that reduced misfires and was equipped with a double-ended ramrod, which meant a soldier under pressure could use either end to ram home the charge, Frederick's favoured tactic was the infantry charge with the bayonet. He was famous for his 'attack in oblique order', the *Schrägangriff*, which was a roundabout way of saying that he would mass an attack against an enemy's flank, where they were generally weakest, roll that up and then attack their centre from the side as opposed to head on. He first used this tactic very successfully at Hohenfriedeberg, which saved Silesia for Prussia. The excellent drill and discipline of his infantry, to whose training he devoted considerable attention, meant that the psychological impact of the tactic was as important as the actual. To stand when being attacked by immaculate ranks of

Prussian infantry, advancing in perfect line at the double and covering 70 yards a minute, was a terrifying ordeal.

Tactically Frederick was the leading field commander in Europe – Napoleon would study his methods carefully and emulate many of them – and he gained considerable kudos from being a king who led his army in person. By the end of the Seven Years' War, despite coming so close to defeat, the Prussian army's transformation after 1714 had proved highly successful. It was also an army that was greatly respected at home. The strength of regional recruiting and the furlough system was that it gave local communities a direct link to their soldiers. When the army was assembled, the government was astute in its billeting policy, accommodating the majority of the infantry in towns where they would not swamp the local population, and although barracks were being built, soldiers would continue to be billeted on families well into the 19th century. The fact that officers, of whom Frederick's wars consumed a very large number – of the 5,500 who fought in the Seven Years' War, 1,500 had been killed, including 120 generals – were drafted alongside ordinary soldiers again lent social cohesion. Frederick did not necessarily believe that you had to be born noble to make a good officer. 'All would be lost in a state,' he wrote, 'if birth were valued above merit';[18] rather, he believed that the structure of Prussian society demanded that nobles must play their part in building that state. Although there was inevitable corruption in how the recruiting officers applied the draft locally, with the burden falling on the poorest, that everyone was liable lent respectability to soldiering, a respectability that would be taken to absurd lengths in the coming century. However, desertion was common, despite being punished harshly with the offender being made to 'run the gauntlet', whereby he had to walk slowly down a double line of his comrades who each beat him with hazel rods. It averaged about 2 per cent across Frederick's reign, although that compared favourably with the 9 per cent in the French army across the same period.[19]

Private soldiers and young officers were not well paid, hence the old soldier's barbed comment to the king at Kolin, but pay increased markedly for senior regimental officers, who also did well from managing their company of battalion accounts. Gratuities for the wounded were initially inadequate, although they improved from 1787. There were genuine attempts to assist wounded veterans such as preferential employment schemes, and an Invalids House, the *Invalidenhof*, was opened in Berlin in 1747, but it was too small to cater for the 200,000-odd who were wounded in Frederick's wars. There was also an orphanage for bereaved children in Potsdam but it could only house 1,250 boys and 750 girls, which was again insufficient. Pensions were introduced for the families of those who had lost their father/husband from 1787, and 2 per cent of the army's budget was devoted to welfare. This may seem a very small amount, but by contemporary standards it was seen as generous and, taken together, these reforms provided a structure for a permanent army that was now accepted as part of the social structure of the nation.

The furlough system meant that the cost of the peacetime army was manageable, soldiers not being paid while they were furloughed, but even so the cost of Frederick's wars was considerable and imposed a severe burden on Prussia. He funded them from income rather than reverting to war loans and bonds, as did other European countries. This was facilitated by his introduction of a new currency from 1750.

Until then the standard currency across the German-speaking world had been the Imperial Thaler. Unwilling to accept the degree of Austrian financial control this implied, Frederick introduced the *Reichsthaler*, subdivided into *Groschen* and *Pfennigs*. A typical labourer's wage mid-century was 1–2 *Reichsthalers* per week, making one *Reichsthaler* worth about £100 in modern British money. This new currency meant that the government could control the content of the coinage, which would be debased five times by 1763 so that they were actually worth approximately one-third of their pre-war value. From 1764 the war circulation coins were withdrawn and new *Reichsthalers* issued with their full precious metal content so that confidence was quickly restored. Frederick would also push as much cost as he could onto conquered territories like Silesia and Saxony and also received generous subsidies from his ally, Britain. It is estimated that the total cost to Prussia of the Seven Years' War was 125 million *Reichsthaler*, of which London contributed 28 million.[20] Inflation, which had been relatively low during the early 18th century, spiralled during the Seven Years' War, with food prices trebling in Berlin. Remarkably, after 1763 the economy recovered quickly, Frederick concentrating his considerable energies on economic reconstruction. That meant that, in general, although the major portion of government expenditure, the army was affordable, at least when it wasn't actually fighting.

By the 1760s the Prussian army therefore met the criteria for a successful army suggested in Chapter One. It had concentrated, ruthlessly, on training and equipping a deployable field army which had been successful on the battlefield. It had established itself as a truly national army, both respected for its professionalism and regarded as part of the fabric of the nation. Its soldiers were valued for what they did and, although their terms of service still left much to be desired, they were no worse off than many people in rural Prussia and they mostly felt they belonged to a community – an important aspect of soldiering which is often overlooked. It was also an army that was designed to be affordable. Yet it was also inherently flawed, which would soon cost Prussia very heavily indeed. Why?

Its problem was that it was an army dominated by one man, a quite remarkable man and an exceptional commander, who could both run his state and deal with the detailed work of tactical command at the same time. An innovator in his early days, Frederick became increasingly isolated and autocratic so that few dared challenge him. He relied on only a handful of generals, men like Schwerin, the Old Dessauer and Ziethen, most of whom were dead by the 1770s – although Ziethen lived on, fighting duels and finally dying in his bed aged 86 – and without a properly functioning war ministry or general staff. This meant that the army atrophied. Frederick was also an astute self-publicist, well aware of the value of his image both on the battlefield and at home. His position within Prussia was unassailable. He retained absolute power and a monopoly of force, which he exercised with an efficient bureaucracy that meant that the nation was well governed. His reputation internationally was considered to be beyond reproach partly because of his liberalism and partly from the kudos he earned from personally commanding his armies in the field. He was seen as the champion of the Protestant underdog who fearlessly took on the Catholic might of Austria and the dictatorial czars of Russia. He was especially popular in England, a nation as intent on benefitting from the Seven Years' War as Prussia, with bonfires lit in London on his birthday and hundreds of pubs called The King of Prussia – although, unsurprisingly, they were quickly renamed in 1914.

Yet by the time of his death Frederick had become something of an anachronism. He was a baroque figure, who spoke in French, and ruled from his charming and intimate rococo villa in Potsdam outside Berlin surrounded by French intellectuals. He despised German culture, regarding German as 'a rude and almost barbarous language'.[21] He also disliked Berlin, only visiting his capital once a year during his last two decades. Meanwhile, the German-speaking world in general, and Prussia in particular, was experiencing a cultural renaissance, an *Aufklärung*, looking back at its history and experimenting with all things Germanic. The movement took its inspiration from a supposed romantic German past, which may or may not have existed, but which suggested a wholesome world of simple people, of mountains and rivers, of heroes and warriors, of a purity since corrupted. Importantly, it heralded the possibility of a German nation, a movement which would grow rapidly in the coming decades until it was given substance in Paris in 1870. While Frederick and his clique were arguing in French and promoting lavish old-fashioned operas, Berlin was experiencing a German cultural revival. In 1778 Goethe visited Berlin, where he premiered his play *Götz von Berlichingen*. Frederick was appalled that Goethe should have produced a play in German, calling it 'an abominable imitation of those bad English plays',[22] while Goethe was fascinated by the king's godlike status and found him more interesting than a god because he 'not only determined human destiny but shared it', while the gods were not involved in the consequences of their decisions.[23] He also witnessed a military parade while he was there, which he described as 'a monstrous piece of clockwork'.[24] His observation was more accurate than he may have realized.

Frederick died on 17 August 1786. Prussia could not quite believe that he was gone. 'A mood of silence, though not of mourning; the people seem numbed rather than sorrowful. One scarcely sees a face that does not wear an expression of relief, even of hope,' thought the French author, statesman and wit, Mirabeau. 'No voice of regret is to be heard; not a sigh, not a word of praise! Is this the sum of so many victorious battles, of such fame and glory? Is this the end of almost half a century of rule, a reign so rich in great deeds?'[25] The doctor who attended the dying king replied with admirable sang-froid, when Frederick asked him whether he had assisted many men into the next world, 'not as many as Your Majesty'.[26]

Having no children, he was succeeded by his nephew, Frederick William II, who ruled for 11 undistinguished years, but years in which Prussia made significant progress internationally, albeit without the army being tested as it had been earlier in the century. The French Revolution meant that the old Prussian hostility to Austria was temporarily suspended and a joint Prussian-Austrian army invaded France in 1792, only to be repulsed at Valmy, but that was expunged by a successful if expedient reaction to Polish attempts to re-establish themselves as a separate nation. Poland was partitioned again in 1795, which allowed the junction of Silesia with East Prussia, thus increasing Prussia's population by 3 million. Formalized at the Treaty of Basel later that year, Prussia agreed to withdraw from the coalition against France in return for French recognition of its gains. France also agreed to return all Prussian territory east of the Rhine.

Meanwhile, the *Aufklärung* was creating a very different world in Prussia, a German world which, while always respectful of Frederick the Great, 'Old Fritz', and his legacy, was beginning to identify with ideas he would have found foreign. Berlin was becoming a cosmopolitan city, where German plays, German music, German architecture and German art were celebrated. In 1767 Gotthold Lessing, a Saxon, had staged the first performance of *Minna von Barnhelm*, a play in which he directly criticized the lack of provision for wounded soldiers. Frederick was infuriated and had it banned so that it moved to Hamburg, subsequently becoming famous throughout Europe. In 1773 Friedrich Nicolai then published his *Life and Times of Herr Magister Sebaldus Nothanker*, a picaresque novel which, while it may not necessarily command attention today, was remarkable in that it was dedicated to 'Germanness' and celebrated introducing solid, honest rural folk into Berlin. Artists like Daniel Chodowiecki drew cartoons satirizing everyday life, although his popular drawings of Frederick were always sympathetic. German artists like Anton Graff and Carl Fechhelm painted street scenes with shops and shoppers, people working and enjoying themselves. To Frederick's particular chagrin, one of the more celebrated artists was Anna Dorothea Therbusch, a woman whose husband ran one of Berlin's ubiquitous *Kneipen*, or local inns.

In 1788 Frederick William II commissioned Carl Gotthard Langhans to design the Brandenburg Gate in Berlin which, together with Johann Gottfried Schadow's famous Quadriga of the Goddess of Victory in her chariot which tops it, has since become a symbol of Berlin and of Germany. It was also seen as representing the *Aufklärung*, an iconic, clean, classical German monument, and a refined, economical and beautiful symbol of 'Athens on the Spree', as Berliners liked to refer to their fast-developing city.

Goethe was not Prussian, nor were many authors and artists living in Berlin, but it was becoming less important whether one was Saxon or Hanoverian, from Bavaria or the Rhineland, as the thread that linked the movements came from the German language and that elusive sense of German romanticism. The 1790s and early 1800s would see an extraordinary flowering of some of the most talented Germans and, unusually, this cultural renaissance would be reflected in the army. Both *Aufklärung* and calls for military reform would grow even stronger as the 1790s gave way to the 19th century.

Frederick's death left a vacuum in command. Nothing, however, changed in the army, which was preserved as Frederick had left it, almost as if it were sacrilege to tamper with the great organization that had given Prussia so many victories. Frederick had done everything himself and had not made any plans for his succession in command, so that the aged generals were those who had fought with him as younger officers. The emphasis remained on a strict replication of the social hierarchy, repetitive training in the tactics of the Seven Years' War and minimal innovation, while in France the revolutionary army was showing that victories could be won by those who stood to lose everything should they be defeated. While French officers worried about being guillotined should they fail, Prussian officers remained supremely confident that the Prussian army was unbeatable, while they drilled and drank toasts to the great Frederick who, by the next time they took to the field, had last fought a battle 43 years before. Promotion in the Prussian army was by seniority in a regiment, so effectively dead men's shoes. In wartime, high officer casualties made for a rapid flow but, once the army ossified in peace, promotion slowed with it.

Once officers had achieved a position which gave them both status and a decent income, they were reluctant to give it up. By 1806 the average age of junior regimental officers was in their 50s, while colonels averaged in their 60s. Generals were mostly ancient. As the French armies expanded, each Prussian infantry company still received 50 pounds of hair powder each month so that they could appear uniformly on parade with their white hair tied back with a black ribbon.

This created a corresponding lack of impetus to modernize tactics and procedures. Frederick had insisted on a military machine that would obey his orders to the letter and in which initiative was discouraged, even penalized. Instead he personalized the thinking and planning in the army alongside those very few trusted staff officers who served him. He had the genius to do so, but once he was gone senior officers, trained in a world where they had only to obey orders, fell back on formulaic and rigid doctrine which was outdated. 'A true strategist of that period,' wrote the cynical General Colmar von der Goltz, 'considered himself incapable of leading three men across a gulley unless he had a table of logarithms' to help him to do so.[27] Even an officer considered a progressive like General Heinrich Dietrich von Bülow insisted that an attack could only be successful if it was mounted at 'an operative angle of at least 60 degrees and preferably more than 90 degrees', a perfect example of how Frederick's attack in oblique order – his concept of attacking in overwhelming force at the enemy's weakest spot – had become translated into some meaningless formulaic procedure.[28] There were a few would-be reformers, such as the Würtemberger von Massenbach, who in 1803 pushed through a partial reformation of the general staff, assisted by a young Hanoverian officer called Gerhard von Scharnhorst.

Massenbach's efforts were doomed to failure – later he would end up in prison convicted of having published state secrets – and it would be left to his assistant to complete the process after 1806.

Frederick William II died in 1797, being succeeded by his son, Frederick William III, who would reign for 43 years. He was a weak man, destined to be indecisive at a time when Prussia called for the firm leadership of his great-uncle Frederick or The Great Elector. Napoleon described Frederick William as 'no less false, than stupid'.[29] His strength, until she died in 1810, was his wife Luise of Mecklenburg-Strelitz, who would become a symbol of Prussian resistance. During his early years in power, Frederick William kept Prussia out of the wars against revolutionary France. Following his father's success at the Treaty of Basel, he capitalized on the Imperial Diet's Treaty of Lunéville which, at French instigation, secularized 70 bishoprics and 45 imperial cities across Germany. Prussia gained Paderborn, Münster, Hildesheim, Erfurt and Essen, amongst other towns, and its population increased by half a million. This policy lasted until 1806 when, alarmed at growing French ambition in Germany, he joined the Fourth Coalition against Napoleon alongside Great Britain, Russia, Sweden and Saxony. Arguably an unwise move just a year after Napoleon's shattering defeat of Austria and Russia at Austerlitz, Napoleon predictably responded by invading Prussia.

Advancing rapidly with an army 180,000 strong organized into six corps together with the Imperial Guard, which was effectively a full corps in its own right, and with a reserve cavalry corps, Napoleon's campaign was one of his most effective. He had perfected the corps system, which grouped infantry, cavalry and artillery together with integral logistic support into semi-independent units, which were coordinated via the genius of his chief of staff, Louis-Alexandre Berthier. Of all Napoleon's many campaigns, his actions in the autumn of 1806 demonstrated his army at the height of its ability and with its most effective commanders: Ney, Davout, Murat, Soult, Bernadotte and Lannes. Although there would be recriminations amongst them, and Bernadotte was criticized for not supporting Davout, it was still unfortunate for the Prussians that they faced Napoleon at his most formidable. He was, in his own self-effacing words, 'in the ascendancy of his genius' and, more importantly, his army was still powerful enough to substantiate his ambition.[30]

The Prussian army in 1806 numbered 247,000. With garrisons in East Prussia facing Russia, and in Westphalia facing west, they still had approximately 145,000 deployable troops, which they grouped in three armies to confront the French. The main army was commanded by the 71-year-old Duke of Brunswick; the second by Frederick Louis, Prince of Hohenlohe, who had no combat experience and owed his position to his royal status, while the third was commanded by Ernst von Ruchel, who failed to move to support Hohenlohe when Napoleon attacked. Of the other senior commanders, Friedrich, Graf von Kalckreuth who commanded the reserve was nearly 70 and Anton von L'Estocq, who had been last active in the Seven Years' War, was 68. Prussian staff work was poor, there appears to have been no coordinated plan, and communication between the armies was woeful. Their muddled deployment was incomplete when Napoleon fell on Hohenlohe's army on the plateau of Jena, above the River Saale in central Germany (and then in Saxony), on 14 October, inflicting over 25,000 casualties – killed, wounded and taken prisoner. Ruchel's reserve, in Weimar, failed to move until it was too late. Although Napoleon thought he had engaged the Prussian main body, it was in fact Davout who, answering Berthier's summons to come to Napoleon's assistance, ran into Brunswick's force nearby at Auerstadt on the same day, inflicting 15,000 casualties. Bernadotte, also nearby and summoned to Jena, failed to join Davout, for which he was heavily criticized and was the first step towards him eventually breaking completely with Napoleon. What was left of the Prussian armies then disintegrated, and although General Gebhard von Blücher managed to retreat to Lübeck with a substantial force which Scharnhorst, his chief of staff, managed to organize into two small corps, he was trapped against the Danish frontier and forced to surrender with 10,000 troops on 7 November.

Consequently, the road to Berlin lay open, and on 25 October it was occupied by the French, Davout being given the honour of leading the victorious army into the shocked city. The idea of the Prussian army being defeated was so extraordinary that the city's marshal, von der Schulenberg, could not bring himself to announce such an unconscionable catastrophe, restricting himself instead merely to say that 'the King has lost a battle. The first duty of every citizen is to stay calm.'[31] Berliners watched in sullen silence as Napoleon paraded down the Unter den Linden on 27 October. Later he led his staff to Potsdam where they stood in front of Frederick the Great's tomb in the garrison church. 'Hats off, gentlemen,' said Napoleon. 'We would not be here today if he was still alive',[32] which may or may not have been true. Frederick William III and his government fled east to Königsberg, but his humiliation still had its course to run. Having grazed the Russians at Eylau in February 1807, Napoleon defeated them decisively at Friedland in June 1807, so that by July he was able to force Czar Alexander to negotiate at Tilsit. His hold on East Prussia was now complete, and Frederick William and Queen Luise were forced to watch from the bank of the River Niemen while emperor and czar bargained away their country. Prussia's western territories became a separate kingdom of Westphalia, to be ruled by one of Napoleon's brothers. Poland was re-established as the Grand Duchy of Warsaw, Danzig made a free city and Saxony and Russia given extensive Prussian land. All Prussia's gains since 1740 were reversed, its population was reduced by half and its revenue likewise. On top of that, the now almost bankrupt nation had to pay France a war indemnity of 120 million francs, or seven times the annual government revenue. Worst of all, the Prussian army was reduced to 42,000, of whom 16,000 were to be at Napoleon's disposal. While this butchery was taking place on a barge moored in the centre of the River Niemen, Queen Luise held the hand of her young son, the ten-year-old William. It was a humiliation he would not forget and one that, 64 years later, he would amply avenge as he declared the German Empire in the Hall of Mirrors at Versailles.

The French now proceeded with an eight-year occupation of Prussia, which was marked more by arrogance and complacency than brutality, although it was undoubtedly at times brutal. It was also remarkably incompetent and allowed the reformers in Prussia to press ahead with reforms to both the political system and the military, which they had long been contemplating. There was never a danger of revolution in Prussia such as France had suffered despite Prussia being arguably a more despotic regime. The government was too efficient, rural life too well ordered, the cities too under-developed and the Prussian character too unresponsive to allow that. There was, however, a lively intellectual debate as to how the country might progress politically, a movement which existed in parallel with the cultural *Aufklärung*, and which now saw its opportunity as the discredited monarch fled. It was a movement articulated by men like Johann Gottlieb Fichte, a philosopher and pupil of Kant who arrived in Berlin soon after Jena. Described as 'having something of Luther about him; Luther's massive intelligence, his rugged honesty, the mixture of professor and demagogue',[33] Fichte articulated an appeal to all Germans to seize the opportunity offered by what he saw as the collapse of old Europe to establish the German nation. He gave a series of lectures in Berlin, which, strangely, French officers attended, possibly confused by whether Napoleon actually stood for the values he espoused rather than the aggressive French nationalism he practised. 'If you continue in your dullness,' Fichte preached, 'all the evils of serfdom await you... by the sacrifice of your nationality and your language, you have purchased for yourself some subordinate and petty place, until in this way you gradually die out as a people.' However, he continued, 'if, on the other hand, you bestir yourself and play the man... you will see in spirit the German name rising by means of this generation to be the most glorious among all peoples; you will see this nation as the regenerator and recreator of the world.'[34] Fichte's legacy was significant. At best it inspired poets like Heinrich von Kleist and works such as Grimm's fairy tales; at its most extreme, it inspired Wagner's music and the mad, magical castles of the mid-19th century. At its worst, it allowed an emphasis on racial purity and the historic wrongs suffered by the *Volk*, the German people, to be corrupted into Nazism.

Yet in the short term it gave encouragement to those who had been debating the future of Prussia and especially to men like First Minister Heinrich Friedrich Karl, Freiherr vom und zum Stein, who, together with his successor, Karl August, Fürst von Hardenberg, now started to reform the Prussian state. Working within the loose confines of French occupation, vom Stein and Hardenberg, after he was forced to resign having been found writing that 'Napoleon was a villain and an enemy of the human race' and that the French Empire was 'a monstrous fabric cemented by the blood and tears of so many millions and reared by an insane and accursed tyranny',[35] overhauled Prussia's economy, its education and, most importantly, its army. That they could have carried out a major military review, and so fundamental a restructuring as they accomplished under the very noses of Napoleon's marshals, says much about why Napoleon's plans for Europe ended in abject failure.

They were also due to the extraordinary talent of a group of military thinkers and reformers who would not only regenerate Frederick's army so that within six years it would comprehensively defeat Napoleon but would also create the army that would go on, for better, and later for worse, to dominate Europe for a century and a half. Working within the intellectual inspiration the *Aufklärung* offered, and with the active encouragement of the king's ministers, they would transform the Prussian army. Their leader was Gerhard Johann von Scharnhorst, a Hanoverian from a small landowning family, who transferred his allegiance to Prussia in 1801. Scharnhorst had studied at the military school sponsored by Count Wilhelm zu Schaumburg-Lippe and was originally commissioned into a cavalry regiment in the Hanoverian army. Later transferring to the artillery, he taught in the artillery school in Hanover and made a name for himself as an instructor by publishing a series of handbooks for young officers; his simply titled *Handbuch für Offiziere in den anwendbaren Teilen der Kriegswissenschaft* – which today we would understand as a staff officer's handbook – was particularly well received. He gained valuable operational experience in the French Revolutionary Wars and was initially approached by Frederick William III in 1797 but turned the offer down. In 1801 it was repeated with twice the pay and a patent of nobility, an offer too tempting to refuse. He had risen rapidly in Prussian service so that he was seconded as chief of staff to the Duke of Brunswick during the Jena campaign where 'he found his advice ignored'[36] and where he realized that it was the muddled staff work that prevented the Prussian armies from concentrating to face Davout. He was wounded at Auerstadt, distinguished himself during the chaotic Prussian retreat, and was with Blücher in East Prussia. He again distinguished himself at Eylau, for which he was awarded the coveted decoration *Pour La Mérite*, originally inaugurated by Frederick the Great and later more widely known as the Blue Max. In the aftermath of Jena even the conservative-minded Frederick William III appreciated that the army's senior commanders had failed, with 103 out of a total of 142 being retired. Scharnhorst became a major general and was appointed to lead the Military Reform Commission, of which Stein was also a member, giving him direct access to the king.

What is notable about Scharnhorst's reforms is that they were inspired by military thinkers who saw the army in the wider context of the *Aufklärung*, as part of Prussia and the wider Germany's expression of nationhood. Of these the best known, and also the most passionate, was Karl von Clausewitz, an officer again with considerable operational experience who would become an acolyte of Scharnhorst's and provided much of the intellectual energy that drove his reforms. Although his famous book *Vom Kriege* ('On War') was published much later, it was largely based on his thoughts and writings as they worked together. Captured at Jena, briefly imprisoned in France, Clausewitz, like Scharnhorst, could not accept Frederick William's alliance with Napoleon and took himself off to work for the czar. He was present at the inconclusive and bloody battle of Borodino and only re-admitted to the Prussian army in 1815 when he was present on the Waterloo campaign. Clausewitz believed Prussians should put king and country above all else. Nothing mattered but the 'glorious struggle for freedom and the dignity of the Fatherland'.[37] The idea of war being a limited affair based on a calculation of relative strengths and mathematical formulae was irrelevant; war was instead the expression of a nation's will, its soul and its dignity. Military defeat, such as Jena, was a terrible national humiliation to which the whole nation must react. Clausewitz observed, 'To be anything at all apart from Fatherland and national honour. Everything I am or might be I owe to those two earthly gods and without them nothing would be left of me but an empty shell.'[38] Clausewitz is more often quoted than read, most staff colleges restricting their study to his rather obvious comment that war is an extension of policy by other means, which undersells the passion and the pivotal role he played in establishing the German sense of nationhood.

Neither was *Vom Kriege* widely read in the years following publication in 1832, the year after he died. It really only came to prominence through the endorsement of Helmuth von Moltke, revered by the German military as the man who would later defeat Austria and France so decisively, who listed it alongside the Bible and Homer's *Odyssey* as being one of the three books that had most influenced him. A German army journal noted in 1873 that 'Clausewitz has earned his place as the foremost authority on military learning in the German army' and that he had shown how 'strong discipline, good weapons, appropriate elementary tactics, good march dispositions, railways, practical supply arrangements and communications determine everything in war', and credited Clausewitz with having discredited the 'formalistic strategy of manoeuvre'.[39] The article was only partially correct, and the reference to railways something of an anachronism, because actually those principles had become commonplace in the Prussian army as part of the post-Jena reforms, but what it illustrates is Clausewitz's other role as director of the Prussian War College. It has been argued that his position there was largely administrative, and it is possible that his later writing reflected what he heard discussed as opposed to being his own original ideas, but he became associated with what came to be regarded as the principles of the Prussian and later German military approach: 'simplicity in planning, energy in execution, and a readiness at all levels to take responsibility'. 'Everyone must hold the conviction that it is better to advance on one's own responsibility than to remain idle waiting for orders.'[40]

Yet his wider influence was arguably strategic as opposed to tactical. Moltke himself paraphrased *Vom Kriege* when he wrote that 'Victory alone breaks the will of the enemy and compels him to submit to ours. It is not the occupation of a slice of territory or the occupation of a fortress but the destruction of enemy forces that will decide the outcome of the war. This destruction thus constitutes the principal object of operations.'[41] Once widely adopted by the German leadership after 1817, and later enthusiastically taken up by the French, Clausewitz's beliefs, forged in the fury and shame of the Napoleonic occupation, came to dominate strategic thought in the last decades of the 19th century and, critically, the first decade of the 20th century. Whereas Clausewitz acknowledged that a limited war was possible, he argued that it was only total war that would decide the outcome of interstate rivalry and, even if there were circumstances in which limited objectives were achievable, the enemy would logically adopt a total war approach to prevent them being obtained. It was therefore incumbent for combatants to be prepared to opt for total war from the outset.

Clausewitz's theories have been credited, or blamed, for the Allies' insistence on Germany's surrender in 1918 and again for the demands for unconditional surrender in 1945. His works would certainly influence Marshall and the U.S. Army leadership in the Second World War and were influential, if possibly less assiduously studied, by the British. Was a limited outcome possible or desirable in either conflict? It is a question that has vexed commentators since and may well come to vex them again in the future. However, what Clausewitz was able to do in 1806, when he returned from captivity in France, which left him with an even deeper loathing of all things French, was to use his by now extensive experience to work with Scharnhorst on Prussian military reform. From that work, however it was arrived at, came the rekindling of that initiative The Great Elector had demonstrated on the Great Sleigh Ride, what has since become known as *Auftragstaktik*, which translates, approximately, as 'mission orientated tactics'.

Moving cautiously, given the ever-present if inattentive French, the Commission began work. A Military Society had in fact existed in Berlin since 1802, started as we have seen by the unfortunate Massenbach, whose members studied reforms in other armies, most notably the French, but had been frustrated by the senior commanders who saw no need for change. Scharnhorst's first move was to centralize authority, also becoming in 1808, although he was not actually known as such, both Chief of Staff and War Minister. Before Jena, 'instead of centralised leadership there was an endless confusion of consultations'.[42] 'By the board went the cumbersome multiplicity of war colleges, military departments, provincial supply departments in Silesia and Prussia, intendancy general, army inspectorate and adjutant generals' office. All these were replaced by a single *Kriegsdepartement*'[43] that answered directly to Scharnhorst. With the machinery in place, he and Stein could move quickly, always aware that they must be ready when the opportunity arose to expel the hated occupiers.

His first moves were to enhance soldiers' self-respect and to re-establish their standing in society, prominent under Frederick the Great but lacking since his death. Corporal punishment was virtually abolished, retained only for serious offences, and a system of merit was introduced for promotion. Although Frederick had maintained that he had also operated a merit-based system, in fact it had only really been effective during the Seven Years' War when his bloodletting of the Prussian noble families had left him short of officers. The cadet school was overhauled, with qualifying exams introduced for promotion, and officers no longer needed to show their *Wappen* to gain advancement, although sadly that would later be subject to reactionary revision.

The major task was to re-organize the field army. Napoleon's army has not been included in this book because ultimately it served no purpose for the French people, but that is not to deny the tactical genius of its inspiration and organization. The creation of the corps system, whereby cavalry, infantry and artillery were grouped together in independent formations with integral logistics, had proved its effectiveness at Austerlitz in 1805 and again at Jena and Auerstadt. Previously, the French army of the *Ancien Régime* had been organized along similar lines to the Prussian army, but now Napoleon introduced a system that was based on mobility, speed, and concentration of force and firepower. Scharnhorst copied it so that next time the Prussian army mobilized in strength it would deploy as a series of corps. They would also be corps supported by a functioning logistic system, now mobile and no longer tied to fixed supply sites. Such was the adherence in the Jena campaign to the old Frederican dictat of not molesting the civilian population that 'soldiers had to freeze and go hungry in camps pitched in the open while the bursting barns and larders of nearby villages could have furnished them with ample provender'.[44] Not only did this cause unnecessary hardship but it mitigated against the idea of the whole population being involved in a war.

Yet for a corps system to work effectively it needed two things. First, commanders who were capable of taking the initiative and second, a field staff system that could manage the planning required to move, supply and concentrate the corps to achieve effect. Scharnhorst's view, reinforced by the chaos of 1806, was that a staff should be able to operate in conjunction with a commander so that he could concentrate on the battle while they dealt with the movement and administration. This required specialist training and the establishment of staff branches, answerable to a chief of staff, and dealing with the functions that an army in the field must manage, from looking after its people, intelligence, operational planning, movement and logistics, to liaising both with the local population and with allies.

Importantly, they would shepherd and move a reserve so that it was available when the commander required it. Again this was an imitation of the Napoleonic system, with Berthier, Napoleon's chief of staff, being the architect of many of his master's victories and noticeably, when absent, for his worst defeat. Yet Scharnhorst, impatient of some of the idiocy he had witnessed from senior Prussian officers, took the concept to the next level, establishing the general staff as a balance and check to ensure that field commanders acted within the dictates of the overall commander's intent. The chief of staff would become the commander's key adviser, whose advice could conflict with his wishes, a situation which would soon be graphically illustrated at Waterloo.

Scharnhorst's development of the general staff was helped by the second of the great reformers, Neidhardt von Gneisenau. A Saxon who had again gained considerable operational experience in the 1790s, he came to prominence in his handling of an infantry brigade at Jena and then by holding the fortress of Kolberg against the French between 1806 and the Treaty of Tilsit. Gneisenau was a liberal and a visionary. He saw the defence of Prussia, and by extension of Germany, as a sacred duty. The nation needed two armies, he maintained – a professional fully trained army but also a universal militia. 'What immense power,' he wrote, 'lies dormant and unexploited in the bosom of a nation! The power of a militia is inexhaustible.'[45] He drew his inspiration from how the Spanish people had risen up against Napoleon, and he argued that the nation also needed a free constitution as indispensable for enhancing its power and its military strength, an attitude which unsurprisingly made him unpopular with Frederick William III who called him 'a wicked and insolent chap'.[46]

However, his ideas chimed with those of Scharnhorst and Stein, and the resultant abolition of the old Frederican cantonment system in favour of universal conscription started from 1808. Controversial with Frederick William and the monarchist clique who surrounded him, and not completed until 1813 once the French had been expelled, the concept of the citizen as a soldier, the duty of every person – interestingly not just men – to defend the Fatherland, was accomplished in one of the most significant revolutions to take place in any European army. Initially they got round the French restriction on numbers by training far more potential recruits than were needed for the 42,000-strong force permitted at Tilsit; this *Krümper* – shrinkage – system[47] therefore produced an excess of men with basic military skills so that when the French were finally expelled in 1812–13, the country had an available pool of manpower on which to draw.

Scharnhorst himself had to leave office in 1811 when Napoleon forced Frederick William into an alliance against Russia, something which the reformers naturally strongly opposed. Napoleon's demands on Prussia for his march on Moscow were large. Prussia was required to supply '480,000 daily rations; 15 million daily fodder rations for horses; 2 million bottles of beer; a similar quantity of schnapps; 44,000 cows, 15,000 horses and 3,600 wagons, all on top of the 77,920 horses, 22,772 oxen and 13,394 wagons directly requisitioned by the French'.[48] Worse was the demand for 20,000 Prussian soldiers, many of whom never returned. It was seen as an even deeper humiliation.

Napoleon's subsequent invasion of Russia and retreat back through Europe would, however, give the reformers the opportunity they needed. As it became increasingly clear that France was now militarily weakened, the pressure within Prussia to act strengthened. There had been the odd previous spontaneous revolt against the occupation. In the autumn of 1808 Major Ferdinand von Schill had led a band of irregulars to help the Austrians before Wagram but had only got as far as Stralsund before he was defeated and he and 11 of his officers executed, all because they had disobeyed their oath to the king who was, of course, under obligation to Napoleon. Senior officers like Blücher, always the loudest and most active in his opposition, called for a general insurrection but Prussia was not ready. However, in 1812 General Graf Yorck von Wartenberg, whose troops had been amongst the unfortunates drafted into the *Grand Armée* for Napoleon's ill-advised venture, decided on his own initiative to desert the French and side with Russia. As the French retreated through Berlin in February 1813, they were pursued by Yorck, quickly followed by a party of Cossacks. Despite the king's disapproval, Yorck became an overnight hero and Frederick William was forced finally to act. On 23 February he made his famous speech *An Mein Volk* ('To my people'), appealing for Prussians to rise up and volunteer for the army. This was the moment the reformers had been waiting for. Scharnhorst returned immediately to Berlin and, together with Gneisenau and General Herman von Boyen from Königsberg – one of the few native Prussians amongst the reformers, again wounded at Auerstadt and a keen disciple of Scharnhorst, and who succeeded him as Minister for War – initiated their mass mobilization.

Scharnhorst had entrusted the poet Ernst Arndt with articulating the appeal to the people, albeit the humiliation of the French occupation had mostly done his work for him. Arndt was virulently anti-French. 'I hate the French carelessness, I despise the French daintiness, I disapprove of

the French loquacity and flightiness,' he thundered and now
he declared, 'Let us hate the Frenchmen, the infamizers and
destroyers of our power and virginity, even more now that we
feel how they weaken and enervate our virtue and strength'.[49]
The French diplomat Lecaro, part of the occupying force in
Berlin, appeared hurt when he noted in 1813 that Berliners
displayed 'such intense hatred and open rage' and 'no
longer concealed their desire to join with the Russians in
exterminating everything French'.[50] Scharnhorst took himself
to the front in the spring of 1813 as the French were being
forced west. Wounded in the foot at the battle of Lützen on
2 May 1813, he died from infection on 28 June, deprived of
the opportunity of witnessing Napoleon's final defeat and the
vindication of his life's work. The plan now enacted by Boyen
and Gneisenau was essentially a version of Frederick William
I's old three-tier strategy, albeit much updated. Formalized
in the 1813–14 defence laws, the first tier was the regular
professional army, for which all military age men were now
liable. Exemptions became severely restricted, applying only
to the clergy, the sick and sole breadwinners, producing
140,000 men. Recruiting was still largely regional, with the
exception of the Guard Corps, the king's personal troops,
but the length of service was reduced from the life sentence
imposed under the Frederican system. The cantonment
system as such was abolished.

The second tier was the *Landwehr*, the reserve which
quickly rose to 113,000. This was not a regular reserve, created
from men in their first two years out of service. Instead the
Landwehr was a 'second phalanx', which deployed its own
units. Veterans were eligible to join after three years, thus
not denuding the regular army reserve. Recruits trained for
four weeks in the first year, then one week a year, with drill

every Sunday afternoon, although increasingly this became voluntary. It had a professional staff of officers and NCOs who conducted the training, ran the administration and helped the *Landwehr* officers. These were selected on merit, but even Boyen appreciated that he needed to acknowledge the still-hierarchical nature of rural society. Men without service in the regular army could become officers if they lived locally and had a reasonable estate or income. They first served for a year as understudies, known as *Einjährige-Freiwillige Dienst*, before commissioning.

The third tier was the *Landsturm*, effectively anyone else, including women and teenagers who were not eligible for the first two tiers. The idea was to create the nation in arms, and the population were encouraged to fight the occupier with any means at their disposal. It was a novel take on the early 18th-century model, substantiating the reformers' mission to mobilize the nation and which frightened the reactionary faction at court possibly rather more than it did the French. It was everyone's sacred duty to defend the Fatherland, not just a few. 'A mass of people may call themselves a state' wrote the philosopher Georg Friedrich Hegel, 'only when they are united in the common defence of all they possess in active struggle.'[51] It is an idea that may resonate with modern governments as they struggle with ways of tackling the 'soft' challenges they face today. It did not last very long, being disbanded by those around the king who thought the concept of a nation in arms too dangerous to exist alongside an absolute monarchy, but the idea caught the imagination of Germany and would be resurrected in the future.

Appreciating that this three-tier model would be unpopular with some of the better off, despite the opportunities offered by *Landwehr* commissions, the government also encouraged the formation of volunteer regiments, *Freikorps*, similar to that commanded by the unfortunate Schill. The most celebrated of these included a well-known Berlin gymnast called Friedrich Jahn, who had defied the laughter of onlookers as he drilled young men during the French occupation, and the poet Theodor Körner, whose poems would later romanticize the volunteer movement. More important as the forerunners of German nationalism than for their military contribution, the *Freikorps* would nevertheless constitute approximately 10 per cent of the army in 1813, and it was their colours of black uniform, red lapels and gold braid that would go on to replace the Hohenzollerns' black, white and red as the national colours of Germany. Fichte also joined, although typically chose to wear a bizarre medieval costume of his own invention, as did the sculptor Schadow, who had designed the Quadriga on the Brandenburg Gate. They would fight at Großbeeren, outside Berlin, in the confused campaigning during 1813 as the French attempted to maintain their hold on Germany.

The French occupation finally came to an end at Leipzig in Saxony that October at the so-called Battle of the Nations. Over two days, the combined armies of Prussia, Russia and Austria defeated a French army commanded in person by Napoleon. With over 130,000 casualties, it was the bloodiest battle of the Napoleonic Wars and led to Napoleon's final withdrawal to Paris and his first abdication in April 1814. After the Bourbon restoration and subsequent year of misgovernment, Napoleon returned from exile in March 1815, leading to the Hundred Days and his final defeat at the hands of an allied army led by Wellington, and a Prussian army led by Blücher at Waterloo.

The Waterloo campaign demonstrated both the speed and effectiveness of the reform programme. There had been a small Prussian force in Flanders while the Congress of Vienna was debating the future of Europe during the winter of 1814–15. The French-speaking provinces of what is today Belgium had been made part of a united kingdom of the Netherlands, something to which many of the population who had either served in the French army or at least been sympathetic to Napoleon were opposed. The role of the Prussians, and a similar-sized British force, was to ensure that there was no trouble. However, once the news broke that Napoleon had landed back in France in March 1815, the European powers mobilized. Russian and Austrian mobilization would take time and their armies had a greater distance to travel than the Prussians. The decision was therefore taken to reinforce the troops in the Netherlands, assemble a British-led allied army in the western half of Brabant, which would include troops from Brunswick, Nassau, Hanover and the Netherlands, while the Prussians reinforced the eastern half, closer to their western provinces. Between the end of March and early June, Prussia had deployed four corps – Bülow's at Liège, Pirch's at Namur, Thielmann's, with Clausewitz, at Dinant, and Ziethen's north of the French border opposite Charleroi – a total of 130,000 troops, a large proportion of which were *Landwehr*, and 304 guns. Blücher was in command with Gneisenau as his chief of staff. The average age of the commanders was much reduced; although Blücher was 72, he was an exception, still remarkably fit and energetic. Bülow was the oldest corps commander at 60, while Pirch was only 52 and Ziethen just 45; several of the divisional commanders were in their early 40s. The deployment had

Central Europe in the Napoleonic Wars

GREAT BRITAIN

North Sea

BATAVIAN REPUBLIC

Amsterdam

Baltic Sea

Vistula

Danzig

Stralsund

Lübeck

KINGDOM OF DENMARK

HOLSTEIN

HANOVER

Hanover

Berlin

Warta

Oder

KINGDOM OF PRUSSIA

Breslau

SILESIA

RUSSIA

Warsaw

Cologne

Rhine

Elbe

Weimar

Auerstedt

SAXONY

Jena

THURINGIAN STATES

HESSE

Frankfurt

Prague

KINGDOM OF BOHEMIA

MORAVIA

Brunn

Kraków

Teschen

Paris

Seine

Loire

Meuse

Strasbourg

FRENCH EMPIRE

NEUCHATEL

BADEN

WÜRTTEMBERG

Ulm

BAVARIA

Augsburg

HELVETIC REPUBLIC

AUSTRIAN EMPIRE

Vienna

TYROL

KINGDOM OF HUNGARY

Budapest

Danube

Draja

SLAVONIA

Sava

CROATIA

DALMATIA

Sarajevo

OTTOMAN EMPIRE

REPUBLIC OF RAGUSA

Rhône

SAVOY

VALAIS

Milan

KINGDOM OF ITALY

Genoa

Toulon

Trieste

Adriatic Sea

PAPAL STATES

KINGDOM OF ETRURIA

Mediterranean Sea

N

0   150km
0   150 mile

The Waterloo Campaign

Brussels

Hal

Forest of Soignes

Waterloo

Mont St Jean

Genappe

Nivlles

Quate Bras

Wavre

Blücher

Ligny

Sambre

Charleroi

Wellington

Napoleon

Ney

Napoleon

Napoleon

Grouchy

18 June

17 June

16 June

15 June

French Army
Coalition forces

N

0   5km
0   5 mile

not been without its problems; some of the units from the Rhineland, from those parts which had been part of Napoleon's *Rheinbund*, proved reluctant and some deserted, but it was still a substantial operational achievement.

Both Wellington and Blücher were unsure whether they would be ordered across the border into France, as had been the case in 1814, or whether Napoleon would attack them first. They had agreed that, should that latter course develop, they would march to each other's assistance so that their combined armies would outmatch the French. In the event that was what did happen; Napoleon judged that he would be able to defeat both Prussian and allied armies individually, take Brussels and then turn to face the gathering menace of the main Russian and Austrian forces. He had massed his best troops, approximately 125,000 men, around Charleroi. He crossed the border on 15 June, attacking Ziethen's corps at Ligny on 16 June. Gneisenau ordered the other corps to concentrate on Ligny, but in the event only Pirch's was able to arrive in time. The ensuing battle was a tactical victory for the French, with the Prussians taking 16,000 casualties and Blücher being wounded, but Napoleon, thinking he had inflicted a major defeat, paused before following up his success. The next day he detached Marshal Grouchy with 30,000 troops to pursue what he thought was the shattered Prussian army towards Namur. In fact, only half the Prussian force had been engaged and even those who had fought were recovered overnight back to Wavre, a position pre-selected to correspond with Wellington's defensive position south of the village of Waterloo, and well west of Grouchy's column. Bülow's corps joined them there, so that by the evening of Saturday 17 June, when Blücher resumed command, he still had 100,000 men at his disposal even allowing for those

'Rhinelanders' who had deserted en route, estimated to be about 8,000. It was a remarkable manifestation of the effect of the Scharnhorst and Gneisenau reforms. Each Prussian corps had 20 staff officers, compared with eight for a French corps, and their ability to recover soldiers from a bloody battle, organize them for a long retreat march and then refit them to fight again on 18 June was remarkable.

As Napoleon subsequently attacked Wellington on Sunday 18 June, Blücher led three corps the 20-odd miles from Wavre to come up on Wellington's left and inflict a crushing defeat on the French. They advanced on two axes, General von Bülow's and subsequently Major General von Pirch's corps attacking the village of Plancenoit to the south while Major General Hans von Ziethen's corps advanced on a northern route, meeting up with Major General Karl von Müffling, the Prussian liaison officer, at Wellington's headquarters as they came onto the battlefield. Ziethen's lead division was commanded by the peppery Major General Karl von Steinmetz. As he arrived, he received orders from Blücher to turn south to join the attack on Plancenoit. Müffling pleaded with him that it was more important to march immediately to relieve French attacks on Wellington's left, which was in danger of being overwhelmed. Steinmetz refused and ordered his division south, at which point Ziethen's chief of staff, Colonel von Reiche, arrived. Reiche, knowing the overall plan and aware of Gneisenau's intent, backed Müffling. A heated argument ensued but eventually Steinmetz agreed to march to join Wellington, a decision Ziethen subsequently endorsed when he rode up. Ironically, the young officer who had brought the orders from Blücher was none other than a von Scharnhorst. That heated exchange, which made a significant difference to the outcome of the battle, was a graphic vindication of the older Scharnhorst's vision. Blücher would later say of his relationship with Gneisenau as his chief of staff that he was 'very reliable, reports to me on the manoeuvres that are to be executed and the marches that are to be performed. Once convinced that he is right I drive my troops through hell towards the goal and never stop until the object is achieved'.[52]

Waterloo ended the French threat to Prussia. The Prussian army had restored the nation's territory and dignity, and in doing so it had reinforced its deep connection with wider Prussian society. A good example of this was the *Eisernes Kreuz*, the Iron Cross, designed by the great architect Karl Friedrich Schinkel. Made of good German iron, and instituted by Frederick William III in 1812, it was the first Prussian award that could be given to people of all ranks, both military and civilian, the first recipient being the late Queen Luise. Once Schadow's Quadriga had been returned from Paris after Napoleon looted it, the goddess's staff was adorned with the Prussian eagle, the oak leaves of victory and an Iron Cross. The army was more the state by 1815 than it ever had been under Frederick the Great.

There was an expectation, now the war was over, that the two movements the reformers had championed for political reform and German nationalism might gain strength. Sadly that was not to be. Stein resigned in 1815, frustrated as the king surrounded himself once more with a reactionary clique. Hardenberg soldiered on until 1822, Frederick William's negotiator at the Congress of Vienna, from which Prussia emerged with significant gains and a population of 10 million people, but without making progress on the nationalist agenda. Outwitted by the infamous Austrian Chancellor Metternich, by then firmly in control in Vienna, the best that could be achieved was the Frankfurt Diet, which acted as a not very effective parliament for the German states, now reduced from 300 to 39. Although Austria and Prussia dwarfed every other state in the German-speaking world – the third was Bavaria, which was only one-tenth of the size of Prussia – Austria was determined that the nationalist movement should be quashed. Hardenberg was persuaded to subscribe to the Carlsbad Decrees of 1819, designed by Metternich to restrict further calls for nationalism by banning student societies and increasing press censorship. Even poor Jahn, the enthusiastic gymnast who had fought with the *Freikorps*, was gaoled for being a member of a student society, a *Burschenschaft*.

The army was not spared. The *Landsturm* was quickly disbanded. Boyen soldiered on, defending the *Landwehr*, until he too resigned in 1819, but Gneisenau went in 1815, although both he and Boyen would later return as Prussia's problems multiplied. Officers with *Wappen* were again preferred by the older generals at court, the so-called *Camarilla*, determined that the defeat of revolutionary France meant that any modernist notions were no longer of consequence. But this was soon to prove illusory. One of the beneficial effects of the peace was that the industrial revolution, held at bay by 23 years of fighting in Europe, was now able to take root in Germany, meaning a rapid expansion of cities. Between 1815 and 1840 the population of Berlin doubled to 400,000, and by 1870 it would be 1 million. With it came economic prosperity but also social misery, and the calls for a more representative government spilled over into violence in Berlin in 1848, much as it did across so many European cities. The calls for a German nation grew alongside. These ranged from a colourful student festival in 1817 at the castle of Wartburg in Saxe-Weimar, where students celebrated the publication of Luther's *Ninety-Five Theses*, and the fourth anniversary of Leipzig, complete with medieval minstrels, a *Sängerkrieg* (song contest) evoking the romantic past and wearing ancient German costumes, to more serious challenges to the Carlsbad Decrees.

But the military structures that the reformers had introduced and proved at Leipzig and Waterloo would endure. The tragedy of 20th-century Germany arguably started before Germany was even created, as later Hohenzollerns, and Bismarck – First Minister of Prussia from 1862 until 1871 then Chancellor of the German Empire from 1871 until 1890 – used the highly efficient army model developed by the reformers to create a nation and an empire, but in doing so removed the checks that men like Scharnhorst and Gneisenau had designed. Germany identified with its army just as much in the latter half of the 19th century as it had in the first, and it must have given Kaiser Wilhelm I great pleasure to avenge the humiliation of Tilsit as he was proclaimed emperor in Versailles' Hall of Mirrors. Adulation of all things military and reverence for uniform and rank reached absurd levels. There is a famous Berlin story of a petty criminal called Voigt who stole an officer's uniform, commandeered a squad of soldiers and demanded that the mayor of a suburb called Köpenick hand over the municipal funds. Made into a play titled *The Captain of Köpenick*, it questioned the absurdity of people obeying someone just because he happened to don a uniform. Bismarck, who understood the restraints under which military power must operate, made the army answerable to him and the kaiser and used it to create the German nation. Once he had been forced from office, the new kaiser, Wilhelm II, could use the enormous power the army represented unchecked.

The Prussian army that Scharnhorst and the reformers designed fits all our criteria for an army that was successful. Not just being supported by the nation, it was at one with the nation; it created a morale and sense of pride and belonging that made it unique, and it rose from a cultural revolution that demanded it. The three-tier system promoted the selection and training of a first-rate field army, while the reserve system, the *Landwehr* and the sadly neglected *Landsturm*, enveloped the whole nation in their own defence. It was an affordable army – at least until expanded to support Bismarck's wars – and it was the instrument that created a great European nation. Admittedly that nation strayed, and an army that had been designed to create then defend that nation was used in ways that its founders never intended. Was that their fault? Whatever you conclude does not detract from the extraordinary military contribution of Scharnhorst, Gneisenau, Boyen and Clausewitz together with Stein and Hardenberg.

Chapter Six

The U.S. Army, 1941

'The United States is a country of machines.'
Joseph Stalin, 1943

Many of the citizens of the United States of America in 1941 came from families who had emigrated from Europe in the previous century – from Ireland, Poland, Germany and Italy, amongst many others. They had mostly emigrated because their original native countries had not offered them the life they sought. In the United States they saw the chance of a new beginning, freedom of conscience and an opportunity to work. Together they had created what by 1890 had become the world's fastest growing economy and, after the tragedy of the American Civil War of 1861–65, a nation that, with the exception of the far west, was peaceful and prosperous, even if that prosperity remained unequally distributed. Why then should American citizens become involved in a European war in 1939 when it looked as if its outcome would have little bearing on their lives, safely out of reach across the Atlantic? It was not a new sentiment. In 1914 their parents had asked themselves the same question. The First World

War looked to many on their side of the Atlantic to be a dynastic struggle between regimes they had been only too happy to escape.

In 1916 the military priority consuming the staff in Washington was the war in Mexico, where an army commanded by General John J. Pershing was engaged in trying to capture the revolutionary leader Pancho Villa. The U.S. supported the Mexican government in their efforts to suppress Villa, who had retaliated by raiding Columbus, New Mexico, resulting in the death of 16 Americans. However, Pershing was possibly too assiduous in carrying out his task as, although he failed to capture Villa, his offensive was not well received by the Mexican government and his troops clashed with their army. In May Villa raided across the border again, this time attacking Glen Springs, Texas, resulting in Pershing mounting a second cross-border expedition. This resulted in an open stand-off with the Mexicans at Carrizal on 21 June, when 23 American soldiers were captured. The popular mood in the United States called for all-out war. President Woodrow Wilson eventually negotiated an agreement with Mexico's president, Venustiano Carranza, which ended open hostilities, although American troops would remain in Mexico until February 1917.

Since the terrible slaughter of the American Civil War, the Army of the United States had been occupied in preventing Native American tribes from hindering the colonization of the western states and in securing the United States' borders. Operations in the Spanish-American War had led to fighting in Cuba and Puerto Rico in 1898 and the Philippines from 1899 to 1902, but otherwise the army's missions were more policing and internal security, which prioritized the role of cavalry. There was a strong feeling that the First World War was a European affair which did not involve the interests of the United States and that there was no reason for them to become involved despite the loss of 128 Americans in the sinking of the *Lusitania* in 1915, when it was attacked by a German U-boat. Isolationism remained the prevalent sentiment. Speaking in Philadelphia after the sinking, President Wilson said, 'There is such a thing as a man being too proud to fight. There is such a thing as a nation being so right that it does not need to convince others by force that it is right',[1] and in 1916 he was re-elected as President under the slogan 'He kept us out of the war'. That September the German government called off their U-boat attacks in the Atlantic.

Yet in February 1917, as Pershing's troops were preparing to return to the United States, Germany reversed its position and once again declared unrestricted submarine warfare in the Atlantic. Wilson was infuriated, severing diplomatic relations with Germany and attempting to get Congress to pass legislation allowing the arming of U.S. merchant ships, a move opposed by anti-war senators. Germany was also making clumsy attempts to persuade Mexico to adopt a more aggressive policy towards the United States. The Zimmerman Telegram was purported to be a telegram from the German Foreign Minister, Arthur Zimmermann, to the German ambassador in Mexico City promising German assistance to Mexico to recover the territory it had lost to the United States in return for active support against the Americans. Later thought to have been a forgery, the telegram was 'intercepted' by the British and forwarded to Wilson. He reacted slowly but by April 1917 felt he had sufficient support to ask Congress to support a declaration of war against Germany. All but six senators supported him, with 82 in favour (the Senate then having just 88 members), and a majority of 323 in the House of Representatives.

This presented the U.S. military with a problem. Wilson's policy shift from neutrality to war had been rapid; only in 1916 the President had forbidden the War Department from working on contingency plans for a general war. Military chiefs now faced three major problems. The first was working with the administration to establish a system that could convert a small force used to guarding the borders and fighting guerillas into an army capable of participating in a modern war and a war in which the combatants now had considerable experience. How, for example, were they to find officers with sufficient experience to organize and lead such a force? The second was purely one of numbers. In April 1917 the U.S. Army numbered 213,557, including both regular army and National Guard, roughly the same size as the combined casualties from the Allied offensive on the Aisne that May.[2] Clearly a massive expansion was required. Their third problem was one of materiel. How could they utilize American industry to produce the equipment modern war demanded, not only the artillery – by 1917 the Western Front was largely an artillery war – but also the ammunition to serve it as well as the aeroplanes, tanks and small arms?

The British and French, naturally keen to see the U.S. Army deployed as soon as possible, suggested simply taking American recruits into their own battalions and training them alongside. This may have been a practical solution but was clearly unacceptable politically. A modified proposal to include an American battalion in each British brigade was also rejected in favour of the U.S. deploying its own American Expeditionary Force, the AEF, which would eventually grow to 2.8 million men. The American formations would be shipped to France, be trained there, and the Allies had to accept a delay of a year until they were combat ready. The AEF was commanded by Pershing, recently returned from Mexico and unfamiliar with the European war. He was a cavalryman by background, impatient of what he saw as Allied hesitancy and a believer in the power of the 'offensive spirit', as the French had been in 1914–15 until their terrible losses caused them to appreciate the power of artillery. To support him a general staff was assembled in the War Department, although again this was not fully functioning until early 1918.

The numbers issue was solved by the passage in May 1917 of the Selective Service Act. This allowed for conscription and under its provisions 24 million men would ultimately be registered. The reaction to the call for recruits was immediate, although there was still a long road before they could be considered as trained soldiers. Pershing believed in large divisions of 28,000, roughly double that of a British or French division, and he had the men to fill them; by contrast, an exhausted Germany could only field divisions of a few thousand. When asked what they most wanted from the U.S., the French had replied, 'We want men, men, men', and the men the Americans sent were 'well-fed, unwearied and unshaken', compared with the European armies shattered by three years of trench warfare.[3]

The issue of ordnance was more difficult to solve. U.S. industry simply did not have the factories able to convert in short order to produce what was needed; employment was high and spare industrial capacity limited. The lack of tanks was a good example. In September 1917 Pershing requested 375 heavy and 1,500 light tanks; by August 1918 he had a tank corps consisting of 2,400 'trained' soldiers, but they had yet actually to see a tank. Eventually the AEF's tank corps was equipped with a combination of British heavy and French light tanks, which they would operate with success – one battalion commanded by Lieutenant Colonel George Patton would distinguish itself in the offensive mounted in September 1918 against the St Mihiel Salient – but the lack of native tank production would set an unfortunate precedent. The same story was replicated for aircraft. The AEF set a target of over 12,000 aeroplanes, arguably a totally unrealistic number. Again, by the time of the armistice the fledgling air service was flying mostly British and French machines; of 6,287 aircraft delivered by November 1918, only 1,216 were produced in the United States.[4]

By the autumn of 1918 the AEF was ready for army-sized operations. On 26 September the U.S. 'First' Army, essentially the AEF, attacked between the Meuse and Reims along a 44-mile front. It was a terrible experience for an inexperienced army. 'Most of us who were young American officers knew little of actual warfare,' wrote Lieutenant Maury Maverick of the 28th Infantry. 'We had the daring but not the training of the old officer of the front. The Germans simply waited, and then laid a barrage of steel and fire. And the machine gunners poured it on us. Our company numbered two hundred men. Within a few minutes about half of them were either dead or wounded.'[5] The AEF fought on through the Argonne until November, taking a total of 117,000 casualties, estimated to be roughly equivalent to their German opponents. They had fought bravely and made a material difference to the war's outcome, but the cost was high. Many in the U.S. thought it was far too high.

American de-mobilization was not managed as efficiently as its mobilization had been the previous year. Those returning to civilian life felt little had been done to help them, especially in the south where there was high unemployment and race riots. The economy suffered as war contracts were halted, and there was a wave of strikes and civil unrest as localities feared they would be swamped by returning soldiers with no work. Coupled to this was a concern, now that Russia was governed by the Bolsheviks, that unemployed ex-soldiers might become sympathetic to communism.

This anti-war mood contributed to a growing sense that America should look to its own and that intervention in other people's wars was a mistake. In 1916 President Wilson had proposed his plan for a League of Nations, summarized in his Fourteen Points, which he saw as creating an international structure that would, at the very least, minimize the risk of future war, if not remove it altogether. Thinking that his move was logical after the recent slaughter, he was disappointed to find it resoundingly rejected by a Congress intent on re-establishing isolationism. The opposition was led by Henry Cabot Lodge, Chairman of the Senate Foreign Affairs Committee, an avowed opponent of the President. He particularly objected to the tenth point which envisaged the League committing military forces against external aggression to its members' territory. He spoke for many when he said in a famous speech on 28 February 1919 that 'we should never permit the United States to be involved in the internal conflict in another country, except by the will of her people expressed through the Congress which represents them.' He was supported by powerful allies such as Theodore Roosevelt, who quipped that the Fourteen Points 'simply added one more scrap to the diplomatic waste-paper basket',[6] while Senator William Borah wished 'this treacherous and treasonable scheme to be buried in hell' and said that if he had his way it would be consigned to

'2,000 leagues under the sea'.[7] Without American support, the President's ambitious plan was doomed, and although it was formally adopted as part of the Versailles negotiations, and Wilson received the Nobel Peace Prize for his efforts, it remained ineffective until it was disbanded in 1946 and replaced by the United Nations.

Similarly doomed to receive a rough ride in Congress was the War Department's proposal to maintain the U.S. Army at 500,000 men. Again fearing Wilson's internationalism, the Army's proposal put forward during the debate on the 1920 National Defense Act was rejected in favour of a far smaller force of 17,700 officers and 280,000 enlisted men, although successive budget cuts meant that by 1923 the actual strength stood at 14,021 officers and 119,222 enlisted. Any idea that the U.S. Army might capitalize on its huge achievements of 1918 was effectively buried. The Army went 'back to normalcy', wrote Major General John S. Wood, who would later command an armoured division. That 'was the post-war slogan, and back to normalcy the post-war army went, struggling to keep alive a flickering flame and faltering spirit of national preparedness, struggling to maintain and modernise its arms equipment, and struggling for its very life to obtain the funds necessary for its meagre existence', a struggle that would become increasingly difficult as the Great Depression gripped America from 1929.[8] And 'isolation from the affairs of Europe' became 'the natural state of things, part of what made America a special country'.[9]

The story of the Army during the 1920s and 1930s is best illustrated by looking at the progress of mechanization, a story that has been traced by David Johnson, a retired U.S. Army colonel and member of the global policy think-tank RAND.

By tracing the development of tanks and aircraft, he has neatly captured the extraordinary debates that surrounded the fielding of arguably the two future battle-winning technologies, tanks and aircraft, that had emerged from the First World War. Tanks had been an almost accidental invention, developed from farm Caterpillar tractors as a means of providing protected firepower to the infantry as they struggled across the cratered moonscape that the European battlefield had become. First deployed – against the advice of their proponents – in a small group by the British on the Somme in September 1916, their performance was disappointing; Sir Douglas Haig, the British commander in chief, had been counselled to wait until he had sufficient numbers and a battlefield that offered easier terrain before committing what some saw as a war-winning weapon. However, as tank design improved so did their effectiveness, and in November 1917 a surprise mass tank attack with 476 machines at Cambrai achieved a breakthrough six miles deep. Although the Germans later counter-attacked successfully, the initial British advance had achieved striking results when compared with the carnage in the mud west of Ypres where the British 2nd and 5th Armies had been unsuccessfully attacking the Passchendaele ridge since July.

Cambrai was being fought as the AEF was training and assembling the nascent U.S. Tank Corps, which, as we have seen, participated in the final offensives of the war in the autumn of 1918. However, their performance had been mixed, with only 16 American tanks remaining operational in November from the 142 with which they had started out just six weeks before. The conclusion of the post-war Superior Board, assembled to evaluate the lessons from the war, was that 'The tank should be recognised as an infantry supporting and accompanying weapon incapable of independent decisive action.'[10] When giving his own post-war debrief, Pershing concluded that 'The Tank Corps should not be a large organisation, only of sufficient numbers, I would say, to carry on investigations and conduct training with Infantry, and I would place it under the Chief of Infantry as an adjunct of that arm.'[11] Under the 1920 National Defense Act all responsibility for armoured warfare was placed in the hands of the Chief of Infantry. While military thinkers across the Atlantic pondered the potential offered by mechanized warfare in general and the tank in particular, the U.S. Army's conclusion was that the arms that had won the war were the infantry helped by the artillery. The AEF had been a formation of mass infantry divisions and had prevailed as such. Future war would be similar; what was important was an ability to raise mass infantry formations and provide them with support weapons. There was almost an element of a comfort blanket in this approach. Congress was adamant that there was no threat to the continental United States. Despite possibly hoping for a third term, Wilson did not stand in the 1920 election, which was won by the Republican senator for Ohio, Warren Harding, by the huge margin of 26 per cent. He had ignored his Democrat rival and fellow Ohio man James Cox, instead campaigning against Wilson's legacy, against intervention and for a return to 'normalcy'.

The 1920s and early 1930s were consequently a period of stagnation for the U.S. Army. However, it certainly wasn't a period lacking in intellectual curiosity; but those who tried to question the accepted War Department status quo – that the United States was not going to become embroiled in another war and, even if it was forced to, it would again be a war dominated by mass infantry formations – were not just ignored but actively repressed. Those officers, including a young Captain Dwight D. Eisenhower and Lieutenant Colonel George Patton, who dared to question the wisdom of disbanding the tank corps and subjugating armoured development to the infantry, were severely reprimanded. Eisenhower was called in front of General Charles S. Farnsworth, the Chief of Infantry, to be told that 'his ideas were not only wrong but dangerous'. He was not to 'publish anything incompatible with solid infantry doctrine' and that if he persisted he would be court-martialled.[12] Patton, an ambitious officer but also someone who wanted to enjoy life, simply went back to a cavalry regiment. In 1927 the Army did, at the insistence of Secretary of War Dwight Davis, establish an experimental mechanized force, organized along the lines of a cavalry regiment. It survived until 1931, when a combination of infantry intransigence and budget pressures forced its closure; it had been forced to operate with antiquated First World War equipment and could only field four relatively modern tanks. With the Depression worsening, the priority was taken to be ensuring continued employment as opposed to new equipment, although the idea of cavalry as armoured formations had sown a seed amongst the more forward thinking who saw the potential for the traditional cavalry role of deep exploitation. This was a debate that would be played out in Europe in 1944.

The future of horsed cavalry also remained, somewhat surprisingly, a contentious issue. The argument of the tank versus the horse has since become something of a stereotypical debate amongst military historians, being used to illustrate a perceived conservatism amongst generals. Actually, the argument for retaining horsed cavalry in the inter-war U.S.

Army was more complex. Horses were a useful and cheap way of patrolling the border and were also a vital part of every army's logistic system. Perhaps ironically, the armies that were most dependent on horses in the 1930s were the German and the Russian. A German prisoner of war, questioned by his American interrogators on Omaha Beach in June 1944, said that he could not believe that D-Day was a real invasion because he had not seen any horses being disembarked and he knew that armies could not move without horsepower. Successive U.S. chiefs of cavalry argued, with less conviction, that the horse still had a combat role, citing the widespread use the Soviets made of cavalry units and, perhaps less presciently, the value the Poles attached to their horsed units. They strongly resisted what would in the late 1930s become an increasing rerolling of horsed units to mechanized units, Major General J.K. Herr, Chief of Cavalry, writing to General George C. Marshall as late as 1942 that 'In the interests of National Defense in this crisis, I urge you the necessity of an immediate increase in horse Cavalry.'[13] Herr believed that there was a 'general hostility against the horse on the part of the War Department General Staff', which 'arose from two classes of people – one, those little brats who had graduated from Leavenworth and who knew nothing about anything, and the other on the part of those Coast Artillerymen and men of that ilk who had never had a dynamic thought'. He reserved his particular ire for General McNair, the chief of staff, who, he believed, 'hates the horse and believes a truck can go anywhere a horse can go'.[14] It may therefore come as no surprise that when the cavalry mobilized as horse-mechanized regiments, they still included a squadron of horses organized into three rifle troops together with horse transporters to carry them forward.

While the U.S. Army was taking a decidedly Stalinist attitude to its inquisitive young officers, its attitude was mirrored to a lesser extent but not so rigorously in Britain and France. There, at least, men like Captain Basil Liddell Hart – a soldier who criticized the conduct of the British Army in Flanders and who argued for mechanization, writing that mass infantry assaults were both expensive and ineffective – and Major General J.F.C. Fuller – who had been on the battle staff who planned the Cambrai offensive, and who proposed the development of tank armies – were able to publish. The country which took notice of their writings was, however, Germany, where the army used the meagre allocation of manpower allowed them under the terms of Versailles to nurture the ideas that Liddell Hart and Fuller promoted. Fuller's most enthusiastic pupil was arguably Heinz Guderian.

One of the capabilities that Liddell Hart expounded was the development of air power, and here, at least, the U.S. Army was forced to take a more proactive approach. The Air Service, as it was termed, was part of the Army and had not been organized into a separate service as it had in Britain, which had created the Royal Air Force. This was to remain a contentious issue – the United States Air Force was not finally created until 1947 – and the best the American Army Air Service could get was to be recognized in the 1920 National Defense Act as a separate combatant arm in the Army's order of battle alongside the infantry, cavalry and artillery. Although they had failed to win institutional recognition, two factors would work to their advantage in the coming decade. First, the civilian aviation industry began to take off so that technological development of aircraft was happening regardless of whether the military sponsored it or not, unlike the tank which, unsurprisingly, had no commercial utility.

By the mid-1920s the United States was the first country in the world to produce more civil aircraft annually than military. Initially the Air Service had to make do with its old war models. These were obsolete, and in 1920 alone they had 330 crashes resulting in the sad loss of 69 pilots. The second factor working in their favour was that the persistent lobbying of their proponents, men like Brigadier General Billy Mitchell, who had strong links to Congress, where representatives were always mindful of the importance of the commercial benefits of the burgeoning aviation industry. Interestingly Mitchell, unlike Patton and Eisenhower, was not prepared to back down in his criticism of the lack of War Department support and was actually court-martialled for insubordination. In July 1926 Congress passed the Army Air Corps Act, which authorized a force of 1,800 aircraft and 16,650 personnel, although it stopped short of authorizing an independent service.[15]

The Air Corps, partly because much of the civilian aircraft development was on multi-engine long-range aeroplanes for civilian transport, and partly because of a deep belief in the ability of air power to win future wars, accompanied by commendable if possibly misplaced crusading zeal, concentrated on what was termed 'bombardment' as opposed to 'pursuit', or long-range bombers rather than fighters. The Air Corps' logic was that the long-range bomber, armoured and with its own protection, was indestructible and could destroy an enemy's means of production as well as the morale of its civilian population, thus rendering land forces unnecessary. Mitchell also argued that for the cost of one battleship, $45 million, it was possible to build 1,000 aircraft, which was an exaggeration, but he made his point by sinking the *Ostfriesland*, a redundant German battleship.

This did not endear him to the Department of the Navy; neither did his argument that the advent of aircraft made the Navy's coastal defence batteries irrelevant. However, it meant that by the late 1930s the one area of the U.S. military that was supplied with capable modern equipment was the bombardment squadrons. 'In this one arm,' said General Douglas MacArthur, who became Chief of Staff in 1930, 'we have not fallen behind in quality… in some types of fighting airplanes our latest models are appreciably better than any others known to exist.'[16]

Another result of the Depression was that officers were reluctant to leave the Army, so that their average age gradually increased. The maximum ages set for each rank were high: a second lieutenant could serve until he was 30 and a captain until 42. By 1939 it was discovered that the average field officer in an infantry battalion, so captains to lieutenant colonels, was 13 years older than his equivalent in 1918, with majors averaging 48.[17] The National Guard fared even worse, with nearly one-quarter of first lieutenants over 40.[18]

In September 1931 the Japanese invaded Chinese Manchuria. In 1933 Hitler came to power in Germany. By 1936 he was confident enough to re-occupy the Rhineland, demilitarized under the conditions imposed by Versailles. In 1937 Japan occupied large parts of eastern China; early the next year Hitler annexed Austria, the *Anschluss*, before moving into the Czech Sudetenland. In September 1939 Germany invaded Poland and Europe was once again at war, while Japan continued its aggressive expansion in South-East Asia. Public sentiment in the USA was decidedly anti-German; a Gallup Poll in October 1939 recorded only 2 per cent pro Hitler, but that did not translate into support for intervention. Frank Knox, who had been the Republican candidate for Vice President in the 1936 election and who had risen from private soldier to lieutenant colonel in the First World War, said in a speech in Cleveland that 'After our experience in the last war, it is simply unthinkable that we will ever again send overseas a great expeditionary force.'[19] Much as Wilson had done in 1914, President Franklin Roosevelt made it absolutely clear that the U.S. would not become involved in yet another European war. 'We are not going in,' he insisted, broadcasting that autumn that 'the United States will keep out of this war... let no man or woman thoughtlessly or falsely talk of America sending its armies to European fields',[20] which was just as well as America in 1939 had no army to send. Its total strength was 172,000 and it had just six operational medium tanks. It ranked 19th in the world, after Portugal and Romania, although slightly ahead of Bulgaria.

On the same day that Germany invaded Poland, General George C. Marshall became Chief of Staff of the Army. Marshall's career had spanned the full breadth of American military experience. An infantry officer, he had served in the Philippines in the Spanish Wars, had been one of the first officers to deploy to France in 1917 on the staff of 1st Infantry Division and had participated in the 1918 offensives. Importantly, he had witnessed the problems caused by the lack of training of the U.S. infantry and the administrative chaos that accompanied the AEF's deployment. One of his first acts as Chief of Staff was to persuade President Roosevelt to ask Congress for a small increase in the size of the Army: up to 227,000 regulars and 235,000 in the National Guard. Marshall felt, correctly, that Roosevelt prioritized the Navy over the Army because it better aligned with his strategic position. Roosevelt also had a strong personal affiliation to the Navy, having served as assistant naval secretary, and his office was decorated with naval prints. He had also taken a strong position in support of the Air Corps when, in January 1939, he had asked Congress for $300 million for the aircraft industry, envisaging a force of 15,000 military aircraft. The Army was being allowed to atrophy while the Navy expanded. 'At least,' Marshall said to the President soon after he was appointed, 'please stop speaking of the army as "them" and the navy as "us".' Marshall concluded that 'as an army we were ineffective'.[21]

Marshall would not have long to wait until the German invasion of France, and that country's rapid capitulation alarmed Congress into authorizing a massive increase in Army funding. On 16 May 1940 Roosevelt put plans before Congress for $1.182 billion. By July this figure had grown to $4.848 billion to fund an army of 1.2 million men, with equipment for a further 800,000, an air corps of 20,000 aircraft and the largest naval expansion in U.S. history. Although there was still opposition, Marshall, possibly testing credulity, justified the appropriations by testifying that the increases were necessary in case of a Nazi attack on South America. Senator Henry Cabot Lodge Jr, grandson of Wilson's nemesis, told Major General Henry Arnold, the Air Corps commander, that 'It is the general feeling of Congress, and as far as I can gather among public opinion throughout the country, to provide all the money necessary for the national defence, and all you have to do is ask for it.'[22]

Roosevelt and Marshall now faced three significant challenges. First, they had to create a national defence framework that would be capable of administering and advising this hugely expanded national capability. 'The US Army had no tradition or machinery of strategic planning.

Its working assumption was that armies were expressions of the national will, generated by political leaders', which offers a thoughtful analysis of what a U.S. army – or indeed any army in a democracy – should be, but which meant that there was a significant gap to be filled.[23] Second, they had to deliver on the Army programme, starting from the very low levels of equipment, training and experience that prevailed. Third, they felt it incumbent, indeed in the national interest, to provide assistance to Britain and what was left of the French forces within the strict confines of the Neutrality Act, which forbade the U.S. from providing assistance to foreign powers in wartime.

The issue of establishing a national capability started with overhauling the War Department, which Marshall found had 'lost track of its purpose of existence... and had become a huge, bureaucratic, red-tape-ridden operating agency'.[24] Sixty-one officers, such as Major General Herr, the very persistent Chief of Cavalry, had direct access to the Chief of Staff, who was expected to preside directly over 350 subordinate commands and departments. The department was, Marshall told his Chief of War Plans, Brigadier General Leonard Gerow, 'the poorest command post in the army and we must do something about it'.[25] Various studies during the course of 1941 reported inconclusively or were shelved as they ran into narrow single arm prejudices and were always open to the Air Corps' lobbying for autonomy.

It was an issue that became more urgent after the Japanese attack on Pearl Harbor in December 1941 when it was clear that poor communication between the War Department's intelligence staff and General Walter J. Short, commanding general in Hawaii, had led to vital warnings of hostile action being overlooked. The subsequent report, together with the next stage of re-armament, worked to Marshall's advantage. In February 1942, working on a report commissioned by Marshall very soon after he had suffered his last harangue from the Chief of Cavalry as to the dangers to national defence of further reducing horse numbers, and prepared by Brigadier General Joseph T. McNarney, an Air Corps officer who had sat on the Pearl Harbor tribunal, Roosevelt signed off a major re-organization. Gone were the chiefs of the various arms, creating instead three commands under the Chief of Staff – Army Ground Forces, Army Air Forces and Services of Supply. Deployed commanders would answer directly to the Chief of Staff, who could now concentrate on strategy rather than inter-department wrangling. The Air Corps would not become autonomous and would remain under the Army but its chief, Arnold, would sit on the Combined Chiefs of Staff Committee as Chief of Army Air Forces. The committee included Marshall, Admiral Ernest King as the Chief of Naval Operations, de facto head of the Navy, and would be chaired by Admiral William Leahy. The idea of an independent chairman was a move Marshall supported. Roosevelt had thought that he would be able to chair the committee himself, a hands-on commander in chief, a move which thoroughly alarmed the pragmatic Marshall. Leahy's role was to be the President's nominee, to act as his representative and brief him as well as preventing inter-service rivalries. Marshall liked the idea of having an admiral, someone who would find it difficult to counter the Army's position and who could not be too overtly supportive of the Navy.[26] Often meeting with Allied representatives, the 'Chiefs' would meet weekly for the rest of the war. A general headquarters was established under Marshall's old confidant, Major General Lesley J. McNair – he and Marshall had shared a cabin on the boat to France in

1917 – whose job was to turn a mass of civilian recruits into a trained army. Interestingly, the U.S. military today still works much along the lines Marshall recommended.

In 1940 Roosevelt also appointed a ministerial team who shared what were rapidly emerging as his concerns over the need to re-arm. He appointed the veteran politician Henry L. Stimson as Secretary of War, or Minister for the Army. Stimson had previously served in the post from 1911 to 1913, had served in the Army from 1917 to 1922 and then been President Hoover's Secretary of State from 1929 to 1933. Consequently, he commanded considerable gravitas in Washington, and, as a Republican, was instrumental in helping to achieve a cross-party consensus in favour of re-armament; he was also, helpfully, very pro-British. The new Secretary of the Navy was Frank Knox, who, as publisher of the *Chicago Daily News*, had now changed his tune and by mid-1940 was urging compulsory military training.

The congressional votes to increase the armed forces in the summer of 1940 required a draft. The 1940 Selective Service and Training Act was signed into law by Roosevelt on 16 September, the first time conscription had been introduced in the United States in peacetime. Like its 1917 predecessor, it required all men aged 21 to 36 to register with their local draft boards, which would later be extended by executive order to those between 18 and 45. There was, after the fall of France, now widespread support for the bill. Sixty per cent of people polled in August 1940 were in favour of extending the draft to include 20-year-olds, while 85 per cent said that they were prepared to pay higher taxes for national defence, a sharp increase since the invasion of France. There was an outpouring of patriotism, with Kate Smith's rendition of 'God Bless America' making it into the charts. Yet there was still strong opposition. The Mothers of America organized nationwide protests under the slogan 'Kill the Bill, Not Our Sons', and some student groups across the nation urged their members to refuse to register. Roosevelt only came out publicly in favour of conscription on 2 August, but by then he was reflecting, not leading, the national mood. As in 1917, an isolationist America, increasingly aware of the impact war in Europe and the Pacific would have on the continental United States, had swiftly changed its national stance.

By November 1940 the first draft recruits were making their way into training centres across the country. McNair's problem in organizing training was twofold. First, he had to set up a system of basic training so that these young men could look after themselves, fire their weapons and survive in the field. But beyond that he was training an army that was woefully lacking in a doctrine of how to fight a modern war, an army which in the 1930s had been consumed with inter-departmental arguments as to whether they should mechanize at all, and if so, who should operate armoured vehicles. What they had not done was to develop a method of fielding them so that they could face both German, and to a lesser extent Japanese, armies who had recently shown how they had perfected the art of bold strategic manoeuvre.

He solved the first problem by instituting a four-stage 13-week progressive standard training package. This started with individual skills, building to 'squad' or 'section' then company training; these stages were evaluated by testing. The standard infantry organization, which had oscillated between 'square' and 'triangular', was now standardized as triangular, with three squads in a platoon, three platoons in a company, three companies in a battalion, three battalions in a regiment and three regiments in a division. The brigade level of command was removed, the functions it would normally have discharged being taken over by the divisional staff. After passing out of this basic training package, recruits were posted to their units for more advanced collective training or 'Special to Arm' training, such as on tanks or as artillerymen. The 18 National Guard infantry divisions were inducted directly into federal service from the date the President signed off the Selective Service Act, so that recruiting was no longer necessarily restricted to men from their parent state, although in practice most National Guard divisions retained a strong local affinity throughout the war. Their place was taken, where it was felt necessary, by State Guards, a quasi-police force answering to the governors.

Despite this well-thought-out programme, training was problematic. The problem was the raw human material, and conscription showed just how damaging the Depression had been to many young American men. Forty per cent of recruits were rejected – the requirement was to be at least five feet tall, weigh 105 pounds, have 12 or more natural teeth and be free of venereal disease and hernias. Nearly 2 million were also rejected for psychiatric reasons.[27] A Gallup poll in October 1940, reflecting a typically reactionary attitude to the nation's youth, found the prevailing view was that they were 'a flabby, pacifistic, yellow, cynical, discouraged, and leftist lot'.[28] Many societies at different times have made the same misjudgement.

A good example of these problems is that of the 82nd Division, which had a distinguished combat record in the First World War but which had then been disbanded. Re-raised in December 1941, it had to be built up from scratch. Seven hundred officers and 1,200 enlisted men were drafted in as a core, but the remaining 90 per cent – some 16,000 – came directly from their induction centres. Luckily, its commander was Major General Omar Bradley, who used the division's history to encourage the recruits that they were coming to an elite unit. Their trains were met on the platform by a brass band, and every soldier was greeted by name and shown to an individual bed space; those who had been mechanics or cooks found themselves in similar posts and great care was taken with the basics such as food, laundry and welfare facilities. He tackled the fitness problem by instituting daily exercise and sport for everyone, himself included. Bradley reckoned that after 17 weeks he had a competent formation. He was, however, an exceptional commander, and the 82nd proved to be an exceptional division which would go on to be the core of U.S. Airborne Forces, but others would take much longer.[29]

By 30 June 1941 McNair's training programme resulted in an army of 1.4 million men; one-third of these – 435,000 – were in the infantry divisions, with just 43,200 in the prototype armoured divisions and 20,400 still on horses. The Air Force now stood at 167,000.[30] Marshall now had to deal with the second of the challenges he faced, which was what was he training this new army for? He had sent officers to observe British training, and although they had reported back favourably on the British battlefield inoculation techniques whereby they subjected soldiers to realistic live-fire exercises, there was scepticism in the U.S. Army as to how effective British armoured formation training was. The Army also faced the unresolved issue of what they thought a tank was there to do. The dominance of the infantry, and the heresy of suggesting that a tank was anything but a weapon to support the infantry assault, had led to a stagnation of thinking as to the tank as an offensive weapon in its own right. Despite the reluctance of General Herr and successive chiefs of cavalry to release horsed regiments to be converted to armour, from the mid-1930s the experimental mechanized force had been re-instituted. Two cavalry regiments, 1st and 13th Cavalry, had been equipped with what had to be called 'combat cars', as opposed to tanks, which would have immediately incurred the fury of the Chief of Infantry. These had combined to form the 7th Cavalry Brigade which, under the inspired leadership of men like Brigadier General Adna R. Chaffee – an officer who would sadly die of cancer too young to have the full impact of his contribution recognized – had quietly worked on armoured tactics and had performed well when tested in the 1936 manoeuvres in Kentucky and Michigan against non-mechanized forces.

The problem was, given its cavalry origins and infantry intransigence, the brigade concentrated on traditional U.S. cavalry roles of scouting, raiding and exploitation rather than on offensive armoured warfare as such. The U.S. cavalry had no history of being a strike force, and the notion of using tank to combat tank, which was the overriding lesson from Russia and North Africa, was not heeded. Instead, the Army would develop regiments of tank destroyers, effectively mobile anti-tank guns, with none of the advantages of mobility and protection offered by a main battle tank; this would cause significant future problems. American tanks, and hence British and Allied, would consequently remain under-gunned throughout the war, the cavalry M3 light tank, for example, initially deploying to North Africa with a 37mm cannon whose rounds simply bounced off even the earlier generation of German panzers.[31]

On 1 July 1940 Marshall had instigated an 'armored force' to accelerate both tactics and vehicle production. It consisted of a corps headquarters and two 'armored divisions', although they were initially lacking in armoured vehicles. Chaffee was given corps command and started work to produce tactics and procedures and to work with industry on tank design. Interestingly, it was at this stage that Patton abandoned the cavalry to return to tanks. In the late summer of 1941 the Army staged large-scale manoeuvres in the southern states to test its new formations and in an attempt to learn some of the lessons of mechanization which had been overlooked. A total of 700,000 troops took part. Marshall used the opportunity, as he explained to a Louisiana senator who complained of the disruption, 'to make the mistake down in Louisiana, not over in Europe, and the only way to do this thing is to try it out, and if it doesn't work, find out what we need to do to make it work'.[32] Two armies consisting of four corps and 18 divisions manoeuvred against each other over 30,000 square miles with over 1,000 aircraft in support. Commanders like Omar Bradley and George Patton distinguished themselves, while Marshall and McNair used it as means of getting rid of those they thought had not made the transformation they required. By the end it was felt that infantry and artillery tactics were sound, while controversy over the role of armour continued. It would subsequently be played out in Algeria and Normandy.

By the fall of 1941, the U.S. Army that Marshall had inherited just two years previously was transformed. It lacked experience and equipment, it was untested in battle and it still had huge administrative issues to overcome – not least where it might be committed and how it would get there – but the speed and energy of its transformation was remarkable and, at least by that stage before Stalin had mobilized the Soviet Union, the fastest mass mobilization in recorded history.

Yet the third of Roosevelt and Marshall's challenges remained: how to help the struggling European nations, especially Britain, not then an ally but regarded by many Americans as soon to become one. The solution Roosevelt devised, urged on both by Churchill and by the many British advocates in Congress, came to be known as 'Lend-Lease' and involved negotiating around the Neutrality Act to be able to send military equipment to Britain. It also had the associated benefit of expanding what was then a very underdeveloped U.S. armaments industry. Lend-Lease needs to be seen against the economic background of the continuing Depression. In 1939 there were 9 million Americans out of work and American industry had considerable spare capacity. Britain and France had been ordering from American firms for some time before the war, the Neutrality Act only applying during actual hostilities. British and French orders had in fact been something of a lifeline for struggling American industry, with over $1 billion in the pipeline when war was declared and with $79 million actually on order which had to be cancelled.[33] Stimson would later go on record to declare that 'Without the head start given to industry by these foreign orders, we would at the present time be in a very grave situation as to the plants and facilities we need for the pending emergency.'[34] Lend-Lease would then benefit the U.S. as well as potential European allies, but even so its instigation was a brave and inspired political move which showed both Roosevelt and Churchill at their most pragmatic and arguably forged the beginnings of a relationship which would be transformational.

Roosevelt's approach in late 1940 was that America should become the arsenal of the free world. 'The nations already contending against Hitler,' he said in his fireside chat on 29 December that year, 'do not ask us to do their fighting.

They ask us for the implements of war... Emphatically we must get these weapons to them in sufficient volume and quickly enough, so that we and our children will be saved the agony and suffering of war which others have had to endure. If Great Britain goes down,' he continued, 'the Axis powers will control the continents of Europe, Asia, Africa, Australasia and the high seas... It is no exaggeration to say that all of us, in all the Americas, would be living at the point of a gun.'[35]

On 6 January 1941 he sent the Lend-Lease Bill to Congress. The debate over the bill, which was numbered 1776 either coincidentally or maliciously – 1776 being the year Congress adopted the Declaration of Independence – aroused strong opposition, especially from Chicago and the mid-west, where isolationism remained strong. But when it came to a vote in March it passed easily through both houses; the 31 senators and 71 in the House who voted against it were nearly all Republicans. Equipment had been finding its way across the Atlantic under various guises throughout the winter, but passage of the bill now made Roosevelt's intent official; Churchill called it 'the most unsordid act in the history of any nation'.[36] Roosevelt had not done everything Churchill wanted. He had drawn the line at providing American naval escorts to the convoys carrying the materiel, arguing correctly that 'escorting could lead to shooting and shooting comes awfully close to war, doesn't it?'[37] He also made Britain pay, so that men like Stimson began to worry that the nation was in danger of bankruptcy.

Eventually Lend-Lease provided the lifeline in armaments that Britain desperately needed to maintain its war effort. Lend-Lease would be later extended to other countries as well, notably the Soviet Union, but of the $50 billion of equipment it provided, about three-fifths went to Britain.

Opposition still continued throughout that summer; the industrialist Henry Ford – isolationist, anti-British, anti-Semitic and holder of the Grand Cross of the German Eagle – cancelled an order to build aero engines in his factories when he discovered they were destined for Britain. They were eventually manufactured in a Packard factory instead.[38]

Much has been made over a 'special relationship' between the USA and Britain, a debate that continues today. Whereas the cynic may believe that at best it is a relationship in which there are times when the interests of both nations converge and that challenges are best met together for mutual advantage, there was in 1940 a significant body of American opinion that was genuinely supportive of Britain and admired Britain's stance against Hitler. A Gallup poll on 25 June that year found 64 per cent in favour of staying out of the war, but by 20 October that position had reversed, with 60 per cent now saying that the United States should help Britain.[39] While Robert R. McCormick, isolationist owner of the *Chicago Tribune*, might rail against Lend-Lease, other newspapers, like the *St. Louis Post-Despatch*, thought that 'Great Britain and the United States have insoluble bonds of language, creed and goal.'[40] The CBS correspondent Edward R. Murrow, who opened his broadcasts with the phrase 'This... is London', did much to familiarize the American nation with the horrors of bombing and the realities of war.

It was a sentiment that deepened when, at dawn on 7 December 1941, 350 aircraft from Admiral Yamamoto's carrier group struck the U.S. Pacific Fleet in Pearl Harbor, Hawaii. On 8 December the USA declared war on Japan, and three days later – after Germany declared war on the USA – on Germany; this time there were no dissenters in Congress. 'Over night the whole temper of our people changed,' recorded Charles F. Zummach, a northern Baptist minister, 'never did a people, or a nation, rally with such swiftness and determination to the challenge and responsibility that confronted them. Our young men volunteered by the thousands.'[41] The strategic logic behind Japan's decision to attack Pearl Harbor remains contentious, as does Hitler's to declare war. That debate is sadly not for this book, but what it reveals is a naïve misappreciation by both countries as to the balance of strategic resources. Joachim von Ribbentrop, Hitler's foreign minister and not normally noted for the perspicacity of his remarks, summarized the situation well when he told Hitler that 'We have one year to cut Russia off from her American supplies... If we don't succeed and the munitions potential of the United States joins up with the manpower potential of the Russians, the war will enter a phase in which we shall only be able to win it with difficulty.'[42] If there had been a logic to Japan's attack then it was to move quickly before the USA could react, something Japanese forces certainly achieved between December 1941 and the summer of 1942 but, as Yamamoto warned, thereafter he had 'utterly no confidence for the second or third year'.[43]

They were both correct. Despite the Depression, which had left 9 million workers unemployed during 1940 and roughly half America's automobile production factories idle, the USA still produced 4.8 million cars against just 331,000 in Germany and 26,000 in Japan. America's mines produced twice as much coal as Germany's; the USA led the world in textiles, electric goods and, critically, in the manufacture of aircraft and ships. In 1941 the US economy, in terms of GDP, was three times that of Germany and five times Japan's.[44] If, as Roosevelt had predicted, the USA was to be the arsenal of democracy, then the USA was in a very strong position to deliver on his pledge and, ironically and unlike in 1917, the existing spare capacity in the US economy meant that the nation could move fast and benefit economically and socially by so doing.

In January 1942, now the USA was at war, the President laid his requirements before Congress. He and Marshall had been working on a 'Victory Program' for the Army since September 1941. A team in the War Department's Plans Division, led by Major Albert Wedemeyer, had the unenviable task of evaluating what the nation would need if it went to war. Wedemeyer, a dedicated officer who had spent 17 years as a lieutenant during the slow promotion years of the 1930s, based his estimates on several key assumptions, one being that the USA would inevitably be at war with Germany and that the first military objective must be the defeat of Germany. He also concluded that the earliest date the U.S. Army could be ready for major combat operations was July 1943 and, to the chagrin of the bombardment enthusiasts in the Army Air Force, that the war could only be won by land forces. Large parts of the plan had, unhelpfully, been leaked to the *Chicago Tribune*, and its owner, McCormick, had led the opposition to Lend-Lease, but now Roosevelt was ready to lay his Victory Program in front of Congress. They were shocked by its scope. 'It will not be sufficient for us and the other United Nations to produce a slightly superior supply of munitions to that of Germany, Japan and Italy,' he briefed. Instead, 'the superiority of the United Nations in munitions and ships must be overwhelming... a crushing superiority of equipment in any theater of the world war'.[45] It called for an army of 8.7 million men in 215 divisions, for the production of 60,000 aircraft in 1942 alone, and a further 125,000 in 1943; 120,000 tanks in the same two-year period,

55,000 anti-aircraft guns and 16 million deadweight tons of merchant shipping. 'And,' the President added, 'I want to make these figures public,' to intimidate Germany and Japan and to make it clear both to them and on the home front that he intended 'to fight a war of machines' rather than men. Ultimately, he would have to fight with both.[46]

The wartime industrialization of the U.S. is a story of extraordinary achievement. The figures are so overwhelming that they can be difficult to grasp. By 1945 the American economy had produced 299,293 military aircraft against Germany's 111,767, Japan's 69,910 and Britain's 123,819; 634,569 jeeps, 88,410 tanks, 2.383 million trucks, 6.5 million rifles and 40 billion rounds of rifle ammunition. Put into more digestible format, by the end of the war, 'every American combatant in the last year and a half of the war in the Pacific islands could draw on four tons of supplies; his Japanese opponent, just two pounds'.[47] The USA was free from bombing, which of course made a big difference, but the scale of production created a benefit of mass which had a military utility in its own right, producing simple, standard designs such as the Liberty ship, the Sherman tank and the B-24 bomber. By way of contrast, Germany sacrificed quantity for quality, putting its industrial effort into delivering well-engineered weapons which were technically advanced, such as the much-vaunted Panzer Mk VI, the Tiger, but it could never produce enough of them nor the complicated spares needed to keep them battleworthy. It took twice as long to produce a Tiger as a Panzer Mk IV, and the greatest number deployed was 671 out of a total production of 1,355; of these deployed tanks there were fewer than 100 operational each month on both Eastern and Western Fronts as they awaited spares.[48] By 1945 Germany was attempting to manufacture

425 different types of aircraft. By 1944 the US economy was producing 60 per cent of the Allies' munitions, and over 25 per cent of Britain's and 10 per cent of the Soviet Union's arms, including 1,966 locomotives.[49] It is no wonder that at Yalta Stalin quipped, with gratitude, that the U.S. was a country of machines.

Such massive industrial restructuring was not without its pitfalls. The process required establishing multiple government agencies – the National War Labor Board, the National Defense Mediation Board, the Office of Production Management and, finally, the War Production Board, which was designed to coordinate them all. It was run by Donald Nelson, an industrialist, alongside General Brehon B. Somervell, Chief of the War Department's Supply Services, 'a man in whom organisational genius and Olympian arrogance were mixed in equal measure'.[50] Initial contracting was chaotic; the Army Air Force bid for 9,000 parachutes in 1941; Robert L. Stevens, a leading textile manufacturer, told them they needed 200,000, being one for each crewmember of the 50,000 planes the President had demanded, so 200,000 were duly ordered.[51]

Gradually a plan emerged, with most business predictably going to the largest existing manufacturers; two-thirds of all contracts went to just 100 firms, with General Motors responsible for 10 per cent of all US war production. Not only did war production soak up the reservoir of unemployed, but competition for skills and overall shortages of people as civilian demand clashed with military recruitment meant that wages gradually started to rise. A shipyard worker in Portsmouth, Virginia noted that his wage had risen from 40 cents an hour in 1940 to $2.75 by 1945. It enabled his family to buy their first home. Increased demand for productivity also helped modernize factory practices, so that by 1945 it was estimated that an American worker was twice as productive as their German counterpart and five times that of a Japanese. An interesting side effect of the drive for war production was the amount of internal disruption it caused to the labour force. Fifteen million Americans left home for military training, but a further 15 million moved their county of residence for work. It is estimated that as many as 8 million moved permanently to another state. There was a major movement from the south to the industrial cities of the north, to Detroit, Pittsburgh and Chicago, but a much larger stream flowed from east to west, to Portland and Seattle, and to Los Angeles, Oakland and San Diego, so that the population of California increased by 72 per cent between 1940 and 1950. It was a permanent shift in settlement that is still very apparent in the USA today.

The growing requirement for civilian labour, combined with a more favourable strategic outlook and Roosevelt's continuing determination to prioritize aircraft production – he demanded 107,000 in 1943, of which 82,000 were to be combat types – also influenced the decision to field a more manageable but arguably dangerous number of 90 divisions instead of the 215 Wedemeyer had originally calculated as necessary. General Lewis Blaine Hershey, director of the Selective Service system, was able to consolidate service manpower requirements – 5.5 million for the army; 2 million for the Air Force; 3.6 million for the Navy, of whom 500,000 were Marines. Overall 16 million people wore a uniform of some sort during the war, and one family in five had someone serving in the forces. It was truly a national effort.[52]

Taking so many civilians and turning them rapidly into soldiers required the Army to think carefully about their welfare, and this was another area in which the USA made substantially better progress than its allies. Marshall's view was that 'the way to placate citizen soldiers and their politicians was by the best possible material conditions',[53] a policy that resulted in the U.S. Army's bases becoming 'oases of abundance'.[54] Marshall also had, from his own long service, an intuitive understanding of the 'citizen soldier' and what motivated him. He was 'ever conscious of the importance of little things to morale' and that 'you had to feel that all your soldiers were readers of *Time* magazine'. He was equally conscious that American soldiers were not fighting 'in defence of hearth and home' and that mostly they were sent to fight and possibly die in places most had never heard of before the war. He devoted considerable staff effort to strengthening morale, commissioning a series of films called *Why We Fight,* and relaunching in-service magazines such as *Stars and Stripes.*[55] He also lobbied for adequate pay rates and, although American soldiers were not well paid compared with their civilian counterparts, especially as the wartime economy took off, their pay was sufficient. A 'Buck' private soldier – a young single man who had just joined – was paid $500 per annum, but if he was married this increased to $1,356. Increments thereafter were reasonably generous and, given that promotion could come quickly – it is estimated that on D-Day half the U.S. Army were non-commissioned officers (NCOs) – so pay increased. British soldiers, by way of contrast, averaged £108 per annum, which they grumbled made them the poor cousins but, given prevailing exchange rates, wasn't in fact that different. What was different was the largesse of U.S. welfare facilities while serving, an area where British governments have habitually failed.

Shocked as senior officers had been by the poor physical and mental state of the nation's youth, the Army's welfare package developed to become the envy of their allies. U.S. Army rations were especially sought after. While British commanders saw it as a virtue to 'muddle through', and of course Britain was suffering from an overall shortage of food and comforts, an American team deployed as a Special Observer Group were appalled by the lack of British medical and dental facilities. An American soldier serving with a British unit In Iceland in January 1943 complained that 'we are on British rations and it's hard tack, hot tea, and sausage for breakfast then the other meal at 4 p.m. is hot tea, Irish Stew (slop) and hardtack', whereas another soldier serving with U.S. forces in North Africa wrote home that they had 'good eats... We have had turkey on two occasions recently, steak tonight, fresh eggs for breakfast. On the whole we certainly have no complaints.'[56] 'It takes a visit to the other fellow to appreciate how well we are fixed,' wrote an officer after visiting a British unit. 'Little things like overshoes, warm gloves, woollen underwear, knit caps to wear under our helmets etc. that we have taken for granted assume a different aspect at 04.00 a.m. in an 80 mile gale; they make all the difference between comparative comfort and misery.'[57]

Medical cover was as good as it could be, the ensuing war being the first in American history when more men were killed by enemy action than by accidents and disease, although this latter figure still amounted to 113,842. Spiritual welfare was seen as equally important. Each division was allocated 15 chaplains, all Christian or Jewish. In 1945 there were 8,141 chaplains serving, of whom 2,278 were Catholic and 243 Jewish. By the end of the war there were two servicemen, and now some servicewomen, in the supporting services for every one in an army combat role in Europe, but in the Pacific that ratio was even higher. Taken across all parts of the military machine, it is estimated that the wartime average was four support troops for one combat soldier.[58]

Yet of all the welfare measures the most innovative and far-sighted was the 'GI Bill' of June 1944. More properly known as the Servicemen's Readjustment Act, Congress legislated to entitle veterans to a whole range of benefits, from free college education and medical care, training, grants and business loans up to $4,000, to assisted house purchase and a year's unemployment insurance. It passed unanimously and was described at the time as 'the most comprehensive piece of social welfare legislation the United States has ever known'.[59] It offered a challenge which other governments largely failed to meet and set a standard of societal care of soldiers which would stand the U.S. Army in very good stead.

One area that was problematic was the employment of Black soldiers, an issue which reflected the racist attitudes that still prevailed in American society, particularly in the southern states. The Selective Service Act specified that there would be no discrimination on racial grounds and the War Department confirmed that African Americans would be posted to all parts of the Army. However, the 'policy is not to intermingle colored and white enlisted personnel in the same regimental organizations'. Marshall also briefed Stimson that he could 'not ignore the social relationships between negroes and whites which have been established by the American people through custom and habit', which resulted in most African Americans being drafted to service and support functions.[60] In fact, discrimination was in-built, with only 250 African Americans sitting on the 6,442 draft boards nationwide and just three in the southern states of Virginia, North Carolina and Kentucky.[61] However, despite ridiculous rules such as the Medical Corps insisting on separate blood plasma for whites and Blacks and a ruling that no 'negro was allowed to hold a rank higher than that held by the lowest-ranking white officer' in a unit, the common cause associated with service was felt by some to have helped reduce racial prejudices. In 1940 African Americans constituted just 2 per cent of the Army; by 1945 they made up 9 per cent, with 6,000 officers. Five thousand African Americans in service units volunteered to fight as infantrymen during the crisis in the Ardennes in the winter of 1944, something Marshall described as 'a very splendid show'.[62]

As this great army grew, there was one area in which, serving a free society, both it and its British counterpart had one significant advantage over the Axis powers – one that would eventually be war-winning. That was the ability to bring together military, science and industry in a structure that both energized experimentation and innovation while equally ensuring armament production was as efficient as it could be. Vannevar Bush, president of the Carnegie Institute in Washington, was a highly respected engineer from Harvard and the Massachusetts Institute of Technology, so well connected with the leading U.S. academic institutions. He had also already helped build an analogue computer capable of solving differential equations with up to 18 variables.[63] In the wake of the panic caused by the Nazis achieving nuclear fission in 1939, he had seen the importance of such collaboration and the need for a national body to harness scientific brains to National Defense. He had discussed this with Harry Hopkins, then Secretary of Commerce, and in 1939 they had together persuaded Roosevelt to set up a body that could coordinate between government, industry and academia. The National Resources Defense Council

(NRDC) was subsequently established in 1939, with Bush at its head, and would work until 1941, when it was subsumed into the Office of Scientific Research and Development (OSRD), again headed by Bush. The achievement of these two successive organizations was to persuade government that research and development should not be done by stressed and largely unqualified civil servants and short-term assigned military officers in government; rather, it was best done by industry, whose commercial future depended on sound research, and in universities where academics specialized in the necessary disciplines. It was arguably the key step towards the USA being able to field war-winning weapons, one of which was of course the atomic bomb, which would end the war in the Pacific when it was dropped on Hiroshima and Nagasaki. Whether that was a desirable outcome or not obviously remains an issue that is fiercely contested, but the point is rather that the United States was able to introduce a system that was capable of producing it.

The NRDC and OSRD structure also gave allies the opportunity to share technology with the USA and again to help in its subsequent development. In 1940 the British government sent Sir Henry Tizard to Washington with details of Britain's latest research, which he was authorized to share. Amongst other devices, he briefed on the cavity magnetron, a microwave generator that allowed the miniaturization of radar so that it could be operated from an aircraft, a concept to which Bush and the OSRD would devote 100 scientific teams.[64] By 1945 there were 1,500 British scientists and technicians working in 45 locations across the USA.

The OSRD also introduced a system of field evaluation of their experiments, so called 'Operational Analysis', a practice that is now commonplace in most armies. The idea was that scientists should deploy into the field and test their ideas in the real world, but it quickly grew to using scientific analysis to examine and help improve other items of equipment and more general military techniques and procedures. OA, as it was known, is credited with contributing significantly to the anti-U-boat campaign in the Atlantic and with improving the accuracy of the Eighth Air Force from a rather frightening 15 per cent – only 15 per cent of bombs falling within 1,000 feet of their aiming point – to 60 per cent by 1945.

So how was this vast, unprecedented expansion of an army affordable? How was a nation recovering from the Great Depression, which had seen tens of millions out of work and caused real social hardship, now able to find the money to pay for this great host of men and the accompanying arsenal of democracy? The total cost of the war to the USA would be about $300 billion, of which just under half was met by direct taxation and the rest by borrowing. Before 1940 Federal Income Tax was 'an utter irrelevancy, or at most a decidedly minor nuisance'. The threshold was $1,500 and as the average national wage was $1,231, only 4 per cent of Americans paid it. In 1942 the threshold was lowered to $624, which immediately snared an extra 13 million taxpayers. By 1945, 42.6 million people were paying at rates from 6 to 94 per cent, and most were paying via their employers, thus making collection easier. These were significant increases, and Congress rejected Roosevelt's attempt to increase the tax take even further in the 1943 Revenue Act, yet the administration was still able to succeed in making the payment of tax a patriotic duty. Irving Berlin was commissioned to pen a catchy jingle which went: 'You see those bombers in the sky/ Rockefeller helped build them and so did I/ I paid my income tax today'.[65]

Yet the reason that the country could afford to pay more tax was because the huge expansion of both industry and the armed services meant that people had more money. Defence spending as a share of GDP rose from just 2 per cent in 1939 to 42 per cent by 1945, a massive 2,000 per cent increase. Government funds were being directly channelled into production, which translated into increased take-home pay and workers enjoying a better standard of living. At the same time, industry was benefitting, and although some of those who had championed Roosevelt's New Deal now saw the irony of taxpayers' money being used to increase the profits of manufacturing corporations, the general mood was supportive. 'You have got to let business make money out of the process,' said Henry Stimson, 'or business won't work.'[66] The issue soon became one of controlling inflation, although its effects took some time to show given the quite considerable existing spare capacity in the economy when war was declared. By 1941 inflation had surged from being virtually negligible in 1940 to 9 per cent, not coming back to a more comfortable 3 per cent until 1943 as higher tax rates and bond sales began to bite. The deficit was made up by selling bonds to both private individuals, about a quarter, but mainly to institutions; between 1941 and 1945 commercial banks increased their holdings of U.S. Treasury stock from $1 billion to $24 billion.[67] America was prepared to pay for its war.

Marshall's original assessment was that this mighty army – now approaching full manning and at least partially equipped with effective modern weapons – would not be ready to fight before July 1943. However, the events of early 1942 would mean that he would be forced to move nine months earlier. The big question was, what should this army do? By the summer of 1942, six months after Pearl Harbor, it had done nothing, leading to populist cries for action. The German campaign in Russia was still progressing in their favour, Japan had completed its lightning conquest of much of South-East Asia, and yet still the USA did not act. Churchill arrived in Washington soon after Pearl Harbor, triggering the Arcadia Conference, which discussed the future direction of the war. There were two fundamental issues to resolve. Should Germany be defeated before Japan and, if so, how should that be achieved? The U.S. Navy was inclined to a 'Pacific first' strategy, but Marshall favoured 'Germany first', as did Churchill. Once the Nazis were defeated, the Allies could turn their attention to South-East Asia. So, if Germany was to be defeated first – and it was in early 1942 by no means a given that it would be despite the USA's involvement – how could that be accomplished? True to Clausewitzian doctrine, the U.S. Army planners favoured the destruction of the German army, combined with a strategic bombing campaign that would simultaneously destroy the German economy and social morale. Even with now just 90 divisions instead of the 215 they originally planned, they thought they had adequate forces to do this, together with Soviet and Allied forces. They would mount an amphibious assault across the English Channel in April 1943, followed by a massive attack on Berlin. 'Through France passes our shortest route to the heart of Germany,' declared Marshall.[68] Known as *Roundup*, there was a branch plan in case the Soviets were defeated by the Germans before the invasion could be mounted, or a sudden weakening of Germany's position, known as *Sledgehammer*, which envisaged a mostly British assault on France to fix the German forces in the west.

The British ultimately wanted the same thing – the total defeat of Nazi Germany – but were, based on bitter experience, convinced that the Allies were still two years away from being able to stage such an ambitious plan. Any cross-Channel assault would require a mass of supporting shipping and landing craft, air superiority if not supremacy, and the assembly of a sufficiently large land force to prosecute the final battle, all interestingly much as Wedemeyer had predicted. Instead, Churchill worked on Roosevelt to stage initial landings in North Africa, where the Axis powers had just six divisions as opposed to the 225 in Europe. Together with the British Eighth Army they could clear the Axis from North Africa, defeat the Vichy French in Morocco who would hopefully swing behind the Allied cause, and then sweep up through the Mediterranean. This would also give an as yet untested U.S. Army valuable combat experience.

The U.S. planners instinctively distrusted this concept. They thought it was too redolent of Britain safeguarding its colonial interests, preserving Egypt and the vital Suez link to India. They also disliked what they saw as the scattering of forces when they should be concentrated for the main objective: the defeat of the Nazis. They also thought it would take too long, would deny an early 'second front' to aid the Soviets, and politically the delay would face considerable criticism in the USA. 'We've got to go to Europe and fight and we've got to quit wasting resources all over the world – and still worse – wasting time,' wrote Eisenhower, now Chief of the War Plans Department.[69]

The issue remained undecided throughout the spring and early summer of 1942. However, in June the U.S. Navy inflicted its first major defeat on the Japanese, sinking four of their carriers at Midway. The same month the Germans captured Tobruk in Libya, taking 30,000 British and Allied prisoners and were pressing their advance towards the Volga, threatening Stalingrad. The prospect of a quick victory in Europe appeared distant. On 25 July Roosevelt opted for North Africa and for the operation to start as soon as possible. Marshall was incensed that the President had listened to the British rather than his own advisers. 'We failed to see,' he later wrote ruefully, 'that the leader in a democracy has to keep the people entertained.'[70] The Democrats still fared badly in the mid-term elections that November but managed to retain control of Congress, albeit with a reduced majority.

It is hard, with the priceless advantage of hindsight, to argue that Marshall was right. When the Allies were finally ready to mount an amphibious assault on France – D-Day – in June 1944, even then its success was not guaranteed despite them facing much reduced and weakened German forces with an almost ineffective Luftwaffe. But the emphasis in mid-1942 now switched to a three-pronged landing operation in Morocco and Algeria, codenamed Operation *Torch*. Task Force West, three divisions under Patton, would sail direct from the USA to land in Morocco and take Casablanca. Task Force Centre, two divisions under General Lloyd Fredendall, would stage via Britain and would land in Algeria to seize Oran, while a third task force, British-led but with U.S. troops under command, would take Algiers. With the three ports in Allied hands, there would then follow a rapid build-up of forces before advancing to take Tunis and hopefully end the war in North Africa.

The landings were chaotic but ultimately successful. The Vichy French obligingly reached an agreement with the Allies but thereafter German resistance, thought to have been seriously weakened after their defeat by the British and

Allies at Alamein in October, proved much tougher than expected. Tunis did not fall until May 1943 and then only after bitter fighting, notably during Rommel's counter-attack at the Kasserine Pass in February. The force build-up proved more difficult than envisaged, again supporting those who had argued that *Roundup* was impractical that spring, and the fledgling U.S. Army suffered 18,500 casualties. Yet the end result was a resounding success, leading to the total surrender of all German and Italian forces in Africa and a quarter of a million prisoners of war.

Despite this strategic success, the U.S. Army's performance in North Africa had not been without its issues. The rapidity of its expansion and the lack of experience of officers and non-commissioned officers, NCOs, inevitably led to problems in what turned out to be a far bloodier and hard-fought series of battles than had perhaps been envisaged. There was a wholesale removal of officers thought inadequate, from Fredendall – who was replaced by Bradley after the Kasserine Pass – to many middle-ranking officers. Tunisia became, according to Brigadier General Paul Robinett, 'a professional graveyard, particularly for those in the upper middle part of the chain of command'.[71] The lack of training also showed in the enlisted men, particularly those drafted in as battle casualty replacements. Of 2,400 men sent to the 34th Division, 80 per cent had not qualified on their basic weapons, and in one batch it was found that nearly half were over 39.

By the spring of 1943, 1,700 men would be admitted to the psychiatric ward of just one general hospital suffering from battle shock, a condition Patton would famously later fail to recognize. The Army struggled with its replacement system throughout the war, so that soldiers felt that they

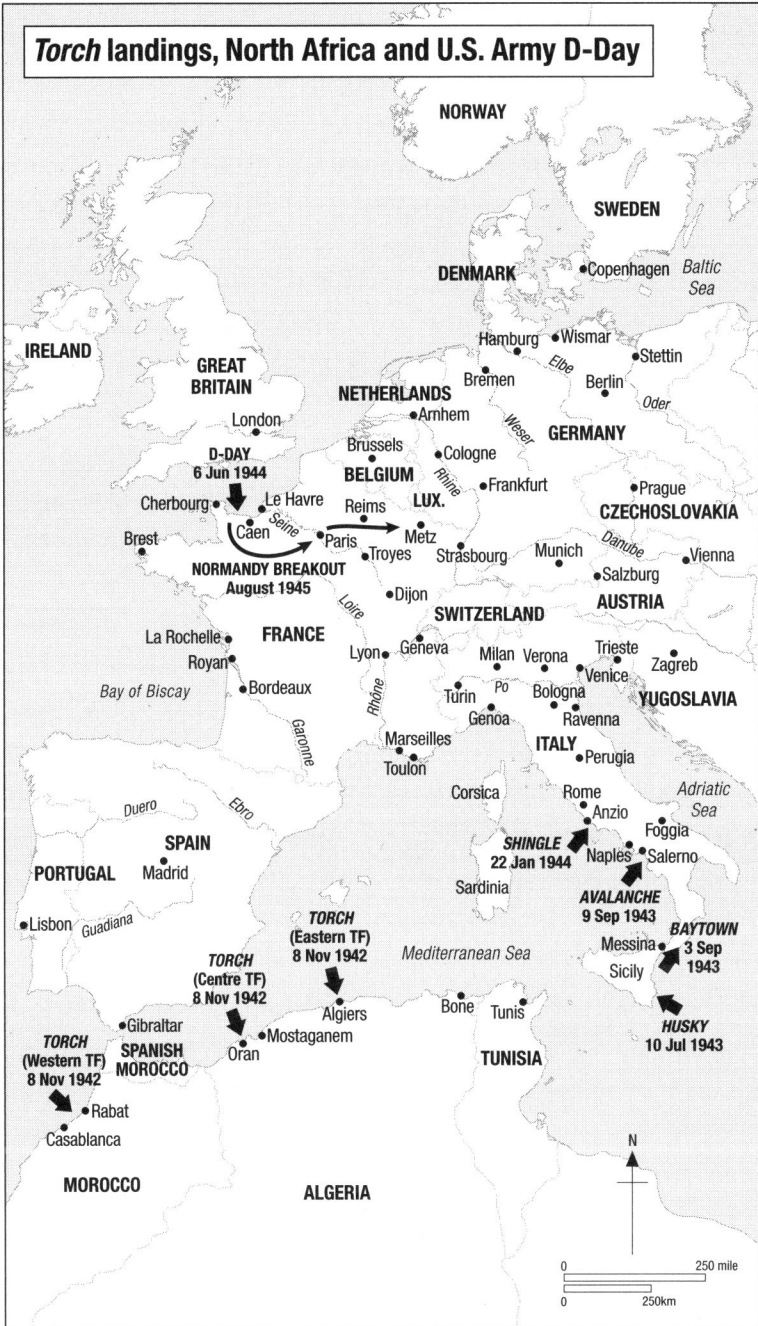

Torch landings, North Africa and U.S. Army D-Day

NORWAY

SWEDEN

DENMARK   Copenhagen *Baltic Sea*

IRELAND

GREAT BRITAIN

NETHERLANDS

GERMANY

Hamburg Wismar
Bremen Berlin
Stettin
Elbe
Weser
Oder

London
Arnhem
Brussels Cologne
BELGIUM
LUX.

D-DAY
6 Jun 1944

Cherbourg Le Havre Reims
Brest Caen Paris Metz Strasbourg
Troyes Munich
Seine *Rhine*
Frankfurt
Prague
CZECHOSLOVAKIA
Danube Vienna
Salzburg
AUSTRIA

NORMANDY BREAKOUT
August 1945

Dijon
SWITZERLAND
La Rochelle
Royan FRANCE
Lyon Geneva Milan Verona Trieste
Loire
Bordeaux
Turin *Po* Bologna Venice Zagreb
Genoa Ravenna YUGOSLAVIA
Bay of Biscay
Garonne
Rhône
Marseilles ITALY
Toulon Perugia

Duero
Ebro
Corsica Rome *Adriatic Sea*
Anzio Foggia
SPAIN
SHINGLE
22 Jan 1944 Naples Salerno
PORTUGAL Madrid
Sardinia
AVALANCHE
9 Sep 1943
Lisbon *Guadiana*
BAYTOWN
3 Sep 1943
TORCH
(Eastern TF)
8 Nov 1942
Messina
Mediterranean Sea
TORCH
(Centre TF)
8 Nov 1942
Algiers
Bone Tunis
Sicily
Gibraltar
Mostaganem
HUSKY
10 Jul 1943
TORCH
(Western TF)
8 Nov 1942
SPANISH
MOROCCO
Oran
TUNISIA

Rabat
Casablanca

MOROCCO ALGERIA

N

0   250 mile
0   250km

were 'handled like so many sticks of wood' and given no unit affiliation or identity.[72] The British got round this through their regimental system, so that a new soldier knew which unit he was destined for even though war-time security usually meant he didn't know where they were serving. 'Perhaps more than any other significant factor, it was this system that was responsible for the weaknesses displayed by the U.S. Army during World War II,' thought military historian Martin van Creveld. 'It possessed a strong inherent tendency to turn men into nervous wrecks.'[73] Major General Ira T. Wyche, who commanded the 79th Division, became so exasperated with the system that he introduced his own divisional organization in which new recruits were given additional training and indoctrination and shepherded by NCOs from the units they would be joining, something which other divisional commanders soon imitated. And the U.S. Army did not have the luxury of simple divisional roulement; those extra divisions Wedemeyer had seen as necessary were instead now translated into aircraft factories. This shortage, particularly of infantry, would return to haunt Eisenhower in 1945.

Battle casualty replacements were sadly always needed. Once the Allies were on the offensive, effectively from the autumn of 1942 onwards, facing German infantry in defence was always going to be costly in terms of human lives. The British had become cautious, some would argue excessively cautious, about the number of casualties they could accept. Most senior British commanders had served in the First World War and were conscious of any tendency to profligacy with their men's lives. Irritating as some American commanders found this, it was a reservation based on sound logic. Britain had almost run out of fighting-age manpower by 1944, and in Normandy the casualties after D-Day, especially in the infantry, were, at 30 per cent, higher than First World War levels. Senior U.S. commanders were less risk adverse. Patton's siege of Metz alone cost 50,000 American casualties, and the fighting in the Hürtgen Forest between September and December 1944 a further 33,000. Ernest Hemingway described it as 'Passchendaele with tree bursts'.[74] This willingness to accept casualties, sometimes heartlessly referred to as 'the devil's bargain' for better pay, equipment, uniforms and food, was epitomized by men like Patton to whom achievement of his battlefield objectives, true to Clausewitzian principles, outweighed all other considerations.

Another issue that had caused significant problems was that U.S. tanks had proved to be seriously under-gunned. Once tank production had got under way, the first models were the M2 light tank and then the M3, the Lee, with a 37mm gun, although later M3 models carried a heavier, but hull-mounted, 75mm gun. The Army had placed much faith in the 37mm gun but, as a tank commander wrote reflecting his frustration after an engagement with a German tank in Tunisia, 'it snapped and popped like an angry cap pistol'. The crew 'pumped more than eighteen rounds at the Jerry... through the scope sight the tracer could be seen to hit, then glance straight up. Popcorn balls thrown by Little Bo Peep would have been just as effective.'[75]

The problem was that the replacement for the M3, the M4 Sherman, which became the workhorse of all Allied armoured formations between 1943 and 1945, was not that much more effective. Its 75mm gun, now turret-mounted, still proved unable to take out the new German panzers, the Mark IVs, the Panthers (Mark Vs) and the Tigers (Mark VIs), unless the crew could manoeuvre for a lucky flank or rear shot. The British, who had been gifted the first batch of Shermans by

Roosevelt after Tobruk, got round this problem by fitting one tank in every troop of four with a 17-pounder anti-tank gun, much as the Germans had fitted their capable 88mm gun into the Tiger. Despite recommendations to the contrary, the U.S. Army did not follow suit. McNair continued to believe in the combination of medium tanks for exploitation and tank destroyers to destroy German armour, an unwieldy solution that reflected the painful history of cavalry conversion that had characterized the inter-war army. As late as 1944 Eisenhower was apparently unaware of the strength of feeling at the inadequacies of the Sherman, but by early 1945 a tank mounting a more powerful 90mm gun, the Pershing, was introduced, although it was only in service for the final weeks of the war.

To U.S. Army irritation, the Allied conference in the newly liberated Casablanca in January 1943 reaffirmed Roosevelt's support for Churchill's 'peripheral strategy', with plans agreed to invade Sicily and Italy as opposed to focusing on a cross-Channel invasion of France and drive into Germany. That would finally take place in June 1944, D-Day, with the subsequent fight into Germany lasting nearly a year, despite the German military prioritizing the Eastern Front. A total of 73,000 American troops landed on two invasion beaches, alongside a similar number of combined British and Canadians. That gave the contemporary British public the notion that Britain and the U.S. remained equal contributors to the war effort, but in reality it was now the U.S. that dominated. Not only was two-thirds of the equipment American but the rapid build-up of American forces would enable them eventually to field 61 divisions in Europe, 1.3 million men, with a further eight in the Mediterranean and 22 in the Pacific. Supreme command was exercised by an American,

Eisenhower, with the largest army group consisting of four armies and an airborne corps. The bitter experience of North Africa had enabled the appointment of a group of exceptional battlefield commanders like Patton who would define the outcome of the war.

However, the persistent problems remained. Eisenhower favoured a broad-front strategy when attacking across the Rhine into Germany, but, despite his 60 divisions, he still lacked the combat power to effect that. Once again Wedemeyer had been proved correct. The issue of under-gunned tanks was at first masked by the bulk of the German armoured resistance in Normandy facing the British opposite Caen, where the British armoured divisions suffered significant setbacks, rather than the Americans, as Patton broke out of the bridgehead in the west and raced for the Seine. It would become more pronounced throughout the winter of 1944–45. Patton's offensive was, in many ways, in the very spirit of exploitation by medium armour that the U.S. cavalry had championed, although McNair's precious tank destroyers were soon jettisoned as the call for an up-gunned main battle tank increased. McNair himself was tragically killed by a misplaced U.S. Army Air Force bombing run during a liaison visit to Normandy.

The U.S. operations in Europe, after several tragic mistakes, also took air-land cooperation to a new level, an area in which the Allies completely over-matched a now almost ineffective German Luftwaffe. Although the Army Air Force was focused on daylight strategic bombing of Germany, together with the British Royal Air Force's night-time raids, close air support of ground operations became axiomatic, mostly carried out by what earlier generation pilots would have described as 'pursuit' aeroplanes, such as the Mustang converted to a fighter-bomber, Typhoons and Thunderbolts. Saturation bombardment was also used in direct support of army missions, such as Bradley's break-out from the bridgehead. Would the U.S. Army have preferred a heavier tank? German commentators after the war cited Allied air power as the battle-winning factor, but operational analysis showed that its actual success rate in destroying ground targets was sometimes limited. However, it had the significant advantage of denying the enemy daylight movement. What was also highly effective was U.S. artillery, regarded as the most professional arm in the Army. This was grouped at divisional level, with 105mm and 155mm guns, many self-propelled mounted on armoured chassis, and a most effective observation and targeting system that made full use of available air power, a concept since developed so that it is an essential part of contemporary offensive support. By 1945 it is estimated that over 30 per cent of the Army was artillery.

Berlin fell to the Russians on 2 May 1945, with the final German surrender coming on 8 May, so-called 'VE Day'. Victory in the Pacific followed in August after the U.S. Army Air Force dropped two atomic bombs. The war was over. How would America react? With celebration, certainly that the killing was over – U.S. casualties in the war totalled over 416,000 killed and over 670,000 wounded. The war had been a truly gigantic national effort. Of the 16 million-odd Americans in uniform, nearly 40 per cent of servicemen had volunteered, as had all servicewomen. The remainder were draftees. Average service was 33 months, and 73 per cent served overseas, for many the first time they had ventured outside the continental United States. Thirty out of every 1,000 had been killed or wounded.[76] Would America retreat to the isolationist stance it had taken until 1917 and then again in 1919? Or would it appreciate that the freedoms and opportunities it offered its citizens depended on a free world and, as that world's most powerful nation, it was better to deter war than having to mobilize all over again? Yet what the war had shown, as well as the exceptional bravery and self-sacrifice of its people, was that wars were won by the nations with the strongest economies. Russia also made terrible sacrifices in the war, losing approximately eight times as many people as the USA – although Russia had been invaded, a fate the USA had obviously been spared – but whereas Russia could produce soldiers, its economy could not produce machines. America could, ending the war by producing the most terrible machine yet invented.

Demobilization came slowly, with troops required to remain in Japan and Europe well into 1947, but by June that year the Army was reduced to 900,000 and by the mid-1950s it was just 590,000 in ten understrength divisions.[77] The provisions of the GI Bill were sorely tested with shortages of housing and welfare facilities. A 1947 National Security Act formalized many of the changes in the higher-level management of defence that Marshall had introduced, and the 1950 Reorganization Act attempted to regulate the structure of the regular army, a reserve component and the National Guard – a triangular structure that would have been familiar to Scharnhorst. Despite opposition, the National Guard was re-instated and would, to the irritation of many, play a full role in internal security in the 1960s. But would America continue to reduce its forces to the point that it had in the 1920s? Two things prevented that from happening. First, in 1949 the USA joined NATO, therefore agreeing to share in the defence of Western Europe against Soviet aggression, a possibility that was now more dangerous since the advent of nuclear weapons. Second, the USA assumed the leadership of what it regarded as the essential struggle against the spread of communism worldwide, first in Korea and subsequently in Vietnam. Military leadership of the 'free world' has since translated into defending the world against extremism and terrorism while still continuing to buttress NATO. To date the lessons and sacrifices of that extraordinary national effort between 1941 and 1945 have not – yet – been wasted.

Chapter Seven

Armies Today

'Fresh thinking is needed on the responsibility of citizens to defend their country.'
William Hague, *The Times*,
21 November 2023

Are liberal democracies worth saving? Some would argue not. An international poll by the Pew Research Center released in February 2024 found that 59 per cent of those polled internationally said that they were dissatisfied with how democracy functioned in their country. Seventy-four per cent thought governments didn't care for them. Polled on alternative forms of government, 25 per cent favoured a 'strong leader' while others favoured government by experts, although in what form is not clear, or direct democracy with far wider involvement of the public in decision making. Rather alarmingly, one-third of those in middle-income nations favoured government by the military, a notion less well supported in the higher-income Western European nations such as Greece, Spain and Germany who have had recent experience of such.[1] A similar poll by Open Society

Foundations across 30 countries found that 42 per cent of people aged 18–35 were 'supportive of autocratic rule' and that 35 per cent of that age group felt a 'strong leader' who did not hold elections was 'a good way to run a country'.[2]

However, overall, judged across results from 24 countries, the Pew poll concluded that 77 per cent still feel that representative democracy is the best way to govern, against the Open Society poll, which found that while a similar number of older voters (71 per cent) agreed, only 57 per cent of the younger age group did. Arguably, the very fact that those polled could speak out so openly suggests that they are enjoying, perhaps without fully appreciating it, the advantages of living in a democratic system. Recent polling in the FGS Global Radar report came up with similar findings; it concluded that 21 per cent of those aged 18–45 favoured government by a 'strong leader'.[3]

The philosopher Alexis de Tocqueville, writing in mid-19th-century France, although basing many of his observations on the USA where he had travelled extensively, and having lived through the aftermath of the French Revolution, thought that part of the reason for people allowing tyrannies to rise up lay in the advance of democracy. It was democracy, he argued, which made it inevitable that individuals will retreat within themselves. His logic was that as equality and wealth spread, there would be many people who, although not powerful enough to have much hold over others, and who probably have no inclination to do so anyway, had enough to care for themselves and as such did not really need anything from anybody. This diminished the virtues of selflessness and responsibility for one's neighbour and allowed tyranny to flourish as no one was really concerned to stop it. He thought democracy encouraged the trading of social responsibility, which had come in the past from village and community life, for material comfort, which, in his generation, the industrial revolution was beginning to provide for many.

This led de Tocqueville to conclude that his contemporaries were 'constantly excited by two conflicting passions; they want to be led and yet they want to remain free'. 'Men are not debased,' he continued, 'by the habit of obedience', but they were 'by the exercise of a power which they believe to be illegal and by obedience to a rule which they consider to be usurped and oppressive'. But by the time they realized that it was, he argued, often too late. Obviously de Tocqueville was long dead by, for example, the time the Nazis came to power in Germany a century later, but what he described applied almost exactly to the German people. 'Soon,' he wrote, 'there will be no middle way between the empire of democracy and the yoke of one man', which neatly describes the rise of Adolf Hitler as it does several contemporary dictatorships today. It is not within the scope of this book to opine on the best sort of government. Interestingly, de Tocqueville, having identified all the drawbacks associated with a democracy, concluded that there was still no better system that he knew given that the concept of a benevolent dictator was a contradiction in terms. Rather, he concerned himself with trying to make democracies function better and to encourage participation amongst those who benefitted so much from enjoying life in a democratic regime to help make that regime work.

A significant number of those polled by Open Societies Foundation expressed major concerns about both international and national insecurity, the climate crisis, and to that list can be added the subsequent social and environmental pressures that arise from them. What this book does therefore try to do is to draw together the lessons from the historical examples in the preceding chapters to see if it is possible to learn from them and to offer some principles that have served previous generations when they have been confronted with similar concerns of insecurity and instability to those the world arguably faces today. It starts with the presumption that currently there is no preferable form of government to representative democracy. It also starts from two further presumptions. First, that representative democracies may be called on to defend both their interests and their way of life and that those who think otherwise may be commendably idealistic but they are also unrealistic. Second, that although nations do not face existential threats continuously, there are times when a combination of pressures means that their society, beliefs and wealth are seriously threatened. The polling cited above would suggest that those living in democracies believe they face such a combination of threats now.

A critic may point out that the book starts with an analysis of two imperial armies. Why not look at the army of the Roman republic, which was probably nearer a representative democracy? That is in itself debatable, the senatorial system in Rome being at best an oligarchy and certainly by the era of Pompey and Caesar it was anything but a democratic army, even though every legionary was a Roman citizen. But this is not a book about democracy. It is a book that aims to look at historical lessons that may be of interest in defending current liberal democracies, and many of the most valuable lessons come from the armies of despots whose policies – conquest in the name of religion – are inimical to those living in Western Europe, or at least hopefully they are to most of us.

The first lesson is that armies are not there to be the agents for, or the experimental vehicles of, social change. Democratic societies will, of course, change, hopefully progressively, but their armed forces should not be used as a laboratory for that. Armies in a democracy are there to defend the society they represent, not to revolutionize it. Maybe taking the example of Cromwell's Protectorate is an extreme way of illustrating this point, but, obvious as this may seem to Western democracies, the army must be subservient to elected authority. When armies try to be both government and defenders of the state, they can do neither successfully. Those alarmingly large numbers of young people, 42 per cent, who told the pollsters that they preferred authoritarian government should be persuaded that it rarely works; the example of living under the rule of priggish Puritans like William Goffe should be enough to persuade anyone of that. Rather, what democratic representatives need to do is to establish with their electorates that future defence, against the myriad new human and physical threats we face, requires, as de Tocqueville pointed out and Lithuania demonstrates, participation from us all.

So how does defence become relevant, or possibly how can it be made relevant, to that large percentage who feel vulnerable? How are they to be defended, or perhaps, following de Tocqueville's logic, we should ask how do they defend themselves? The second lesson which emerges from all the examples examined in this book is that nations need a core professional army to defend them when they are threatened, either acting on its own or, more likely, as the basis on which to build a larger force. Where that is neglected, as in the USA after 1918, nations develop an inherent weakness that takes an enormous effort to correct and they pay a heavy price when war does come. The lesson that the reforms Constantine launched in AD 306 teaches us is that the principal role of an army is to fight rather than man border posts, collect taxes, build walls, decorate palaces and all the other manner of nefarious tasks that the late 3rd-century Roman army had accumulated and which had rendered it militarily ineffective. Constantine was successful because he separated out his field army, the *comitatus*, and trained and equipped them for high-intensity battle, relegating the supporting governmental tasks to the *limitanei* or *ripenses*. To achieve the unity he sought he realized that he would have to fight and that he needed to have a force capable of winning. He also realized that it would take time to select, train and equip a field army; he would not commit them to a major battle for six years. This again was a revolutionary policy. Previously Roman armies had been raised and almost immediately sent off on campaign in reaction to some emergency or senatorial ambition. Admittedly, warfare was common in the 1st and 2nd centuries so there was usually a supply of seasoned veterans to call on to train new recruits, but Constantine's approach was different. He created a professional army that would stay in being, an experienced army, and soldiers' careers and welfare would be managed to facilitate that. He appreciated that if he was to bring stability to the empire then he needed that consistency – a permanent, highly trained combat army as opposed to raising and disbanding armies ad nauseam. He also needed a command structure to lead it.

Mehmet arrived at the same conclusion, appreciating that for an army to be capable of assimilating and developing new techniques and managing revolutionary equipment, it had to be not only permanent but under the direct control of the central government, in other words, the sultan. There was no point investing in the latest cannon and muskets if they were to be distributed amongst the *timars*, relegated to some barn or attic until they were next needed, in which case there would be nobody who knew how to use them.

Obvious as this may seem today, the concept of a permanent regular and professional force was not taken up by the European armies the Ottomans confronted, with the odd exception, for another two centuries.

For Cromwell and Scharnhorst, the issue was not so much one of creating a field army but rather of training and motivating the one they had. The principle was the same – to succeed the army needed to be overhauled, new leaders promoted, re-equipped, given moral purpose and be deployed to battle in such a way that it could win. Both had the incentive that failure would have dire consequences, personally as well as nationally. And the United States in 1941, having finally committed to fight, put its quite extraordinary energy and resources into creating a field army almost from nothing and doing so with all the advantages of being the world's leading economy, yet also motivating its soldiers who were not 'fighting for hearth and home' to risk their lives overseas for a concept with which many probably found it difficult to identify. It is an army that is still in being today.

Today we lack the clarity of thinking that men like Constantine and Mehmet, Cromwell, Scharnhorst and Marshall displayed. Armies – by no means not all but a significant number – are seen more as a useful last resort for problems such as dealing with environmental disasters, providing essential services, delivering vaccines and the like so that their training for warfighting is neglected. For example, when the poor people of Valencia were so badly flooded in November 2024, they said that they had been let down by the army. That is a curious position to take. Armies may have the structure, equipment and communications to help with flooding, but surely there is a better way of dealing with environmental catastrophes? Why do you go to the expense and effort of recruiting, equipping and training an army only to use it to fill sandbags? It is a debate which is perhaps at its most intense in Australia. The Australian Army, fundamental to the security of a nation in what may become one of the more dangerous parts of the world, has spent a considerable amount of its time in the last two years dealing with natural disasters instead of training. It has been used to put out bush fires, and to assist with hotel quarantine and vaccine roll-out during the COVID-19 pandemic and with relief operations during the 2022 flooding. This 'has led to raised expectations among the general population of the ADF (Australian Defence Forces) being used as a first response unit, and states have come to rely on ADF support rather than on their own emergency services. As a result, during the recent floods, increasing pressure was put on the federal government to deploy the military to disaster zones, and disappointment was great when this did not happen as quickly as desired.'[4] There is a muddled way of thinking that lies behind this approach. It runs along the lines of: we'll prepare an army to fight if we have to, but for the time being it is too difficult and anyway we don't really believe that it is going to come to combat. Therefore we will use the army for all the other things that a government has to do, as equipment and training are expensive and paying for them can be controversial. It is an understandable position to take in a democracy, and there are times when at least part of an army can be so employed, an argument developed below, but it is also dangerous.

One of the threads that links all the armies this book has described is that when faced with a crisis, or in Mehmet's case, the need to expand so his empire survived, their leaders were all prepared to take radical decisions to reform their armies. They were also clear thinking as to how their forces should be organized. Most Western democracies today make great play of staging regular defence reviews, but these have mostly – not entirely – become the formulaic reproduction of procedure, lacking any fundamental changes or improvements. They tend to repackage existing force structures and are often used by governments to disguise a savings exercise, what are referred to euphemistically as 'efficiencies'. Arguably it takes a major crisis, a genuine existential threat such as the United Kingdom faced in 1939, to push government to think more deeply. By that stage, as the United States found in 1941, it is often too late, and both the human and financial costs of such a tardy reaction can be huge. Governments must, though, of course balance their priorities, and those more hard-line politicians who regularly call for massive increases in defence spending may be misguided. What a nation must do is to spend enough to maintain what all the armies examined have judged to be critical – in other words, a fully effective combat force – and there are times such as the present when that is not happening across Europe. Spending profligately on defence when there is no immediate threat is wasteful, as the Soviet Union discovered in the 1980s; armies that become routinely unaffordable do not survive. By 1989, the year the Berlin Wall fell, the USSR was estimated to have been spending upwards of 27 per cent of its GDP on its armed forces.[5] The New Model Army had, by 1660, made itself not only deeply unpopular but an unacceptable financial burden. However, not spending adequately on defence when there is an acknowledged threat is irresponsible government. There can be little point in prioritizing social programmes if the beneficiaries of that well-intentioned spending are on the point of being overwhelmed.

The third lesson we can draw from these historical examples is the need for an army to be seen as part of the nation, not separate or superior to it, as in Cromwell's Protectorate, in Germany and Japan in the 1930s, or in Iran today. There needs to be an ongoing national debate about defence across European nations, initiated and led by government but not dominated by it. Obviously this is happening dramatically in Ukraine and in front-line states like Lithuania but other countries need to do the same. This debate should lead cash-pressed governments to look at ways of widening the burden of defence throughout society both to seek greater support and to reduce costs. How might that work? One idea would be by following the examples set by those who have developed what emerged as the Prussian triangular system, arguably perfected by the USA. The argument starts, as articulated by de Tocqueville, in that, whereas all citizens in a democracy benefit from being defended, only a few are actively involved in delivering that security because the system of government under which they live allows them to opt out. There was no such choice under the Anglo-Saxon *fyrd* nor the Prussian *Landsturm*. This emphatically does not mean a form of military service for all young people as was practised in Germany and France until relatively recently. Again, hard-line politicians frequently call for that, citing rather doubtful evidence that it can be socially cohesive and teach a coming generation values and skills. Whereas there may be some truth in that, it is militarily unworkable given the need outlined above. There is a place for national service, but it is not in the form that it is commonly portrayed in the Western media as some sort of universal boot camp.

What armies may need, however, is more soldiers than they can recruit voluntarily, and societies need to look at ways of providing those people, bearing in mind that number may increase. About 70 countries still have a form of national service on their statute books, with about 22 actively using it, including Norway, Sweden, Denmark, Greece and Switzerland.[6] However, in most countries it is managed so that there are alternative forms of service available or it only applies to very few people as enough volunteers come forward. In Switzerland it is a core part of the country's defence policy. In 2013 a referendum was held to abolish it, but 73 per cent of the population voted for its retention. In some countries, like Norway and Israel, it applies to men and women. An extreme example is, predictably, North Korea, where men selected must serve ten years and women seven years. Carefully managed, some form of national service can therefore be made to work, but models like the Swiss system warrant careful study.

Most, if not all, of those full-time professional combat armies also need a reserve element that is deployed as necessary to give the professional army capabilities it does not need to employ full time. Nations also need a part-time force, a combination of Scharnhorst's *Landwehr* and the *Landsturm*, a force which is community based and which may need to be dedicated to community support. It is definitely not a 'Third Force', somewhere between the army and the police, rather like the Italian *carabinieri*, although it could fulfil a community policing function, and the term *Landsturm* can be misleading in that respect as it had different meanings in Austria and Prussia.

Looking at these three elements in more detail, the combat army, the professional core, has been discussed above. However, armies need now to think whether they really do need to restrict recruiting to a narrow age bracket. This is a classic repetition of historic norms, when only men of a certain age were judged physically fit enough for the demands of soldiering. As populations live longer, have better medical care and are generally fitter, the argument for not recruiting older people, both men and women, weakens. Ukraine is a good example of this as discussed in Chapter One. Recruiting and training soldiers is expensive and difficult in economies which offer attractive alternative careers. It is therefore sensible to retain soldiers in service for as long as they can do the job. The infantry is the arm generally regarded as requiring the highest degree of physical fitness, but infantry represent on average about 40 per cent of modern armies. Older people possess skills which are becoming increasingly valuable. You don't need to be 20 to launch a drone.

An associated lesson that our historical examples show is that it is critical for the combat army to be trained to perform the most demanding operations. Armies can scale back their performance, and frequently have done so, especially as operations transit from high-intensity combat to, for example, becoming an army of occupation in post-Second World War Germany, but it is time consuming and demanding for an army to scale up, as the British Army found to its cost in France in 1940 or in the Western Desert. As technology delivers increasingly complex weapons to the battlefield, the need for demanding training and the simulation of combat conditions intensifies. Cromwell's army is a classic example of an army that was quarantined, re-organized, re-equipped and then trained ruthlessly until it became effective, and despite being committed to combat before it was fully ready it got away with it because the Royalist army was in an even worse state.

The reserve element of the combat force should be those capabilities which it needs to operate but which it doesn't require full time. Historically, armies, like the Prussian army after Jena, have used those who have recently left full-time service in the combat army, arguing that they can be utilized for a period while their training is still current. Others with specialist roles, such as medics, linguists, cyber analysts and the like, can continue to do their military training in parallel with vocational training. The British Army's system of medical support is a very good example of how this can be made to work. In the past, the British Army had its own hospitals with full-time teams of surgeons and nurses. Gradually this came to be counter-productive. As the army reduced in size, the surgeons did not have enough work to ensure that they could keep their skills current, and the proliferation of surgical specializations meant that it would be impossible to keep pace with modern medical practice. Despite well-intentioned but misplaced campaigns to retain full-time military hospitals, the preferred solution was to make an arrangement with the British National Health Service so that the army could draw on the specializations it needed, nurse soldiers together in one central hospital – important psychologically especially when nursing those wounded on operations – and deploy surgeons on operations for short periods as required, which gave them valuable experience.

Reserves can be organized as individuals or as units but they must have clear roles and be trained and equipped for them. This may sound obvious, but in practice few armies make the reservist system work efficiently; were one to ask army headquarters across Europe to list all their available reserves, their contact details, their medical fitness and their current state of training, it is unlikely that they could all do so. What is important, as demonstrated so clearly by Constantine, is that there is a clear distinction between a reservist who has a role in the combat force and one who is a member of a second-line organization – the *ripenses*, the *Akıncı*, the *Landwehr* or *Landsturm*, the militia or Territorial Army or the National Guard. This is a distinction which has become muddled, particularly in the United Kingdom.

So the next lesson we can draw is that as the threats nations face change and, as discussed, become as much from the environment, from disease and from civil disorder, then nations should adjust to cope with them. Here is where the concept of national service does become relevant. Given the pressure on national budgets, the problem is that establishing a separate force to manage these threats is expensive. If the professional army is deployed, it ceases to be an available combat force and few police forces have the necessary capacity. The Anglo-Saxon *fyrd* principle, later the militia, should therefore apply in that if people are to benefit from the protection of the state then they may have to contribute to providing that protection. A city or county would be tasked with establishing a force with a range of skills, be they technical, mechanical, cyber, medical etc. that would utilize, to take the United Kingdom as an example, the extensive existing Territorial Army infrastructure. It would be part time, with a small regular staff, much as the current Territorial Army is organized, with people asked to volunteer to cover a specified range of skills. Were insufficient volunteers to come forward then the government would have the power to select. People would be required to carry out a certain amount of training and then be on call. Pay would be on a pro-rata basis and the emphasis should be on volunteering as opposed to second careers. There is an argument for asking people to serve *pro bono* given that their work is for the community. Were you to ask a cross-section of, say, a British town if they were prepared to serve in the Territorial Army, most would probably say no; were you to ask them if they were to join a body dedicated to helping others in their community, then many would say yes. The skills required are omnipresent in each community, often amongst those retired from full-time employment or working part time. It is an issue of re-focusing existing structures and sentiment to meet contemporary needs and utilizing a system which has long been present in British society, albeit recently neglected. De Tocqueville would argue that it is ultimately inevitable that those who live in a democracy and benefit from the defence of their community must participate in its protection – otherwise society reaches a point with absurd levels of government interference and subsequent taxation. It is a similar system to the one that Scharnhorst instituted. He focused the *Landsturm* on being a military-type force, almost guerrilla bands, dedicated to fighting what was then the main threat to the Prussian community, the French. Today he would have applied that principle to these new threats.

It is encouraging that the need for such a force was acknowledged in the recent British Defence Review; the question now is whether the government has the resolve to take its recommendations forward and, if they do, whether the British bureaucracy is competent enough to execute them. Certainly in the United Kingdom many of the elements of such a force exist already within communities, such as the Civil Defence Corps. It is more a question of drawing them together to give coherence and centralized control. Once established, the range of what such a force could achieve is variable, from straightforward community tasks such as emergency deliveries, to assistance with severe weather or flooding, to roles when national security is threatened much as the Civil Defence Force carried out before 1945.

Why bother if the existing system seems to be working? For two reasons. First, the pressures and threats look set to grow so that government and communities need a capability to respond. Second, if we believe that the world is becoming more dangerous, and threats are becoming more serious, in this particular example to the United Kingdom, then having an embryonic structure in place that can be tailored to future requirements is sensible. So, for example, in Ukraine the need for such a system of community involvement is obvious, as it is rapidly becoming so in other front-line states such as Lithuania. Does that mean that it should have a military role, a sort of contemporary Home Guard? Very possibly, if the need arises and its capabilities can be adjusted accordingly. And how should it work with the police? Again, using the United Kingdom as an example, where community trust in policing is at a historic low, inventive police forces must be able to improve their performance by working with a force rooted in local communities, especially in areas such as crime prevention and intelligence. It strikes many military people as strange that (and this applies across Europe) many of the excellent data and community analytical tools developed for military operations seem to be unavailable to domestic police forces. Governments like to reassure the public that they are already doing things like that but, if so, they are not doing them very well, and many find it strange that the police seem unable to harness the huge resource available in communities who are only too keen to reduce crime in their areas.

Many people living in democratic countries think that their armies are remote. They seldom see soldiers in their daily life, which is both a function of how small many armies now are and that their activities tend to be concentrated away from where the public can see them, an obvious exception being ceremonial soldiers but, reassuring as they are, their role is subtly different. Historically, governments imposed recruiting quotas on different regions so that there was always a representation in an army from across their society; the idea of locally raised regiments is one example, and another is the Prussian cantonment system. Recruiting for modern combat armies is already difficult in societies where the skills and motivation required are at a premium, so the idea of imposing regional quotas on geographical areas is probably unhelpful. However, the concept of a community force would allow a more direct regional linkage and reinforce the idea that defence is present and relevant. Successful armies have kept their support within their nations strong.

The USA is a good example of how the system can work. It already has a complete structure that delivers this in the United States Army, with its strong reservist support, and the National Guard. The National Guard answer to their state, and are used by governors to perform support tasks for policing – for example, in March 2024 the New York National Guard were deployed to patrol the subway system following violent attacks on a train conductor and a cellist travelling home after a concert.[7] However, National Guardsmen can be deployed in support of federal forces and frequently were in the military operations which followed 9/11, much as they were after 1941. The federated structure of the United States, with more power residing at the state level as opposed to the federal level than is common with most democracies, makes this structure more straightforward to deliver, but equally it offers a good example of how citizens are more involved with their own defence.

Another constant thread which runs through the five armies described in this book is that they all appreciated the need to innovate both in terms of equipment and tactics, and they involved many different elements across society to help them to do so. Arguably, Constantine's success was as much due to his introduction of new ideas and the technology – such as the style of mounted warfare and the use of armour he had experienced from fighting the Persians – as it was to his generalship. Mehmet's early appreciation and exploitation of gunpowder, well ahead of his European counterparts, gave him and his successors a technical advantage which it took the Hungarians and later the Hapsburgs a century to equal. Cromwell's ability to realize the battle-winning tactics in the British civil wars, and to structure his army accordingly, even though he was not responsible for the introduction of any great technological developments, was what gave his army tactical superiority. It was a similar story with the Prussian army. Although the French were the most innovative in terms of introducing new procedures and equipment, such as horse artillery which could accompany cavalry, Scharnhorst's ability to make the Prussian army adopt them and train with them was what enabled them to defeat Napoleon at Leipzig and later at Waterloo. After the Treaty of Versailles, when Germany's military was severely capped, the decision of the general staff was to ensure in the inter-war years that they kept those officers who could innovate, thus allowing their experimentation with armoured forces and the development of the blitzkrieg concept.

Yet perhaps the most important lesson comes from Roosevelt's establishment of, first, the National Resources Defense Council, and its successor, the Office of Scientific Research, with its accompanying emphasis on operational analysis. Instead of working on the assumption that government had a monopoly of wisdom in knowing what technical innovation was required, Harry Hopkins and Vannevar Bush appreciated that the real thinking was taking place in the research and development departments of American industry and in its universities. The idea that such intellectual horsepower could be matched by civil servants and army officers in the federal government was, they appreciated, naïve. Some of the war's great battle-winning technologies, including, for better or worse, the atomic bomb, were delivered through this process. Yet since 1945 governments have let this collaborative working arrangement slip. Military requirements are still set by government staffs, working without industry involvement and often unaware of what else might be technologically possible to solve their needs. The wartime sense of mutual trust and cooperation has been replaced by a more confrontational arrangement in which the requirement is developed in great secrecy and then issued to potential manufacturers, most of whom could have saved the government a great deal of time and money had they been involved earlier in the process. Governments across Europe will say that they have to act like this due to commercial sensitivities and the need to secure the best financial deal. Really? It worked very well in the Second World War with all its stress and hovering danger, especially in the USA and United Kingdom, so it seems strange that it cannot be made to work today. If we are facing a similar threat then we need to adopt similar measures to prepare to meet it. The result of the present system is that equipment that armies badly need invariably arrives late, sometimes ridiculously so, over budget and without the specifications needed.

It also means that armies are unable to take advantage of the most advanced technologies. A good example of this is space, which offers opportunities for communications, intelligence, targeting and a host of other technological advances that, as satellite capacity and capability increase, save both personnel and money. Yet space exploitation by governments is in its infancy, largely because they lack the officers and officials who are familiar with the possibilities that space offers. It is a classic example of how collaborative working with industry could make a major difference to budgets and capabilities.

An associated lesson, and one again which these historical examples teach us, is the need to establish and nurture an industrial capability that can supply an army. This has become progressively more complicated for two reasons. First, the complexity and cost of weapons and, second, the international nature of the defence market. It was relatively simple for Constantine to establish his factories and workshops, his studs and his forges. Not only did he exercise sufficient economic control but the materials he needed for his weapons and equipment – the metal, leather, fabrics and horses his army used – were being produced anyway as they were the commercial staples of 4th-century Europe. The position became more complicated for Mehmet, who found he had to establish specialist workshops, cannon and gunpowder not being everyday items in the Ottoman lands in the 15th century, yet his army's success was because the empire was able to produce significant quantities of both. Cromwell was able to supply the New Model Army, whose material needs were actually not that different from Mehmet's, because the Parliamentary forces controlled not only the major ports but also what were then the economic centres of England, including London. The Prussian example is particularly interesting, because in Frederick William I, Prussia had a king who specifically linked military supply to commerce, making the army contribute to the economy by ensuring that all supplies were purchased locally and regularly re-ordered. Scharnhorst and the reformers were able to supply their new army precisely because the network of factories established across Prussia meant they could do so without importing and thus arousing French suspicion on their borders. Again, the materials needed were widely available across the country, meaning that they could be obtained from multiple sources. Although military demands were slowly becoming more technical – the Waterloo campaign was the first in which the telegraph was used, in which soldiers were inoculated against smallpox and in which howitzer shells were used in artillery as well as the traditional cannon balls – warfare was still using the same basic ingredients of metal, wood, fabric, leather and countless horses much as it had done for centuries. That changed with the industrial revolution, the emergence of technologies that allowed the rapid development of artillery with its enormous appetite for shells and the percussion cap that required the more complicated manufacture of bullets rather than the lead balls that had been fired from muskets for 500 years. The production of military equipment has continued to become increasingly complex, to require vast numbers of components and to become more and more international.

It was the Second World War which established the supremacy, as opposed to the advantage, of industrial might. However much the Japanese may have hoped that Pearl Harbor could bring them a quick victory, once America declared war the outcome was never, as Ribbentrop warned Hitler, in serious doubt. As long as the American people retained the will, then the USA's economic might would ensure Allied victory. In fact, as we have seen, America's ability to harness its industry to the war effort would result in it producing nearly two-thirds of the total equipment used in the war by all sides. The USA's economy may have changed significantly since 1945, but its economic capability still means that it can outproduce any other military power with the possible exception of China, although we have insufficient knowledge of Chinese military production to be able to derive firm conclusions from that contention. Yet when compared with Europe, the USA's capacity is revealing and perhaps best articulated by studying a recent report by the Stockholm International Peace Research Institute (SIPRI). Published in December 2024, this concluded, unsurprisingly given increased world tension, that in 2023 sales of arms and military services increased by 4.2 per cent from 2022 levels to reach $632 billion. The top 41 of the world's leading 100 defence companies were based in the USA, including all the top five, and between them they recorded half the world's defence sales by revenue. By contrast, in 2023 European companies recorded revenues of just $133 billion, reflecting the smallest increase over 2022 figures of any global region – and this despite increased orders as a result of Russia's invasion of Ukraine. Interestingly, it was estimated that nine of the top 100 companies, those that were based in China, saw a smaller year-on-year increase to a total of $103 billion.[8]

March 2024 saw the publication of a much-heralded 'First ever European defence industrial strategy to enhance Europe's readiness and security'. This specified that by 2030 EU countries should purchase at least 40 per cent of the defence equipment in partnership, spend at least half their defence procurement budgets on products made in Europe, and trade at least 35 per cent of defence goods between EU countries as opposed to with other countries.[9] It is an ambitious political target, but it could well be that if it is not met other countries could find themselves in the position of Ukraine since 2022 where a shortage of munitions, from 155mm artillery shells to complex missile systems, threatens their survival as a nation. Europe's attempt to come up with a strategy is brave; unless you are the USA or possibly China, how do you otherwise guarantee your munition supply in war? The lesson from history is that each nation needs to have evaluated its own defence industrial strategy, which is not, as so many are, just platitudes about working with industry, but detailed and constantly updated spreadsheets of what sustainment is needed over a given time period with a fall-back strategy for when those initial holdings are exhausted. Would Ukraine, for example, have planned on still being engaged in high-intensity conflict three years after the Russian invasion? Could it ever have held sufficient stocks to sustain its army at its current consumption rates? In 1997 the author was tasked with writing the United Kingdom's reconstitution policy to restore fighting capability should there have been a major war – in other words, how do you reset having expended existing stocks? There is an element of *reductio ad absurdum* here; it is arguable that you should hold such enormous stocks that you would never run out, but quite clearly that would rapidly consume the whole defence budget.

The answer has to lie in nurturing an industrial capacity to produce at least some of what is needed. That in itself is difficult, partly because government must therefore cover some of industry's costs in preserving that capacity but also because, as discussed in Chapter One, we live in a world where defence is seen in some way as immoral. In 2024 an attempt by a small United Kingdom company engaged in defence-related activities to open an account with two of the major British clearing banks resulted in outright rejection before there was even a proper discussion, based simply on the nature of the business. One bank wrote back saying they would not deal with companies engaged in 'pornography, gambling or defence'. On 8 May 2024 *The Daily Telegraph* reported that two clearing banks had closed 300 accounts as they had links to defence companies. The newspaper concluded that this put national security at risk, yet the Bank of England, ultimately funded by the United Kingdom's taxpayers, continues to provide facilities for both those banks to trade. It is a problem mirrored in Europe, where European defence industry leaders complain that banks are 'taking an activist stance against defence companies', citing ESG (environmental, social and governance) concerns.

The figures would seem to support their case. In May 2023 the *Financial Times* reported that UK investment funds had cut their holdings in large UK defence companies such as BAE systems and QinetiQ by an average of 9 per cent since the start of 2022.[10] 'Britain's vital and successful arms industry is being unfairly shunned by investors' ran a *Times* leader in September 2023. 'Fund managers who insist on treating the defence sector as a pariah to appease fashionable sensitivities insult its workers and the servicemen and women who rely for their survival on its excellence. How long would their careers, or freedom, last if they championed ESG in Russia and China?'[11] There is clearly a need for European nations in general, and the United Kingdom in particular, to produce a defence industrial strategy that reaches beyond platitudes and instigates active measures to promote the industry that allows the defence of its citizens.

The pattern of respect for their soldiers amongst the armies we have looked at is uneven, as is the associated provisions for their care and well-being. De Tocqueville thought that the respect with which societies treated their soldiers depended on whether they had a 'military spirit'. He thought that when that 'forsakes a people, the profession of arms immediately ceases to be an honour, and military men fall to the lowest rank of public servants; they are little esteemed and no longer understood'. This happens, he argues, in democracies, concluding that 'it is then no matter of surprise that democratic armies are often restless, ill-tempered, and dissatisfied with their lot although their physical condition is commonly far better, and their discipline less strict than in other countries'. In *Democracy in America*, he goes on to make his familiar point that it was all so much easier in 'aristocratic ages', and lack of respect for the military was another problem associated with democratic government.[12] He had a point. In societies like the late Roman Empire, the way to advancement was through the army, especially if one had imperial ambitions. The senior levels of government in all areas tended to be dominated by military men. Constantine himself used his *candidati*, men with whom he had served closely on campaign, to fill the top posts as both generals and, bearing in mind he divided military from civilian authority, as *vicarii*. The same pattern was true of the Ottomans, helped by the *devşirme* system being used for both military and palace appointments. In a society where the way to advancement lay in service to the sultan, the army was seen as offering a route to both senior appointments and to wealth. Both empires consequently cared for their soldiers well, reinforcing the link between saying they respected their soldiers and introducing reforms so that they could actually do so.

Constantine's improvements to his soldiers' terms of service between AD 306 and 312, and especially his reforms of 326, were continuing a long-established Roman tradition.

Modern readers of Roman history puzzle over how rival commanders such as Octavian and Mark Anthony managed to make their legions fight each other so fiercely when they were actually fighting their fellow Roman citizens and quite possibly men whom they had served alongside in former wars. Fighting the Gauls or Barbarians was understandable, but the savagery of the seemingly endless civil wars can be hard to comprehend. A part of the answer must lie in the advantages they perceived in being on the winning side and the potential rewards of victory. Veterans expected to be looked after and to be given land; the provision of farms for ex-soldiers was one of the key issues in the Catiline conspiracy on which Cicero declaimed with much force. Constantine knew that the stability of the empire depended on his veterans receiving a generous settlement, not least if he was going to use them to provide structure to society by placing them in a whole range of local administrative posts. The laws he passed in AD 326 gave retiring soldiers a very good package indeed. Similarly, the Ottomans needed soldiers as both settlers, to take over the lands they had conquered, and to administer them as *timars* while also using the grants as a system of reward. The continual expansion of the empire meant that this system lasted well into the 17th century, and in some areas well beyond. The advantage was that it came at little cost, and the structure of the imperial administration was preserved alongside adherence to Islamic orthodoxy.

The position changed, as de Tocqueville pointed out, in modern armies. The case of the New Model Army is, again, illustrative. The soldiers were adequately paid, always allowing for the fact that pay was often late partly through Parliamentary design and partly due to incompetence. In their glory days of the 1650s they were able to demand regular increases so that the pay of a private soldier in the foot rose by about 15 per cent between Naseby and the Restoration, when it was ten pence per day or a bit more than an agricultural labourer's wage. The horse, who of course had to feed their horses from their pay, went up by around the same percentage so that a trooper's pay rose from two shillings a day to two and threepence.[13] Officers were well paid, colonels earning a pound per day, which made them well off, and the most junior officer, a cornet, was on five shillings by 1660. Parliament was also generous in handing out rewards to senior officers. Fairfax was awarded £10,000 and an estate worth £4,000 a year while Essex was given an estate worth £10,000 a year. The major generals, like Whalley, took a bonus of £500 a year and Lambert got £1,000. Parliament were less generous in handing out what Constantine's legionaries would have recognized as 'donatives', although soldiers who had particularly distinguished themselves were given cash awards. The men who captured Royalist standards at Marston Moor and Dunbar were given ten shillings each, and after Dunbar Parliament declared that every soldier was awarded a medal with Cromwell's head on one side, although there must be some doubt as to whether they were all issued because very few now survive.

Yet the soldiers of the New Model Army would appear to have had high morale, even allowing that the more zealous would presumably have felt inspired that they were doing 'God's work'. The military spirit was certainly present and commanders like Cromwell and Ireton understood the importance of social respect for their men. The difficult economic circumstances after the Restoration meant that army service continued to be highly valued, with men 'purchasing' places given that they carried a guaranteed and secure income. This would translate into the much-criticized 'purchase system' by which officers bought their commissions. Much ink has been spilled criticizing the apparent inequity of such a system but in fact it served the British government very well indeed, as it ensured that the army was officered by men of property who, having made a substantial investment in its stability, were unlikely to overthrow it. The unfortunate side effect was to widen the already fairly substantial gulf between officers and soldiers, with the former being well respected, and the latter often derided. It was a position that would endure in the British Army until well into the 19th century.

Respect for the military in Prussia and later Germany was always strong, despite the harsh conditions under which the soldiers lived perhaps suggesting otherwise. The cantonment system meant that every locality had 'their' soldiers, the identification of the army with German nationalism ensuring that this deep national respect endured after the Napoleonic Wars even though welfare provision was at best adequate. In fact, respect for uniform became absurd, as demonstrated by *The Captain of Köpenick*. The two world wars only heightened this further and, despite some wavering in 1918, it was not until 1945 that the army became discredited. But it is to the U.S. Army after 1941 that we should look to really learn how a society can both honour and care for its soldiers. The enthusiasm to serve in 1917, mirrored in 1941, despite the fact that roughly half the army was conscripted rather than volunteered – interestingly, initially the U.S. Navy and Marine Corps only took volunteers – gave service a respectability and ethos that found an echo in the traditional U.S. pride in nation and state. Service in many countries in wartime was, of course, seen as honourable, although in many it was a question of national survival. In the United States it was more fighting for a belief and it wasn't until Vietnam, when many Americans felt that belief to be a tarnished concept, that the Selective Service Act, still administered by Hershey until February 1970, came to be seriously questioned. But what really helped the U.S. Army's position was Roosevelt's revolutionary GI Bill, very much a modern reincarnation of Constantine's welfare reforms of AD 326. Here was a government honouring its soldiers, both its professionals and its citizens who had answered the call, and doing so effectively. The U.S. Army continues to look after its servicemen and women very well today, probably better than any other army. Military spirit, which often comes in reaction to a threat, needs to be matched with measures that substantiate the sentiment it articulates and allow soldiers to live decently on a par with their society. It is a lesson all governments should note.

How do modern armies match up to these criteria? Some well, some less so. Every nation faces threats in this unstable era but some threats are more imminent than others. That is especially true of the Baltic States. Lithuania is one of them, the other two being Estonia and Latvia. Lithuania became independent from the Soviet Union in 1990 but remains a nation under threat from Russia, its nervousness obviously heightened when Lithuanians saw what happened to Ukraine. They fought the Russians in the 1940s and have every intention of doing so again should the menace materialize. Despite the Russians' dire performance in Ukraine, and the fact that they have lost almost an entire generation of middle-ranking and junior officers whom it will take them several years to replace, their army could still swallow up tiny Lithuania, just 2.8 million people with the Russian enclave of Kaliningrad to their south and Belarus to their east. Lithuania has armed forces of about 23,000 including navy, air force and para-militaries. The army itself is around 13,000, part regular and part active reservists. In 2015 it was felt that insufficient numbers of men were coming forward for military service so conscription was introduced. All men between the ages of 18 and 26 must serve for nine months. Names are selected annually at random by computer. Once they have completed their service they form part of a national reserve. Lithuania now feels like a nation that is mobilized with citizens from all walks of life contributing; Russian speakers, for example, ring people in Russia to explain the realities of Putin's war in Ukraine.[14] Yet despite this impressive show of strength, Lithuania knows it could not long delay a determined Russian invasion were it not for its NATO membership. Having joined the alliance in 2004, Lithuania could find itself dependent on NATO for its survival. Since 2017 the alliance has stationed a battlegroup there – a battlegroup is a battalion-sized force made up of different combat elements and about 1,000 strong. Known as NATO Enhanced Forward Presence (eFP), there are similar battlegroups in Latvia, Estonia and Poland. There is overwhelming popular support for Lithuania's military posture; a recent poll showed NATO support at 86 per cent.[15] It is hardly surprising. De Tocqueville would applaud the military spirit. Lithuania has prioritized a professional combat army with a strong active reserve; it has a developing national reserve capability, spends over 3 per cent of GDP on defence, and its army enjoys overwhelming popular support. Innovation has come from working with its allies, and defence equipment is imported. It is hard to see what more a small nation could do – but it is a very small nation.

To the south of Lithuania, originally part of the same kingdom and sharing a short land border as it also does with

Kaliningrad, lies Poland. Of all European nations Poland enjoys one of the most distinguished military legacies and yet has suffered more than most from some terrible defeats. Originally the centre of one of Europe's great medieval kingdoms, and a nation whose territories ran from the Baltic to the Black Sea, it was the intervention of the Polish army which saved Vienna from the Ottomans for the Hapsburgs in 1683. Subsequently carved up by successive Prussian and Russian governments, by 1793 it had ceased to exist as a separate nation. Briefly revived under Napoleon, it did not become a nation again until 1918 when it was promptly re-invaded by Russia. Invaded by Hitler in 1939, it was then partitioned yet again between Nazi Germany and the Soviet Union. Poland suffered a tragic war and found little relief when it became part of the Soviet empire in 1945. It was not until 1989 that it was finally able to shake off its neighbours and re-establish itself as a European nation. Hardly surprisingly, then, that the Polish Chief of Defence, General Wiesław Kukuła, should say that 'Everything is indicating that we are the generation who will stand up in arms to defend our country. And neither I nor any of you intend to lose this war.'[16] Poland's military expansion has been truly impressive so that it now ranks as the leading European military power. Its army of around 200,000 is the third largest in NATO after the United States and Turkey and will soon be able to deploy three armoured corps; to put that in perspective, the United Kingdom can currently field just part of one armoured division, so Poland can field about seven times what the United Kingdon can. With its planned purchases, it will have over 700 main battle tanks, a large proportion being the American Abrams. It is also buying a range of other off-the-shelf items including attack helicopters, and it has a burgeoning space industry.

It doesn't have conscription at present but it has the legal framework should it be necessary and it calls reservists up for regular training. It is rapidly expanding its Territorial Defence Force, a recent innovation, for which recruitment is strong. Defence spending rose by 51 per cent between 2022 and 2023 and is now somewhere between 3.5 and 4 per cent of GDP, with aspirations to raise it to 5 per cent. Poland is the NATO country that spends the highest proportion of its GDP on defence; Estonia is second, with Lithuania sixth.

There are significant problems in fielding such a large force that has been assembled so quickly: training, all arms interoperability, logistics, infrastructure, command and control all need to be developed, but again de Tocqueville would admire the spirit that General Kukula has articulated. Support for Poland's initiative remains strong; in 2024 90 per cent supported NATO membership and 70 per cent thought their armed forces were doing well.[17] It is, however, expensive and is placing strains on the national finances. Poland is one of 12 EU member states whose finances are under scrutiny by the European Commission for running an excessive deficit. A question must remain as to how sustainable this rate of build-up is should it be required for an extended period – but then a more pertinent question might be, what is the point in being solvent if you are not free?

Poland again hosts a NATO forward battle group and, despite its impressive forces, NATO membership remains the basis of its defence planning. And currently NATO means the USA. The U.S. Army remains, as do the U.S. Armed Forces in the round, in a league of their own in terms of capability and in meeting those criteria we have examined. The U.S. spends approximately 3.5 per cent of its GDP on defence, the third highest in NATO but in absolute terms massively outstripping Europe (with Canada), at $755 billion to $430 billion. The U.S. spends $2,239 per capita on defence; the next highest in NATO is Norway at $1,754. The U.S. Armed Forces number over 1.3 million people.[18] The USA's decision not to withdraw into isolationism in 1945, as it did in 1918, and its decision to combat the spread of communism by forward defence in Europe, and its subsequent international campaigns against terrorism and totalitarianism, has meant that the army that Roosevelt and Marshall built has not been wasted; the U.S. Army today is fundamentally the same army, albeit obviously much changed on the surface. The U.S. looks after its servicemen and women, it leads the world in innovation and military research, and the U.S. Armed Forces enjoy considerable respect both at home and throughout NATO. The U.S. Army is the most powerful in the world, arguably the most powerful the world has ever seen given that modern technology compensates for those huge number of soldiers fielded after 1941. In terms of what an army should be it is difficult to beat, yet no other nation, with the possible exception of China, enjoys similar wealth and aptitude.

All this may change should the US. decide to withdraw some of its support for NATO. European nations have, since 1941, benefitted hugely from U.S. involvement in Europe, both militarily and commercially. The USA now rightly expects them to pay for more of their own defence, if not the totality. Hopefully that does not mean that the U.S. will withdraw completely from Europe, repeating the mistakes of 1918 which had to be corrected at such a huge cost in 1941. Given the global strategic context, and the need for nations to interact and trade, it is hard to see how isolationism can serve American citizens providing that Europe at least shares the defence burden. Were European nations to have to replicate all the capabilities that the USA provides for NATO then they would have to develop a political structure that allows them to do so. Currently this does not exist, and when and if it does, it will take time to develop the defence infrastructure necessary.

There are many other armies that this book could have studied. Hopefully some readers may get back to me suggesting others – that would be good, as it will show that they have read this far! Equally, there are self-evidently many, many other modern armies that could be used to illustrate the application of the same timeless principles. This can never be an exhaustive study but I hope it has achieved its purpose in asking people to think about what an army is and to accept that armies are as relevant today as they have always been. The principles on which they operate are unchanging. It is an arrogant generation which ignores history.

'There are two thousand years of experience to tell us that the only thing harder than getting a new idea into a military mind is to get an old idea out.'
Captain Sir Basil Liddell Hart

Endnotes

CHAPTER ONE: WHAT IS AN ARMY?

1 Leon Trotsky, *Letter to Albert Goldman Jun 1940*. There is some debate as to what Trotsky actually meant by this pronouncement but it is generally accepted to be as quoted here.

2 Such as Kenneth Waltz's *Man, the State and War: A Theoretical Analysis* (Columbia, 2001).

3 From Earandel Reporting No. 29 5–12 Feb 2024. Actual given figure is 49cm. Russian losses during 2023 are estimated at *c.* 1,000 per day.

4 The global total of military personnel is estimated to have fallen from 29 million in 1989 to 9 million in 2005. By 2021 that figure had risen to 28 million. Quoted in Peter Wilson, *Iron & Blood: A Military History of the German Speaking Peoples since 1500* (Penguin, 2022), p. 629.

5 For a good description of how Lithuanians see the current situation, see Simon Kuper, 'How Lithuanians are preparing to stop Putin', *Financial Times Magazine 4/5* (November 2023), p. 14.

6 There are very few proven historical exceptions to this norm despite the imagination of Hollywood.

7 Wellington allegedly said this before Waterloo. He also used the phrase in a letter to Lord Bathurst from Spain on 2 July 1813.

8 The *fyrd* was an Anglo-Saxon system by which communities had to supply a number of men to the army for a defined period based on their size and prosperity. Used extensively by the rulers of Wessex to fight the Vikings, the system was remodelled under Alfred the Great and provided the basis of the army until Hastings in 1066. It required communities to keep a core of trained men available who could be supplemented by untrained locals as necessary.

CHAPTER TWO: THE ARMY OF CONSTANTINE, 312

1 Shapur, Saphor, Shabuhr or Sapor was the second king of the Sasanian dynasty who ruled Persia from about AD 240–270.
2 Edward Gibbon, *The History of the Decline and Fall of the Roman Empire* (London, 1794). This edition reproduced by Palatine Press, 2015, Vol. 1, Ch. X, p. 151.
3 Gibbon, Vol. 1, Ch. X, p.168.
4 Gibbon, Vol. 1, Ch. XIII, p. 5.
5 Lactantius, *The Manner in which Persecutors Died* (Edinburgh: T & T Clark, 1871).
6 There is endless controversy over the exact date Constantine was born. Some historians suggest it was as early as 272, although this seems unlikely given comparative ages in the Roman world. For a fuller debate on this subject see David Potter, *Constantine the Emperor* (OUP, 2015), p. 28.
7 Potter, p. 63.
8 Georges Depeyrot, 'Economy & Society', Chapter 10 in *The Cambridge Companion to the Age of Constantine*, edited by Noel Lenski (CUP, 2006).
9 Gibbon, Vol. 1, Ch. XIII, p. 84.
10 Gibbon, Vol. 1, Ch. XIII, p.107.
11 Lactantius, p. 181.
12 Lactantius, p. 180.
13 Part of the huge Roman city of Carnutum, home to the Danube fleet, has been expertly restored by the Austrian government.

14 For a good analysis of his approach see Paul Stephenson's *Constantine: Unconquered Emperor, Christian Victor* (Quercus, 2009).

15 A very detailed breakdown of Gallienus' army is in Ilkka Syvanne, *The Reign of the Emperor Gallienus* (Pen & Sword, 2019).

16 A full list of Constantine's restructured provinces can be found in the *Laterculus Veronensis*, thought to date from *c.* 314.

17 The best detailed description of this system is Hugh Elton, 'Warfare & the Military' in Lenski, ed., *Cambridge Companion to the Age of Constantine*, pp. 325–346, Ch. 14.

18 For a full list, see Edward Bocking, ed., *Notitia Dignitatum Et Administrationum Omnium Tam Civilium Quam Militarium In Partibus Orientis (1853)* (Kessinger Publishing, reprint, 2009).

19 C.E.V. Nixon and Barbara Saylor Rodgers, eds, *In Praise of Later Roman Emperors: The Panegyrici Latini* (University of California Press, 1994), Panegyric IV – Nazarius, p. 376.

20 C.P. Scott, trans., *Codex Justinianus* (Cincinnati, 1932), Book 12, Title 48.

21 For a good analysis see Hugh Elton, *Warfare in Roman Europe AD 350–425* (Clarendon, 1997).

22 Figures taken from Ross Cowan, *Roman Legionary AD 284–337* (Osprey, 2015), p. 14. The following pages contain some excellent examples of individual soldiers' pay and the amount of their donatives.

23 Figure taken from Robert C. Allen, *Quantifying the Roman Economy* (Oxford Academic, 2009), Ch. 16. There are many different views as to exchange rates and the value of coin but this seems to be the most realistic.

24 Figures come from contemporary records displayed, along with a huge hoard of denarii, in the Trier Museum.

25 Elton, 'Warfare & the Military', p. 335.

26 *Codex Justinianus*, Book 12, Title 47 and Potter, p. 219 quoting the *Codex Theodosianus*.

27 Depeyrot, 'Economy & Society', p. 229, quoting *Codex Theodosianus*.

28 Ian Hughes, *A Military Life of Constantine the Great* (Pen & Sword, 2020), p. 35, quoting from the *Notitia Dignitatum*.

29 See Cowan, *Roman Legionary*, pp. 31–32. Lactantius also describes military equipment in some detail.

30 *Codex Justinianus*, Book 12, Titles 51 & 52.

31 Depeyrot, 'Economy & Society', p. 246.

32 Cowan, *Roman Legionary*, p. 27.

33 See Note 19 above. *Panegyrici Latini*, Panegyric of Constantine delivered at Trier probably in AD 309, Verse 12.

34 Lactantius, pp. 194–195.

35 They are now in the excellent Turin Archaeological Museum.

36 Lactantius, p. 170.

37 Ross Cowan, *Milvian Bridge AD 312* (Osprey, 2016), pp. 43 & 48.

38 Cowan, *Milvian Bridge*, p. 45.

39 Potter has a good analysis of the symbology, p.143.

40 Eusebius, *Ecclesiastical History* 9.95, quoted by Hughes, p. 129.

41 Eusebius, 10.5.4, quoted by Hughes, p. 140.

42 Listed by Hughes, p. 142.

43 See Note 19 above. Nazarius pp. 365–66.

CHAPTER THREE: THE OTTOMAN ARMY OF MEHMET THE
CONQUEROR, 1453

1 Konstantin Mihailović, *Memoirs of a Janissary* (Marcus Wiener, 2011), pp. 79–80.

2 Colin Imber, *The Ottoman Empire 1300–1650* (Palgrave, 2002), p. 134.

3 Imber, p. 135.

4 Mihailović, p. 80.

5 Halil Inalcik and Suraiya Faroqhi, *An Economic & Social History of the Ottoman Empire 1300–1914* (CUP, 1994), pp. 88–89.

6 Imber, p. 258.

7 Much of the information in this and succeeding paragraphs
   is taken from Mesut Uyar and Edward Erickson's excellent
   A Military History of the Ottomans (Praeger Security
   International, 2009).

8 Gábor Ágoston, *Guns for the Sultan: Military Power and the
   Weapons Industry in the Ottoman Empire* (CUP, 2005), p. 24.
   This excellent and thoroughly researched work is, to my
   knowledge, the only comprehensive study of the Ottoman
   armaments industry.

9 Mihailović, p. 83.

10 Imber, p. 260.

11 Rhoads Murphey, *Ottoman Warfare 1500–1700* (UCL Press,
   1999), p. 45.

12 Imber, p. 271.

13 Murphey, p. 45.

14 Ágoston, pp. 195–198.

15 Mihailović, p. 74 & p. 89.

16 Mihailović, p. 90.

17 Uyar & Erickson cite 40,000 by the mid-15th century, but
   other estimates are much lower. See also Incalik and Faroqhi,
   p. 89.

18 Mihailović, p. 96.

19 Murphey, pp. 36–37.

20 Murphey, p. 161.

21 Incalik and Faroqhi, p. 89.

22 Mihailović, p. 99.

23 Franz Babinger, *Mehmed the Conqueror and his Time*,
   translated by William C. Hickman (Princeton University
   Press, 1978), p. 40.

24 Babinger, p. 40.

25 David Stacton, *The World on the Last Day* (Faber & Faber,
   1965), p. 138.

26 Marios Philippides, *Mehmed II The Conqueror: And the Fall
   of the Franco-Byzantine Levant to the Ottoman Turks: Some
   Western Views and Testimonies* (Arizona Center for Medieval
   and Renaissance Studies, 2007), p. 97.

27 Stacton, p. 160.

28 Babinger, p. 91.

29 Stacton, p. 216.

30 The *kerkoporta* is still there and can be found on the walls just behind the well-preserved shell of the palace of Constantine Porphyrogenitus.

31 Pope Pius II, 'A Brief Treatise on the Capture of Constantinople' in Philippides, pp. 112–113.

32 Babinger, p. 93.

33 Imber, pp. 141–142, quoting Kochi Bey.

34 Murphey, pp. 40–41.

35 Mihailović, pp.86–87.

CHAPTER FOUR: THE NEW MODEL ARMY, 1645

1 C.H. Firth, *Cromwell's Army*, 2nd Edition, 1911, reproduced by Naval & Military Press, p. 13.

2 Firth, p. 17.

3 Firth, p. 26.

4 Oliver Cromwell letter to Colonel Valentine Walton, 5 July 1642.

5 Ian Gentles, *New Model Army: Agent of Revolution* (Yale, 2022), p. 3.

6 Glen Foard, quoting D. Wolfe, *Leveller Manifestoes of the Puritan Revolution* (1944), p. 2, in turn quoting John Milton, *The Second Defence*.

7 Gentles, p. 7.

8 Gentles, pp. 10 & 14.

9 Firth, p. 36.

10 Barney White-Spunner, *Horse Guards: The Story of the Household Cavalry* (Macmillan, 2006), p. 11.

11 Lord Orrery, cavalry commander, *The Art of War* (1677), pp. 198–199, reproduced by Firth, p. 401.

12 *The History of the War in Ireland from 1641 to 1653*, by a British officer in the regiment of Sir John Clotworthy (1873), p. 49.

13 Firth, p. 72, quoting Lupton, *A Warlike Treatise on the Pike*.

14 Firth, p. 89.

15 Orrery, p. 80.

16 Thomas Micel, *The Last Newes from the Armie* (Printed for James Neale, 20 June 1647).

17 There is an excellent short history – *Colonel John Pickering's Regiment of Foot* by Glenn Foard (Whitstable & Walsall, 1994) – from which I have taken much of this information.

18 Gentles, p. 21.

19 Quoted by Firth, p. 44.

20 Firth, pp. 186–187.

21 Trevelyan Papers quoted by Firth p. 118.

22 For an excellent short account of how the army was fed on the Naseby campaign, see Aryeh Nusbacher, 'Civil Supply in the Civil War: Supply of Victuals to the New Model Army on the Naseby Campaign 1–14 June 1645', *The English Historical Review*, Volume CXV No. 460 (February 2000).

23 Gentles, p. 70.

24 Denzil Holles, *Memoirs of Denzil Lord Holles, Baron of Ifield, 1641–1648* (Hard Press Classic Series, 2019), p. 149.

25 Gentles, p. 81.

26 Geoffrey Robertson, *The Levellers* (Verso, 2018), p. x.

27 Gentles, p. 131.

28 Gentles, p. 167.

29 Cromwell, quoted by Gentles, p. 173.

30 See, for example, *The Resolutions of the Private Souldiery of Colonel Scrope's Regiment of Horse* of May 1649 (University of Michigan Library), A91704.

31 Jonathon Riley, *The Colonial Ironsides* (Helion, 2022), p. 25.

32 Christopher Durston, *Cromwell's Major Generals: Godly Government during the English Revolution* (Manchester University Press, 2001), p. 16.

33 Durston, p. 33.

34 Durston, p. 22.

35 Durston, p. 45.

36 White-Spunner, *Horse Guards*, p. 20,

37 White-Spunner, *Horse Guards*, p. 20.

38 White-Spunner, *Horse Guards*, p. 20.

39 White-Spunner, *Horse Guards*, p. 42.

40 White-Spunner, *Horse Guards*, p. 43.
41 White-Spunner, *Horse Guards*, p. 60.
42 White-Spunner, *Horse Guards*, p. 81.
43 White-Spunner, *Horse Guards*, p. 103.
44 Wayne Stack, *Rebellion, Invasion & Occupation: The British Army in Ireland 1793–1815* (Helion, 2021), pp. 25–27.

CHAPTER FIVE: PRUSSIA, 1806

1 Scharnhorst, quoted by Brendan Simms, *The Struggle for Mastery in Germany 1779–1850* (Macmillan, 1998), p. 78.
2 Andreas Gryphius, *Tränen des Vaterlandes*, quoted by Barney White-Spunner, *Berlin: The Story of a City* (Simon & Schuster, 2020), p. 66.
3 Frederick Schiller, *The Thirty Years War* (Jefferson Publications, 2016), p. 4.
4 Geoff Mortimer, *Eyewitness Accounts of the Thirty Years War 1616–1648* (Palgrave, 2002), p. 47.
5 White-Spunner, *Berlin*, p. 65.
6 Derek McKay, *The Great Elector* (Longman, 2001), p. 22.
7 White-Spunner, *Berlin*, p. 106.
8 Peter Wilson, *Iron and Blood – A Military History of the German Speaking Peoples since 1500* (Penguin, 2022), p. 243.
9 White-Spunner, *Berlin*, p.115.
10 White-Spunner, *Berlin*, p. 126.
11 Johann Friedrich Heyde, *Der Roggenpreis* (Akademie-Verlag Berlin, 1988), p. 35.
12 Wilson, *Iron and Blood*, p. 193.
13 Frederick II, *Memoirs of the House of Brandenburg* (Forgotten Books, undated), p. 247.
14 White-Spunner, *Berlin*, p.117, with figures taken from Christopher Clark, *Iron Kingdom* (Penguin, 2006), p. 157.
15 Professor Benjamin Marschke, *La Charactière Bizarre: Princes' Power, Aristocratic Norms and Personal Eccentricities: The Case of Frederick William I of Prussia 1713–1740*, German Studies Association Annual Conference Report (San Diego, 2007), p. 49.
16 White-Spunner, *Berlin*, p. 122.

17 David Fraser, *Frederick the Great* (Penguin, 2000), p. 353.

18 Fraser, p. 213.

19 Wilson, *Iron and Blood*, p. 342.

20 Wilson, *Iron and Blood*, p. 355.

21 Frederick II, p. 223.

22 Tim Blanning, *Frederick the Great, King of Prussia* (Penguin, 2016), p. 343.

23 John Mander, *Berlin: The Eagle & The Bear* (Barrie & Rockcliff, 1959), p. 38.

24 Mander, p. 38.

25 White-Spunner, *Berlin*, p. 148.

26 Mander, p. 39.

27 Gerhard Ritter, *The Sword and The Sceptre: The Problem of Militarism in Germany, Vol. II The Prussian Tradition 1740–1890* (Allen Lane, 1972), p. 42.

28 Ritter, p. 42.

29 White-Spunner, *Berlin*, p. 152.

30 Barney White-Spunner, *Of Living Valour: The Story of the Soldiers of Waterloo* (Simon & Schuster, 2015), p. 64.

31 White-Spunner, *Berlin*, p. 156.

32 White-Spunner, *Berlin*, p. 157.

33 White-Spunner, *Berlin*, p. 160.

34 White-Spunner, *Berlin*, p. 161.

35 White-Spunner, *Berlin*, pp. 163–164.

36 Wilson, *Iron and Blood*, p. 286.

37 Ritter, p. 54.

38 Karl von Clausewitz, Letter to his Fiancée, 3 October 1807, quoted by Ritter, p. 48.

39 Michael Howard, *Clausewitz* (OUP, 1983), p. 59.

40 Howard, p. 61.

41 Howard, p. 60.

42 Ritter, p. 165.

43 Ritter, p. 166.

44 Ritter, p. 41.

45 Ritter, p. 72.

46 Ritter, p. 104.

47 Wilson, *Iron and Blood*, p. 299.

48 Wilson, *Iron and Blood*, p. 358.
49 Ernst Arndt, *Geist der Zeit* (Leipzig, 1806), vol. 4, p. 148.
50 White-Spunner, *Berlin*, p. 170.
51 Hegel, *Die Verfassung Deutschlands* (1802)
52 Mark Adkin, *The Waterloo Companion* (Aurum, 2001), p. 110.

CHAPTER SIX: THE U.S. ARMY, 1941

1 Howard Jones, *Crucible of Power: A History of U.S. Foreign Relations Since 1897* (Rowman & Littlefield, 2001), p. 21.
2 David E. Johnson, *Fast Tanks and Heavy Bombers: Innovation in the U.S. Army 1917–1945* (Cornell University Press, 1998), p. 20.
3 Johnson, p. 21.
4 Johnson, p. 45.
5 Peter Hart, *The Great War* (Profile, 2013), p. 457.
6 *Metropolitan Magazine*, January 1919.
7 Cited in Ivo Daalder and James Lindsay, *America Unbound: The Bush Revolution in Foreign Policy* (Washington: Brookings Institution Press, 2003), p. 7.
8 Johnson, pp. 219–220.
9 Norman Moss, *Nineteen Weeks* (Aurum, 2004), p. 10.
10 *The Role of Tanks in Modern Warfare* 1, 2, quoted by Johnson, p. 38.
11 Johnson, p. 39, quoting U.S. War Department *Acts and Resolutions December 1st 1920*, p. 436.
12 Johnson, p. 75
13 Johnson, p. 106.
14 Memorandum Chief of Cavalry dated 5 February 1942, quoted by Johnson, p. 181.
15 Figures provided by the National Museum of the United States Air Force.
16 Douglas MacArthur, *Annual Report of the Chief of Staff*, quoted by Johnson, p. 114.
17 Harvey S. Ford, *The American Army* (George, Allen and Unwin, 1941), p. 66.

18 Rick Atkinson, *An Army at Dawn* (Little Brown, 2003), Vol. 1, p. 10.

19 Moss, p. 222.

20 David M. Kennedy, *Freedom from Fear: The American People in Depression and War 1929–1945* (OUP, 1999), p. 427.

21 Johnson, p. 176.

22 Moss, p. 117.

23 Nicholas A.M. Rodger, *The Price of Victory* (Allen Lane, 2024), pp. 478–479 offers a good analysis of this approach.

24 Johnson, p. 177.

25 Johnson, p. 178.

26 Walter R. Bornemann, *The Admirals: Nimitz, Halsey, Leahy and King – The Five Star Admirals Who Won the War at Sea* (Little Brown, 2012), pp. 270–271 has a good analysis of Leahy's appointment.

27 Atkinson, *An Army at Dawn*, p. 9.

28 Atkinson, *An Army at Dawn*, p. 9.

29 Alan Axelrod, *Bradley* (Palgrave MacMillan, 2008), pp. 75–78.

30 Ford, p. 26.

31 Major Louis A. DiMarco, *US Army's Mechanized Cavalry Doctrine in World War Two* (Fort Leavenworth, Master's Thesis, 1995). Chapter 2 is an excellent study of this problem.

32 Niall Barr, *Yanks and Limeys: Alliance Warfare in The Second World War* (Jonathan Cape, 2015), p. 148.

33 Moss, p. 64.

34 Moss, p. 66.

35 Franklin D. Roosevelt, *The Public Papers & Addresses of Franklin D. Roosevelt* (Random House, 1938–50), Vol. 1940, pp. 633–644.

36 Warren F. Kimball, *The Most Unsordid Act: Lend Lease 1939–1941* (John Hopkins Press, 1969), p. 236.

37 Kennedy, p. 474.

38 Moss, p. 238.

39 Barr, pp. 30 & 113.

40 Tim Bouverie, *Allies at War: The Politics of Defeating Hitler* (Bodley Head, 2025), p. 355.

41 Michael Snape, *God and Uncle Sam: Religion and America's Armed Forces in World War II* (Boydell Press, 2015), p. 29.

42 Barr, p. 113.

43 Kennedy, p. 615.

44 Statista, 'World War Two Annual GDP of Largest Economies 1938–1945', www. Statista.com.

45 Kennedy, p. 618.

46 A good analysis of this debate is to be found in Kennedy, p. 619.

47 Kennedy, pp. 655 & 668.

48 Tom Jentz and Hilary Doyle, *Tiger 1 Heavy Tank* (Osprey, 1993), p. 13.

49 Kennedy, p. 654.

50 Kennedy, p. 621.

51 Moss, p. 238.

52 Kennedy, p. 636. Hershey would stay in post until 1970, managing the draft for both Korea and Vietnam.

53 Snape, p. 42.

54 Snape, p. 42.

55 Snape, p. 42.

56 Barr, pp. 210–211.

57 Barr, p. 334.

58 Snape, p. 58.

59 Snape, p. 41.

60 Snape, p. 43.

61 Figures are from Snape, p. 43.

62 Snape, pp. 44–45.

63 Kennedy, p. 661.

64 John Whiteclay Chambers II, *The Oxford Companion to American Military History* (OUP, 1999), p. 642 and see also Mark A. Stoler, *Allies in War: Britain and America against the Axis Powers 1940–1945* (Hodder, 2005), p. 48 and Moss, p. 250 for a fuller explanation.

65 Kennedy, p. 625.

66 Kennedy, p. 622.

67 For a fuller explanation see Kennedy, pp. 622–626.

68 Atkinson, *An Army at Dawn*, p. 11.

69 Atkinson, *An Army at Dawn*, p. 11.

70 Atkinson, *An Army at Dawn*, p. 17.

71 Atkinson, *An Army at Dawn*, p. 399.

72 Martin van Creveld, *Fighting Power: German and US Army Performance 1939–45* (Greenwood Press, 1982), p. 77.

73 van Creveld, p. 79.

74 Barr, pp. 418–419.

75 Freeland A. Daubin, *The Battle of Happy Valley* (USAMHI, 1948), p. 8, quoted by Johnson.

76 Figures taken from The National World War Two Museum in New Orleans.

77 Whiteclay Chambers II, pp. 53 & 209.

CHAPTER SEVEN: ARMIES TODAY

1 Pew Research Center, 'Representative Democracy', released 28 February 2024.

2 Open Societies Foundation Poll, 'Can Democracy Deliver', published September 2023 and quoted here by Jon Henley in *The Guardian*, 11 September 2023.

3 Melanie Phillips, 'Loss of faith in Democracy endangers us all', *The Times*, 13 January 2025, p. 22.

4 *The Future of the ADF: Geopolitical Considerations and Disaster Relief*, 25 March 2022, persicopekasaustralia.com.

5 CIA Directorate of Intelligence, *Defense in the 1989 Soviet state Budget*, June 1990.

6 For a full list see article 'Army Conscription' in *Daily Express*, 24 January 2024.

7 *Financial Times*, 'National Guard Troops Called In To Patrol Subway System', London, 9 March 2024.

8 The Stockholm International Peace Research Institute, *Top 100 Arms-producing and Military Services Companies 2023*, December 2024.

9 European Union Directorate General for Communication, *First-ever European defence industrial strategy to enhance Europe's readiness and security*, Brussels, 5 March 2024.

10 Quoted by *The Banker*, 27 June 2024.

11 'Editorial', *The Times*, 14 September 2023.

12 Alexis de Tocqueville, *Democracy in America* (Bantam Classics, 2002), p. 805.

13 For a full breakdown see Firth, Chapter VIII.

14 Taken from Simon Kuper, 'How Lithuanians are preparing to stop Putin', *Financial Times*, 4/5 November 2023.

15 Lithuanian Ministry of National Defence website.

16 Brussels Signal 7 October 2024, quoting General Wieslaw Kukula.

17 Ministry of National Defence Warsaw, *25 Years of Poland in NATO*, 2 February 2024.

18 All these figures are taken from NATO's Public Diplomacy Division Press Release, 'Defence Expenditure of NATO Countries 2014–2024'.

Further Reading and Ideas
for Exploration

The problem with writing a book like this, where I have taken five historical examples of great armies, is that there is only space to write a chapter about each, whereas they all merit considerably greater study and deserve at least a volume in their own right. However, had I written this book in five volumes, then I rather doubt anyone would have published it, nor would many readers have been brave enough to buy it. Below I have put together some recommendations and ideas for those who would like to learn more about each of the armies I have introduced and, as ever with history, learning can be by visiting as well as reading.

All the books recommended below can be found, together with publishers' details and dates, in the Bibliography on pages xx–xx. Many are out of print but can easily be sourced online on sites such as abebooks.com.

THE ARMY OF CONSTANTINE

The problem with studying Constantine the Great is that there is no objective biography of him, nor much contemporary history which wasn't written from a particular bias. The Christian authors praised him and bestowed all sorts of accolades on him, many of which were possibly undeserved, while later commentators reviled his legacy. The two most famous books about Constantine are Lactantius' *De Mortibus Persecutorum* or *On the Death of the Prosecutors*, often translated as *The Manner in which the Prosecutors Died*. It's quite a short book but allowed Lactantius to vent his fury at the likes of Galerius. It is usually included in volumes of Lactantius' wider writings which include his *Institutiones Divinae*, the *Divine Institutes*, essays on how he saw God. Originally a pagan, probably from Numidia, he was converted at Diocletian's court and later became tutor to Constantine's son Crispus, hence the possibility that he was not totally objective. The date of his death is unclear but it is probable that it was before Nicaea.

The other work is Eusebius' *Vita Constantini*, his *Life of Constantine*, intended specifically as a eulogy. Even contemporary sources said that the author had allowed his religious and personal reverence for the emperor to cloud his historical judgement. He includes a work meant to be by Constantine himself, *An Oration to the Assembly of the Saints*, probably written after the defeat of Licinius. It is from Eusebius that we get the story of the vision before the Milvian Bridge, which he maintained Constantine told him personally, but then it is clear that towards the end of his life Constantine may have come to believe that he talked to God on quite a regular basis. Eusebius, Bishop of Caesarea, was nevertheless an important historian of the early church, his *Ecclesiastical History* becoming a standard work. He was probably an Arian and certainly knew Arius well; he had taken refuge with Eusebius when he was first cast out of Alexandria. However, he should not be confused with Eusebius, Bishop of Nicomedia, a Syrian and close to Constantine and who was definitely a follower of Arius.

Otherwise there is the revisionist work of Zosimus, a pagan who lived in Constantinople about one hundred years after Constantine's death, who was, with possible justification, fiercely critical of how Constantine had encouraged the Christians to persecute the older religions. Then there are the panegyrics – the *Panegyrici Latini*, a series of the stylised speech made in praise of the emperors. The first one in praise of Constantine is one probably delivered at Trier in 309 and the last is the *Panegyric of Nazarius*, given in Rome in 321, which includes a description of the Milvian Bridge. Other interesting works are the *Notitia Dignitatum*, the list of both the military and civil offices of the empire, actually published sometime after Constantine's death but much influenced by his reorganisation, and both the *Codex Theodosianus* and the *Codex Justinianus*, compendiums of imperial law, both again compiled long after Constantine's death, but many of the laws they record date from his reign.

Gibbon's monumental *Decline and Fall of the Roman Empire* is of course a classic, although he seems to have made the existing sources go a long way when discussing Constantine. Chapters 13 to 21 are the most relevant.

Then there are some excellent modern books about Constantine. *The Cambridge Companion to the Age of Constantine*, edited by Noel Lenski, is a particularly good series of essays covering a wide spectrum of his life and rule. Perhaps the best complete biography is David Potter's *Constantine the Emperor* while Ian Hughes' *A Military Life of Constantine the Great* is an excellent study of his army and how it operated. Ross Cowan's *Milvian Bridge 312* is a very clear short explanation of the battle, and his *Roman Legionary AD*

284–337 an equally helpful more general military history and particularly thorough in its research of inscriptions, which adds the colour of the individual to the life of the soldier.

However, perhaps the most interesting way of learning more about Constantine is to visit Nis, York, Cologne, Trier, Turin, Milan, Rome and Istanbul, where careful exploration of monuments and museums reveals so much about the man and his life.

THE OTTOMAN ARMY OF MEHMET
THE CONQUEROR

The same can be said about exploring the life of Mehmet, and any visitor to Istanbul is immediately immersed in the Islamic city he created on top of Constantine's foundation. The Turks have a habit of taking over the buildings they want, such as turning Aya Sofia into a mosque, but leaving everything else much as it was. Until fairly recently this meant that you could trace the actions during the siege quite easily, although the pressure of population and visitor numbers is beginning to make this more difficult. However, you can still walk much of the Theodosian Walls, see the *kerkoporta*, find the Edirne Gate through which Mehmet entered the city on that fateful Tuesday and follow his route down the *mese* to Aya Sofia. Rumeli Hissar still dominates the European shore of the Bosphorus to the north of the city, and is open to visitors. Aya Sofia itself remains one of the world's most atmospheric and impressive buildings. Having been turned into a mosque by Mehmet, it was briefly made a museum by Ataturk in 1935 before being recently turned back into a mosque by the current Turkish government; many felt this was a retrograde step and a set-back for wider religious understanding.

In terms of reading, Caroline Finkel's masterly *Osman's Dream* is the best overall history of the Ottomans, and Colin Imber's *The Ottoman Empire* is an excellent companion volume which dwells more on the institutions of empire as opposed to the straight history. Those interested specifically in the more detailed military history can do no better than read Mesut Uyar's and Edward Erickson's *A Military History of the Ottomans* and Rhoads Murphy's *Ottoman Warfare*. Gábor Ágoston's *Guns for the Sultan* is a fascinating, if quite detailed, account of how Mehmet and his successors developed the Ottoman arms industry. Konstantin Mihailović's *Memoirs of a Janissary* is a first-hand account of what it was like to serve in that elite corps, together with a broad resumé of Ottoman history as he saw it. It's a unique account and interesting also because it shows how those recruited through the *devsirme* system did not all become willing servants of the sultans. For a gripping account of the siege itself, turn to Simon Mayall's *House of War*.

THE NEW MODEL ARMY

Marxists believe that the British Civil Wars were a bourgeois revolution, what they see as an inevitable step on the progression from feudalism to communism. Whatever one may think about the failure of the Marxist model, there is at least some truth in this assertion. Those who benefitted from the wars were the men of property, those on both sides who believed in the right of parliament, representing their class as it did, to exercise power as opposed to a monarchy. They were those who initially fought the king but then became alarmed as the New Model Army attempted to turn their victory into a social revolution, in other words trying to complete the next stage of Marxist dogma at the same time. The Restoration came about because they wanted to protect their interests and saw a constitutional monarchy as the best way of achieving this. The Civil Wars and the Interregnum are therefore arguably one of the most pivotal periods in modern British history where the outcome established the order of British society for the next four hundred years, preventing a further violent revolution and establishing political control over the army which has stood the country in good stead ever since. Now neglected by history departments in schools across the United Kingdom, who prefer to concentrate on more socially fashionable issues, and because its politics are complicated, a proper understanding of the wars is essential to making sense of how British society developed. I could have taken the late-19th century British army as an example. I nearly did, as so much of how the British Army now operates stems from the reforms of Cardwell in the 1860s to 1870s and Haldane in the first decade of the 20th century. Yet the basis of the army lies in the 1650s and it is the New Model who, unwittingly as it turned out, gave us its structure, its organisation, its constitutional niceties and its fighting – as opposed to its religious – spirit.

Again, there is so much to learn from visiting museums and battlefields. Both Marston Moor and Naseby are easily visited and there are monuments at both. Should you ever alight from the London Underground at Turnham Green, you are standing where the City's Trained Bands turned back the Royalists after Edgehill. The National Army Museum in Royal Hospital Road and the Household Cavalry Museum on Horse Guards Parade both have fascinating Civil War artefacts; the Household Cavalry Museum has a pot and a front and back from Monck's Life Guard, complete with a proof mark where a musket ball was shot at the front to prove it was up to task.

The classic works on the period are C.V. Wedgwood's Civil War trilogy – *The King's Peace 1637–1641*, *The King's War 1641–1647* and *The Trial of King Charles I* – or in one volume *Christopher Hibbert's Cavaliers and Roundheads*. Christopher Hill's biography of Cromwell, *God's Englishman*, is an equally excellent one-volume history.

Turning specifically to the New Model, the most comprehensive study is C.H. Firth's *Cromwell's Army*, first published in 1902 and recently re-published by the Naval and Military Press. A recent study by Ian Gentles, *The New Model Army*, is another very good starting point. For those interested in life under the Protectorate, Anna Keay's *The Restless Republic* is an excellent and entertaining account and Christopher Durston's *Cromwell's Major Generals* is a very good description of just what an extraordinary system of government they represented. For more detail on individual regiments and the stories of individual soldiers, try Glen Foard's excellent short history of Pickering's regiment – *Colonel John Pickering's Regiment of Foot* – or my own *Horse Guards, The Story of the Household Cavalry*, which covers the events between 1660 and 1688 in detail and, as the title suggests, tells the story of the Life Guards, The Blues and The Royal Dragoons in detail.

PRUSSIA 1806

If you look in a book shop for titles on German history, the chances are that most of what you will find covers the period from 1933 to 1945, the Nazi era, or the Cold War, possibly with a few books on the First World War. This is depressing, as that great arc of German history before 1914 tends to be ignored. The best place to start with Prussia is to read Christopher Clark's *Iron Kingdom*, his justifiably well-known history of Prussia from the time the Hohenzollerns began to transform the insignificant Mark of Brandenburg into what would become the Kingdom of Prussia and eventually the German Empire. There is a real shortage of books in the English language about 17th-century Prussia, the Great Elector and that bizarrely effective king, Frederick William I. Immodest as it may appear to recommend my own book, my *Berlin: The Story of a City* covers the period and the development of the army. There is then a plethora of books about Frederick the Great. Tim Blanning's biography is the best overall story of his life but David Fraser's book is best on the military aspects. Fraser was Vice Chief of the General Staff so this is not surprising. Both books are simply entitled *Frederick the Great*.

For an overview of Prussian and wider German military history, Peter Wilson's recently published *Iron and Blood* is the definitive work (and is also available on Audible). Annoyingly much of the history of the early 19th century otherwise tends to be told from the Napoleonic perspective, but Brendan Sims' *The Struggle for Mastery in Germany 1779–1850* is excellent, as is Charles White's biography of Scharnhorst. It is in two volumes: the first covers up to 1801 and is widely available but the second, from 1801 to 1805, is difficult to source. There are numerous biographies of Clausewitz; Hew Strachan's *Clausewitz's On War: A Biography* and Michael Howard's *Clausewitz* are two of the best and both equally readable.

It is more difficult to connect with the Prussian military, again because so much of its later history became subsumed by

Nazism. However, the German History Museum on the Unter den Linden in Berlin has good military coverage and a visit to Potsdam still, despite the crowds, allows you to get a feel for Frederick the Great. Sans Souci is much as it was, despite the old East German government having ruined the view from the terraces with apartment blocks, and the old town, badly damaged in the war, is slowly being restored. However, much the most interesting is to visit Frederick William I's country house, Königs Wusterhausen, where he lived the life of a country squire while governing Prussia. Spared by the Soviets in 1945, despite being on the path taken by the 5th Shock Army, it is still much as he left it with the furniture in his *Tabakskollegium* and the portraits of his generals. It is easy to get to, being the last stop on the eastern S-Bahn line.

Leipzig is a difficult battlefield to visit. The unfortunate city was very badly bombed in the Second World War and is as confusing now as the Allied generals found it in 1813. Waterloo is of course now a major tourist attraction and the Prussian movements can be followed quite easily, including Ligny where there is a small museum and the two approach marches to Waterloo itself, but, again, it is a battlefield more about Napoleon with a bit about Wellington and very little about Blücher. There is just a small memorial in Plancenoit where so many of those who volunteered for the *Landwehr* fell. The Waterloo campaign was the proof of the effectiveness of the Prussian Army's reforms and it is sad that it does not make sufficient acknowledgement of their sacrifice.

U.S. ARMY 1941–45

In 2000 David Kennedy, an American historian, won a Pulitzer Prize for *Freedom from Fear: The American People in*

Depression and War 1929–1945. It is an excellent place to start when trying to understand this difficult period of American history and is particularly good at analysing how the nation moved from isolationism to its massive strategic intervention in the Second World War. A hefty read, at over 900 pages, it is nevertheless fluent and absorbing. Equally excellent, although on a lesser scale, one of the very best books of military analysis written this century is David Johnson's *Fast Tanks and Heavy Bombers*. Johnson charts the U.S. Army's uneven path from 1917 through to 1945, explaining both its structural faults and the illogical nature of much of its procurement. Immaculately researched using original sources, it should be a must-read at all staff colleges.

Rick Atkinson's *An Army at Dawn*, which also won a Pulitzer Prize, is a fast-moving account of Operation *Torch* and the North African landings and taking Tunis. Atkinson wrote two further books – *The Day of Battle* about the war in Sicily and Italy and *Guns at Last Light*, the story of the liberation of Europe. Martin van Creveld, the well-known Israeli historian, has written an excellent comparison of the U.S. and German forces in his *Fighting Power* while, for those with a more detailed interest, Niall Barr's *Yanks and Limeys* is a really good analysis of the more involved aspects of coalition warfare.

Visiting the U.S. Army's North African battlefields can be a bit complicated but Sicily and Italy are easy to reach. However, what really brings home the achievement and sacrifice of the U.S. Army is to follow the route of some of their formations from the Normandy D-Day beaches south and then west. A visit to Omaha Beach with its accompanying cemetery – the American policy was to gather all their fallen and bury them together in one place, whereas the British tended to prefer local cemeteries close to where the soldiers had fought – has to be a must for those interested, especially as the world enters another dangerous period. It is then easy and interesting, if sobering, to trace the breakout from the beach head as Bradley and Patton drove south before trapping a large part of the German forces in the Falaise Pocket.

Bibliography

GENERAL

de Tocqueville, Alexis, *Democracy in America* (Bantam, 2004)
Waltz, Kenneth M., *Man, the State and War: A Theoretical Analysis* (Columbia, 2001)

THE ARMY OF CONSTANTINE

Abdy, Richard, *Legion: Life in the Roman Army* (The British Museum, 2024)
Barnes, Timothy, *Constantine: Dynasty, Religion and Power in the later Roman Empire* (Wiley Blackwell, 2014)
Béyodère, Guy de la, *Gladius: Living, Fighting and Dying in the Roman Army* (Abacus, 2020)
Bocking, Edward, ed., *Notitia Dignitatum: Et Administrationum Omnium Tam Civilium Quam Militarium In Partibus Orientis (1853)* (Kessinger Publishing, reprint, 2009)
Cowan, Ross, *Roman Legionary AD 284–337* (Osprey, 2015)
Cowan, Ross, *Milvian Bridge AD 312* (Osprey, 2016)
Dági, Marianna and Zsolt Mráv, *The Seuso Treasure: The Splendour of Pannonia* (Hungarian National Museum, 2020)
Dahm, Lambert, *Trier: Die Stadt der Römer* (Geschichte und Kultur, 2014)
Dudley, Dean, *History of the First Council of Nice* (The Book Tree, 1999)

Elton, Hugh, *Warfare in Roman Europe AD 350–425* (Clarendon, 1997)

Eusebius of Caesarea, *Vita Constantini* (Limovia, 2013)

Fischer, Thomas and Marcus Trier, *Roman Cologne* (J.P. Bachem, 2014)

Gibbon, Edward, *The Decline and Fall of the Roman Empire* (Wordsworth Classics, 1998)

Grant, Michael, *The Emperor Constantine* (Weidenfeld & Nicholson, 1993)

Hughes, Ian, *A Military Life of Constantine the Great* (Pen & Sword, 2020)

Jost, Dr. Cliff Alexander, *Welterbe Limes: Der Limes In Rheinland-Pfalz* (Schnell & Steiner, 2014)

Kulikowski, Michael, *Imperial Triumph: The Roman World from Hadrian to Constantine AD 138–363* (Profile, 2018)

Lactantius, *The Works of Lactantius*, translated by William Fletcher, 2 volumes (T & T Clark, Edinburgh 1871)

Lenski, Noel, ed., *The Cambridge Companion to the Age of Constantine* (Cambridge University Press, 2006)

MacCulloch, Diarmaid, *A History of Christianity: The First Three Thousand Years* (Penguin, 2010)

Nixey, Catherine, *The Darkening Age: The Christian Destruction of the Classical World* (Pan, 2017)

Nixon, C.E.V. and B.T. Rodgers, *The Panegyrici Latini* (University of California Press, 1994)

Ottaway, Patrick, *Roman York* (History Press, 2011)

Potter, David, *Constantine the Emperor* (Oxford University Press, 2013)

Renatus, Flavius Vegetius, *The Military Institutions of the Romans*, translated by John Clarke (Must Have Books, 2023)

River; Charles, ed., *Legends of the Ancient World: The Life & Legacy of Constantine the Great* (Harvard, undated)

Stephenson, Paul, *Constantine: Unconquered Emperor, Christian Victor* (Quercus, 2011)

Syvänne, Ilkka, *The Reign of Emperor Gallienus: The Apogee of Roman Cavalry* (Pen & Sword, 2019)

THE OTTOMAN ARMY OF MEHMET
THE CONQUEROR

Ágoston, Gábor, *Guns for the Sultan: Military Power and the Weapons Industry in the Ottoman Empire* (Cambridge University Press, 2005)

Babinger, Franz, *Mehmed the Conqueror and his Time*, Bollingen Series (Princeton, 1978)

Chalkokondyles, Laonikos, *The Histories*, translated by Anthony Kaldellis (Harvard, 2014)

Finkel, Caroline, *Osman's Dream: The Story of the Ottoman Empire 1300–1923* (John Murray, 2005)

Finkel, Caroline, *The Administration of Warfare: The Ottoman Military Campaigns in Hungary 1593–1606* (VWGÖ, 1988)

Imber, Colin, *The Ottoman Empire* (Palgrave Macmillan, 2002)

Incalcik, Halil, *The Ottoman Empire: The Classical Age 1300–1600* (Phoenix, 2000)

Incalcik, Halil and Suraiya Faroqhi, *An Economic & Social History of the Ottoman Empire 1300–1914* (Cambridge University Press, 1994)

Kaldellis, Anthony, *A New Herodotos: Laonikos Chalkokondyles on the Ottoman Empire, the Fall of Byzantium and the Emergence of the West* (Harvard, 2014)

Mayall, Simon, *The House of War: The Struggle between Christendom and the Caliphate* (Osprey, 2024)

Mihailović, Konstantin, *Memoirs of a Janissary*, translated by Benjamin Stolz (Marcus Wiener, 2011)

Murphy, Rhoads, *Ottoman Warfare 1500–1700* (UCL Press, 1999)

Philippides, Marios, ed., *Mehmed II The Conqueror: And the Fall of the Franco-Byzantine Levant to the Ottoman Turks: Some Western Views and Testimonies* (Arizona Center for Medieval and Renaissance Studies, 2007)

Stacton, David, *The World on the Last Day* (Faber, 1965)

Uyar, Mesut and Edward Erickson, *A Military History of the Ottomans* (Praeger International, 2009)

THE NEW MODEL ARMY

Calvert, Giles, *A Word for the Army and Two Words to the Kingdom* (M. Simmons at The Black Spread-Eagle, 1647)

Clotworthy, Sir John, an unidentified officer in the regiment of, *The History of the War in Ireland from 1641 to 1653* (McGlashan & Gill, Dublin, 1873)

Durston, Christopher, *Cromwell's Major Generals: Godly Government during the English Revolution* (Manchester University Press, 2001)

Esson, D.M.R., *The Curse of Cromwell* (Leo Cooper, 1971)

Firth, C.H., *Cromwell's Army* (1911; reproduced by Naval & Military Press)

Foard, Glen, *Colonel John Pickering's Regiment of Foot 1644–45* (Pryor Publications, 1994)

Gentles, Ian, *The New Model Army: Agent of Revolution* (Yale, 2022)

Hibbert, Christopher, *Cavaliers and Roundheads: The English at War 1642–1649* (Harper Collins, 1994)

Hill, Christopher, *God's Englishman: Oliver Cromwell and the English Revolution* (Penguin, 1990)

Holles, Denzil, *Memoirs of Denzil, Lord Holles, Baron of Ifield in Sussex 1641 to 1648* (Hard Press, 2019)

Jones, Serena, ed., *Britain Turned Germany: The Thirty Years War and its Impact on the British Isles 1638–1660*, Proceedings of the 2018 Helion and Co. Century of the Soldier Conference (Helion, 2019)

Keay, Anna, *The Restless Republic: Britain without a Crown* (Harper Collins, 2022)

Micel, Thomas, *The Last Newes from the Armie* (Printed for James Neale, 20 June 1647)

Murtagh, Harman and Diarmuid Murtagh, *The Irish Jacobite Army* (Four Courts Press, 2024)

Nusbacher, Aryeh J.S., 'Civil Supply in the Civil War: Supply of Victuals to the New Model Army on the Naseby Campaign 1–14 June 1645', *English Historical Review*, February 2000

Peacock, Edward, ed., *The Army Lists of the Roundheads and Cavaliers* (Chatto & Windus, 1874)

Riley, Jonathon, *The Colonial Ironsides* (Helion, 2022)

Robertson, Geoffrey, *The Levellers: The Putney Debates* (Verso, 2018)

Wedgwood, C.V., *The Thirty Years War* (Methuen, 1981)

Wedgwood, C.V., *The King's War 1641–1647* (Penguin, 1955)

Wedgwood, C.V., *The King's Peace 1637–1641* (Fontana, 1958)

White-Spunner, Barney, *Horse Guards: The Story of the Household Cavalry* (Macmillan, 2006)

PRUSSIA

Adkin, Mark, *The Waterloo Companion* (Aurum, 2001),

Blanning, Tim, *Frederick the Great, King of Prussia* (Penguin, 2016)

Boyen, Generalfeldmarschall Herman von, *Denswürdigseiten und Erinnerungen 1771–1813*, 2 volumes (Robert Lutz, Stuttgart, undated)

Brouwer, Jap Jan, *The German Way of War: A Lesson in Tactical Management* (Pen & Sword, 2021)

Büsch, Otto, *Military System and Social Life In Old Regime Prussia, 1713-1807* translated by John G. Gagliardo (Humanities Press, Boston, 1997)

Clark, Christopher, *The Iron Kingdom: The Rise and Downfall of Prussia 1600–1947* (Penguin, 2006)

Fraser, David, *Frederick the Great* (Penguin, 2000)

Frederick the Great, King, *Memoirs of the House of Brandenburg* (Forgotten Books, undated)

Friedrich, Karin, *Brandenburg-Prussia 1466–1806* (Palgrave Macmillan, 2012)

Greene, Joseph, *The Living Thoughts of Clausewitz* (Cassell, 1945)

Heyde, Johann Friedrich, *Der Roggenpreis* (Akademie-Verlag Berlin, 1988

Howard, Michael, *Clausewitz* (Oxford University Press, 1983)

Mander, John, *Berlin: The Eagle & The Bear* (Barrie & Rockcliff, 1959),

McKay, Derek, *The Great Elector* (Longman, 2001)

Ritter, G., *The Sword & the Sceptre: The Problem of Militarism in Germany – Volume II: The Prussian Tradition 1740–1890* (Allen Lane, 1972)

Simms, Brendan, *The Impact of Napoleon* (Cambridge University Press, 1997)

Simms, Brendan, *The Struggle for Mastery in Germany 1779–1850* (Macmillan, 1998)

Stoker, Donald, *Clausewitz: His Life and Work* (Oxford University Press, 2014)

Strachan, Hew, *Clausewitz's on War: A Biography* (Atlantic, 2007)

White, Charles Edward, *Scharnhorst: The Formative Years 1755– 1801* (Helion, 2020)

White, Charles Edward, *The Enlightened Soldier: Scharnhorst and the Militarische Gesellschaft in Berlin 1801–1805* (Praeger, 1989)

White-Spunner, Barney, *Berlin: The Story of a City* (Simon & Schuster, 2020)

White-Spunner, Barney, *Of Living Valour: The Story of the Soldiers of Waterloo* (Simon & Schuster, 2015),

Wilson, Peter, *Iron and Blood: A Military History of the German Speaking Peoples since 1500* (Penguin, 2022)

Wilson, Peter, *The Thirty Years War: Europe's Tragedy* (Harvard, 2009)

THE U.S. ARMY

Atkinson, Rick, *An Army at Dawn* (Henry Holt, 2002)

Atkinson, Rick, *The Day of Battle* (Abacus, 2013)

Atkinson, Rick, *Guns at Last Light* (Little Brown, 2014)

Axelrod, Alan, *Bradley* (Palgrave Macmillan, 2008)

Barr, Niall, *Yanks and Limeys: Allied Warfare in the Second World War* (Jonathan Cape, 2015)

Borneman, Walter R., *The Admirals: Nimitz, Halsey, Leahy and King – The Five-Star Admirals Who Won the War at Sea* (Little, Brown and Co., 2012)

Elberton-Smith, R., 'The Army and Economic Mobilization',
    United States Army in World War II (Office of Chief of Military
    History Department of the Army, 1959)
Fairchild, Byron and Jonathan Grossman, 'The Army and
    Industrial Manpower', *United States Army in World War II*
    (Office of Chief of Military History Department of the Army,
    1959)
Ford, Harvey S., *The American Army* (Allen & Unwin, 1941)
Hart, Peter, *The Great War* (Profile, 2013)
Jentz, Tom and Hilary Doyle, *Tiger 1 Heavy Tank* (Osprey, 1993)
Johnson, David E., *Fast Tanks and Heavy Bombers: Innovation in
    the U.S. Army 1917–1945* (Cornell University, 1998)
Kennedy, David M., *Freedom from Fear: The American People
    on Depression and War 1929–1945* (Oxford University Press,
    1999)
Kimball, Warren F., *The Most Unsordid Act: Lend-Lease 1939–1941*
    (Johns Hopkins University Press, 1969)
Macdonald, Callum, *The United States, Britain and Appeasement
    1936–1939* (Macmillan, 1981)
Moreira, Peter, *The Jew Who Defeated Hitler: Henry Morgenthau
    Jr, FDR and How We Won the War* (Prometheus Books, 2014)
Moss, Norman, *Nineteen Weeks* (Aurum Press, 2004)
Neumann, William L., *America Encounters Japan: From Perry to
    MacArthur* (Johns Hopkins University Press, 1963)
O'Brien, Phillips Payson, *How the War Was Won: Air-Sea Power
    and Allied Victory in World War II* (Cambridge University Press,
    2015)
O'Neill, William, *A Democracy at War: America's Fight at Home
    and Abroad in World War II* (Free Press, 1993)
Roberts, Andrew, *Masters and Commanders* (Allen Lane, 2008)
Rodger, Nicholas A.M., *The Price of Victory: A Naval History of
    Britain 1815–1945* (Allen Lane, 2024)
Snape, Michael, *God and Uncle Sam: Religion and America's
    Armed Forces in World War II* (Boydell, 2015)
Stoler, Mark A., *Allies in War: Britain and America against the Axis
    Powers 1940–1945* (Hodder, 2005)

Van Creveld, Martin, *Fighting Power: German and U.S. Army Performance 1939-1945* Greenwood Press 1982

Weigley, Russell F., *The American Way of War: A History of United States Military Strategy and Policy* (Indiana University Press, 1977)

Whiteclay Chambers II, John (ed.), *The Oxford Companion to Military History* (Oxford University Press, 1999)

Acknowledgements

This book has been hugely interesting and enjoyable to write but I could not have embarked on it without the immensely valuable assistance of Tash Llewellyn, who did so much to research Constantine, and Andrew Rollo, a most talented young researcher, who covered the U.S. Army in 1941. I am deeply indebted to them both.

Huge thanks also to Philip Mansel for his counsel and especially for introducing me to Caroline Finkel to whom I am most grateful for her help on the Ottomans.

Many thanks also to Professor Michael Clarke for all his advice and especially for pointing me in the right direction on the New Model Army. Equal thanks to Bill Rollo, Justin Maciejewski, Simon Mayall and my daughter, Florence, for all their wise counsel. And, as always, the staff at The London Library have been as helpful and knowledgeable as they always are.

My thanks one again to Fiona Petheram and the team at PFD, and a huge thank you the Bloomsbury/Osprey team and especially to Marcus Cowper, Rachel Nicholson, Gemma White, Stewart Larking and Serena Kerrigan-Noble.

Index